ALICE WONG
Year of the Tiger

Alice Wong is a disabled activist, media maker, and research consultant based in San Francisco, California. She is the founder and director of the Disability Visibility Project—an online community dedicated to creating, sharing, and amplifying disability media and culture—and the editor of the anthology *Disability Visibility: First-Person Stories from the Twenty-First Century* and *Disability Visibility: 17 First-Person Stories for Today* (Adapted for Young Adults). Alice is also the host and coproducer of the *Disability Visibility* podcast and copartner in a number of collaborations such as #CripTheVote and Access Is Love. From 2013 to 2015, Alice served as a member of the National Council on Disability, an appointment by President Barack Obama. She is currently working on her next anthology, *Disability Intimacy*, forthcoming from Vintage Books.

@SFdirewolf
disabilityvisibilityproject.com

EDITED BY ALICE WONG

Disability Visibility: First-Person Stories
from the Twenty-First Century

Disability Visibility: 17 First-Person Stories for Today
(Adapted for Young Adults)

Year
of the
Tiger

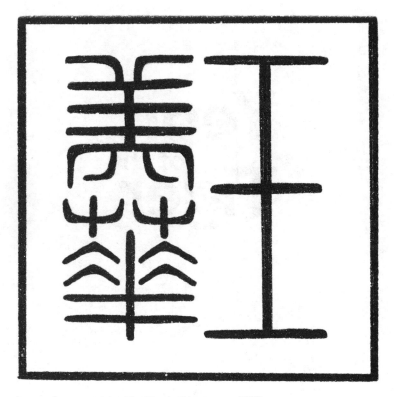

A square frame containing Alice Wong's Chinese name, 王美華, written in seal script, an ancient style of writing Chinese characters. Artwork by Felicia Liang.

Year
of the
Tiger
An Activist's Life

ALICE WONG

VINTAGE BOOKS
A Division of Penguin Random House LLC
New York

A VINTAGE BOOKS ORIGINAL 2022

Copyright © 2022 by Alice Wong

All rights reserved. Published in the United States by Vintage Books, a division of Penguin Random House LLC, New York, and distributed in Canada by Penguin Random House Canada Limited, Toronto.

Vintage and colophon are registered trademarks of Penguin Random House LLC.

Pages 373–76 constitute an extension of this copyright page.

Cataloging-in-Publication Data is available at the Library of Congress.

Vintage Books Trade Paperback ISBN: 978-0-593-31539-2
eBook ISBN: 978-0-593-31540-8

Book design by Debbie Glasserman

vintagebooks.com

Printed in the United States of America
10 9 8 7 6 5 4 3 2

FOR THE DISABLED ORACLES OUT OF TIME;
I JOIN YOU IN THE CHORUS OF OUR WISDOM.

Contents

STORYTELLING

PANDEMIC

FUTURE

Introduction

The book you are reading is from the future, as am I. I have traveled a long way to be with you and have much to share. Spending several decades on Earth has been quite a thing for this disabled Asian American woman in a hostile and unforgiving climate. Clawing, hissing, and fighting through a pandemic, against inequities in vaccine access and eugenic policies and attitudes that consider certain groups disposable, have given me the need to pause and reflect on all that I've been through. I have fought these battles for the bare minimum of existing in the same space with you all.

I realized in 2020 that the time to tell my story was now or never. That's what being a high-risk ventilator user who was deprioritized by the State of California for lifesaving vaccines will do to you. Sheltering in place with your seventy-plus-year-old parents, who are also high risk, for over a year amid anti-Asian violence and hate will do that to you, too. Instead of having a mediocre white man's midlife crisis and buying a combustible self-driving Tesla or investing in cryptocurrency for "true freedom," I decided to write a memoir at this age—the age I was never supposed to reach, during a time I was never supposed to occupy. I will never have children, but my work, stories, and relationships are my legacy, and this book you are reading is the latest contribution to the Canon of Alice.

Did I dream of becoming an activist? No, but it's probably what I'm most known for. Ableism conscripted me into activism. Other people have the luxury to opt in and out of activism like earning extra credit for a project, but not me. What I have learned about creating change and staying true to myself from childhood up to now is yours for the taking. Getting your needs met, being part of a community, stirring up shit, and sharing information: these are examples of my activism, and there are many ways to be an activist whether you use the word to describe yourself or not. How and where I do it is as important as why and whom I do it with. Being agitated and dissatisfied is an activist mood. Activism is undervalued, unsustainable, and unrelenting. Hypercapitalism, white supremacy, and ableism create the structural conditions that undermine activism and other attempts at changing the status quo. Finding the joy, pleasure, and generative possibilities of organizing is part of my long-term unlearning of what activism is supposed to look like. Unlearning and building anew is activism as well.

Living under multiple existential threats, I've seen how marginalized communities care for one another and find solidarity across movements, because at the end of the day no one will remember and save us except us. I say this as a longtime resident of San Francisco who cannot remember the last time there was a torrential thunderstorm but who's had to deal with rolling power outages and days of smoke-filled air from wildfires several years in a row. And in the face of what feels like impending doom, mutual-aid collectives emerge and organizations such as Mask Oakland distribute free N95 masks in anticipation of and response to environmental and public health crises. We can and will do better if we follow the principles of disability justice as outlined by Patty Berne, the cofounder and artistic and executive director of Sins Invalid who believes interdependence is a strength as we meet one another's needs, all bodies are whole and perfect as they are, our freedom is tied to the freedom of others, and people whose lives are most enmeshed in systems are the experts who should lead.

Year of the Tiger is divided into seven sections: "Origins," "Activism," "Access," "Culture," "Storytelling," "Pandemic," and "Future." It is a collection of original essays, previously published works, conversations, graphics, photos, commissioned art by disabled or Asian American artists, and more. I hope you will find this book fun and something you will color in, mark up, highlight, scribble on, fold into dog-eared pages, and give to others. I liken it to a mash-up of scrapbook, museum exhibit, magazine, creative writing assignment, and diary, just without the glitter gel pens or stickers. I contain multitudes, and this is a small, playful sample of who I am.

There are many kinds of writing in *Year of the Tiger*, but essays are my jam. Whether I publish an op-ed for *Teen Vogue* or a blog post on my website, I am taking the time and doing the labor to express what I care deeply about. The economy of an essay forces a writer to be a ruthless, streamlined shark with their ideas. Restraint and precision are part of an essay's elegance along with its structure. An essay doesn't have to be in response to or a critique of something else; it can reveal, subvert, wonder, provoke, analyze, celebrate, and poke fun.

Aside from social media, essay writing is my activist tool of choice, my peak creative and intellectual practice, where I layer, condense, finesse, and coax a thought into a Thing. A story from a personal, overlooked perspective can reach more people than a rally and change more minds than a policy paper. For some publications, I have to summon all that I am into eight hundred words or less, which is some damn fine magic. In Dr. Tressie McMillan Cottom's newsletter *essaying*, she wrote, "Beneath all the prose and the argument, an essay is a public. The best essays build a public through process and form, driven from creative impulse to address a social problem. . . . The best scholarship and the most invigorated publics have this in common: They channel massive amounts of creativity. Into relationships. Into methods. Into networks. Into discourse." It is my intention for every chapter to be in conversation with the others and to ripple out through a mycelial network that builds, shares, and connects My Things to New Wondrous Things, tendrils of making, reaching high and low, in the shade and under the sun.

In writing the proposal for this memoir, I collected some of my past works and was stunned by the volume and the variety. Reviewing cringe-inducing pieces from my high school and college days, I realized every single piece has led me to where I am supposed to be right now. It is a privilege to trace these seeds that grew into sequoias and to highlight the communities that supported me. I planned to have maximum fun in the writing, editing, and assembling process because book stress can always use a chill friend. I tried to let go of my anxieties about memoirs and purposefully did not read an extensive number of them or research comparable ones because I knew it would just mess with my head. This probably goes against most professional advice, but I want to be transparent with you about my process and approach.

Curating myself in words, images, and objects, I was unsure if I had anything new I urgently wanted to write, and why *yes, yes I did!* But I also took this opportunity to throw some shade and to lean into my pettiness. I do this not purely for vindictive reasons but as examples of real experiences (with Joan Collins–level receipts) from my everyday life. My redacted texts, rage, and callouts are my truths as much as my activism and storytelling. And for anyone who does not enjoy profanity, consider yourself warned.

Memoir, as a book category, is beset with a number of unique expectations by both the author and the reader. You will not find any pithy themes from this memoir, but that's what blurbs are for! I resist and challenge the idea that a memoir needs to be neatly digestible with sentimental generalizations about the meaning of life. Since this is my first time writing about myself at length, you should know the following:

- This is not a book that aims to please or center whiteness and nondisabledness.
- This is not a singular success story about overcoming odds, about perseverance or resilience; this is not a "diverse" or "intersectional" book.
- This is not a meditation on identity and pride—that is, whether I am too Chinese or disabled enough—nor a caught-between-two-worlds or my-immigrant-parents-don't-understand-me story. I am actually not Chinese enough and am very, very disabled, and I am hella okay with that. Haven't we all seen enough of these types of memoirs, anyway?
- This is not a "harrowing" yet "triumphant" account of discrimination, ableism, humiliation, and pain. I've got a bunch of these stories, and you're going to get only a sliver. I will not excavate my innermost secrets and traumas for your consumption. A memoir can provide only a glimpse of a person, and I am presenting one that is framed by me for nefarious purposes that you may discover one day if you dare.

One of my concerns when writing *Year of the Tiger* was about the publishing industry's propensity to publish memoirs by disabled people as opposed to other types of books they might prefer to write. I don't have any numbers, but it seems there are more disabled people with memoirs than with graphic novels or cookbooks, with books of photography or poetry, or in genres such as speculative fiction, romance, children's literature, and *every single other category*. Why is that? Is it because readers expect disabled people to have an interest only in explaining disability rather than focusing on their other talents and passions? Is it because disability is more easily understood as an individual phenomenon without broader social and cultural contexts? Is it because it's more palatable and "humanizing" to learn about one person and the presumed challenges and adversities in their life? Is it because the reader expects a catharsis and warm, empathetic after-school-special fuzzies by the last page? *Is it because they sell?* This is not about the authors but about the publishing industry's estimation of what makes a book attractive and salable—and, in doing so, the power a handful of corporations exerts to decide which disabled people's stories are worth telling. Like other disabled writers and editors, I am entangled in this web, too.

I've read abstracts for a lot of disability memoirs that made my eyes roll all the way to the back of my head. And while I get that audiences vary and there should be a wide range of memoirs, I would venture to say that a majority of them are inspirational, exceptional, heroic, angelic, tale-of-adversity, or courageous narratives. I present to you instead an impressionistic narrative comprising irregular dots that fade, drift, and link rather than a soaring, symmetrical arc. Still, it unsettles me to be in this category and makes me mindful of how my book will be perceived, reviewed, and marketed to the public. *How will the public receive my publics?* I await this answer with cautious optimism.

Are memoirs by disabled people the zoo exhibit of the publishing world, allowing the reader (assumed to be a default white, nondisabled, cisgender, heteronormative person) to peer into a life they find equal parts fascinating yet unimaginable? A twenty-first-century spectacle? A reader who wants to feel proud and deserving of diversity points for being a "good" ally after completing it? Whatever reason led you to pick up *Year of the Tiger*, I welcome you to question everything when you are done.

Memoirs are valuable because remembering allows us to access our imagination and power. I have willed myself into existence time and time again, and the power of memory is linked with the ability to manifest one's future. Tiger Power (and caffeine) fuels my travel through portals—it takes a lot of big cat energy to leap into unknown situations, roar against injustice, claw open new spaces, make stealthy moves, and swipe at all who annoy me across the multiverse. For now, I am here at this moment with you and will hold on for as long as I can.

A lot of things remain that I want for me, and there are even more things I want for us. Manifestation requires desire, ambition, sensitivity, and creativity. Each book or story by a disabled person holds a piece of a spell . . . eventually when enough pieces come together and fit, there will be a collective harmonic conjuring. Ripples of energy propelled by momentum, our truths undeniable and irresistible, our messages reverberating far and wide with hidden frequencies just for us. By conjuring our power and manifesting infinite dreams together, the world will finally see us as we are.

Origins

Cats rule the world.

—JIM DAVIS, CREATOR OF *GARFIELD*

Tell me, everybody's pickin' up on that feline beat,
'Cause everything else is obsolete.

—AL RINKER AND FLOYD HUDDLESTON, "EV'RYBODY WANTS TO BE A CAT"

A Mutant from Planet Cripton

AN ORIGIN

The Nerds of Color blog (April 3, 2014)

In 1974, a baby arrived in the suburbs of Indianapolis, Indiana, from the planet Cripton. She looked like the offspring of two Chinese immigrants, Ma and Pa Wong, but something was different.

Earth's gravitational force made it difficult for this baby to raise her head. She couldn't crawl and went straight from sitting to walking. Perplexed, Ma and Pa Wong took their baby to the doctor and found out: she is a mutant from Cripton!

This is her origin story.

This baby alien learned the ways of the Normal quickly; by watching *Sesame Street* and reading books, she immersed herself in the cultural mores around her. She communicated and moved in ways that wouldn't scare the kids on the playground; she knew how to talk to adults when they routinely poked and prodded her. Eventually she grew up and realized that she was not alone, that there were other mutant Crips!

As she came into the age of ascension, Alice (her Earth name) embraced her identity and found power in the community of fellow Crips around her. Scrutinized and labeled deviant by the authorities, Alice and her Siblings of Cripton continue to fight for social justice and equality for mutants and nonmutants alike, even as they face discrimination and oppression for being the Other.

. . .

So that is my mash-up nerd biography. It's true, I was born in 1974 to immigrants from Hong Kong, and I am a crip. It's an understatement to say my love of all things science fiction and cartoons intensely informed my identity as a disabled Asian American woman.

I actually do have a mutated gene—I was "born different" from most babies with a type of muscular dystrophy. I grew up hearing terms such as *weakness*, *congenital*, *defect*, *pathology*, and *abnormal* associated with me. I didn't realize the way it assaulted my personhood. Those words transformed into sources of power and resistance as I fell into my imagination through reading, writing, and watching a whole lot of television.

I stopped walking around the age of seven or eight. This separated me from most of my peers who took part in activities that I couldn't keep up with. Television and the library became my sanctuaries. I distinctly remember being the first person up every Saturday morning because my favorite cartoon, *Super Friends*, was on at 7:00 a.m. I think it was my first time seeing an Asian character, Samurai, in a cartoon (and no, *Hong Kong Phooey* didn't count), flying around with his cyclone torso. It was the first time I saw a superpower as a "special" ability. *Super Friends* was a unique minority that was valued yet not fully understood.

In elementary school I read Madeleine L'Engle's *A Wrinkle in Time*, and it blew my mind. Many books later, I discovered Octavia E. Butler, and then my mind really became blown. In the trilogy Lilith's Brood, the Oankali are incredibly perceptive and sensitive aliens. They do not understand humans' fear of difference. To them, genetic variation is a positive, not a negative.

Like with *Super Friends*, I developed an affinity for ensembles such as *Star Trek: The Next Generation*, *Star Trek: Deep*

Space Nine, and, of course, *X-Men: The Animated Series*. To have one of the most powerful mutants of them all, Charles Francis Xavier, be a man in a wheelchair absolutely delighted me when I started watching the show in 1992. It was like, "Fuck yeah, just try to talk down to me. I'll implode your mutant-hating heart." Actually, that's more like Magneto's attitude. Professor X keeps things calm and cool. He commands respect, and his competence is never questioned.

Themes and characters in the X-Men universe resonate with so many communities: LGBTQ+, immigrants, and people with disabilities. The story lines ask a lot of complex questions about assimilation, identity, morality, militarism, and diversity.

There's something incredibly affirming about seeing yourself reflected in popular culture. In the science fiction, fantasy, and comic book worlds, we may identify with characters like us, characters unlike us, or characters we want to become. Professor X is someone I identify with and aspire to be (although my temperament is a bit more like Magneto's).

Nerd culture—in books, movies, and television—filled

Me holding an issue of *Storm #1*, an X-Men comic from 2014 written by Greg Pak with art by Victor Ibáñez and color by Ruth Redmond.

me up and transformed the way I viewed my disability since my nascent origins. Who are nerds if not those left out, ridiculed, neglected, and undervalued by dominant society? Who are nerds if not those who embrace difference, seek community, and support the powerless?

Lessons from a Chinese School Dropout

When I was growing up in Indianapolis, Sunday nights were filled with last-minute attempts to finish homework and thoughts of dread about going to school the next day (Garfield was right about hating Mondays and loving lasagna). Sunday was the day for another activity that I was not good at: Chinese school, which took place in the afternoon after Sunday school and lunch. The church was the center of my Chinese American universe, where I learned about community, identity, and culture.

My sisters, Emily and Grace, and I grew up with a small gaggle of second-generation Chinese Americans close in age: Amy, Wayne, Ellen, Simon, Sang, Ming, Mark, Jeff, Jemie, Iris, and a few others. Summers were marked with the moms gathering together for 婦女会 fù nǚ huì, a women's group that met for Bible study and social hangouts, where they would learn to make things together such as Auntie Anita's (Ellen and Simon's mom) 花卷 huā juǎn, magical steamed buns with green onions folded into delicate, petal-like layers of dough. The kids (except me) ran wild like feral hogs, and Auntie Jean (Jemie's mom) gave us ice pops in long clear plastic packets that were basically tubes of frozen sweetened water in artificial rainbow colors. She would cut the top off the plastic tubes, and voilà! Oooh, they hit the spot. Garage sales, potlucks, birthday parties, home perms and haircuts (oh, the humanity, such experimental horrors on thick Asian hair), and weekly Friday-night Bible study at Amy's house with the kids hanging out in the basement are some of my most indelible memories from childhood.

The church first started out with mostly Chinese immigrants and graduate students who gathered at homes for Bible study in the 1960s and '70s. As the population grew, the group had services at Northminster Presbyterian Church, a large brick building with a tall white steeple on Kessler Boulevard, on the northeast side of Indianapolis, that from my point of view as a kid looked like a church for rich white people. Afterward, people would connect and socialize at a lunch where a pay-what-you-can meal would be served: white rice with one dish, such as braised beef stew with carrots and potatoes or sautéed ground beef with mixed frozen vegetables—something simple and filling for large quantities of people, cooked by a cadre of women volunteers, who also cleaned up and washed dishes afterward. Auntie Rosario regularly made this huge rectangular angel food cake with whipped cream and crushed pineapple. She would cut it into small square pieces, each topped with halves of maraschino cherries, so that there would be enough for everyone. It was such a luxurious treat!

Years later, the elders of our community purchased a church of our own at 5614 Broadway Street. It was an old building with a steep staircase in the back going down to the basement. The basement had a kitchen, a stage, classrooms, and a large meeting space in the center where all activities took place, aside from morning worship services for the adults upstairs in the main sanctuary. The aunties, mostly moms, organized everything from Chinese school to summer vacation Bible school to Sunday school in that basement. Mom or Dad would hoist me down the scary staircase lined with cobwebs and dust in precarious ways that could only happen in the 1970s and '80s. Maybe this was when I developed my fear of spiders . . .

A Christmas program featuring children from our Chinese community church. On the far right side of the stage, I am sitting on a folding chair, dressed as an angel and with a grumpy expression.

It became more difficult and exhausting for me to walk around holding on to tables and chairs for dear life once I got down to the church basement. I wonder if that was a subconscious factor in me quitting both Chinese and Sunday schools or if I simply wanted to stay home for some quality Me Time in front of the T.V., my first true safe space. Being alone, by choice or social exclusion, left me time to use my imagination. I was meaningfully included in my family life, but I also had the freedom to opt out of things when they became untenable. Either way, my parents did not force the issue or make me feel like a failure. This is a form of autonomy, now that I look back on things. Apparently I have never been nor will ever be anyone's model minority.

Auntie Ling-Ann, mom of Amy and Wayne, was the principal of our Chinese school for many years. One year, Uncle Paul, the dad of Ellen and Simon, was my teacher in a class that included Ellen and Emily. For some reason I can remember only that year of classes with Uncle Paul. We had workbooks with lessons featuring a character called 王大中 Wáng Dà Zhōng, a silly everyperson name akin to John Doe, generic and devoid of meaning. The books were numbered, and I did not advance past the fourth one. I ended up learning a few characters, 注音 zhù yīn (a transliteration system for Mandarin Chinese, most commonly used in Taiwanese Mandarin, also known as Bopomofo) sung to the tune of the alphabet song, and my name. Here are a few lessons that remain with me to this day.

Lesson one: There is a certain order to writing a character.

王 Wong is my surname, a hella common name that means "king." It is blessedly a very simple one to write, requiring only four strokes. There are three horizontal lines, starting left to right, from top to bottom, with the vertical line going down the center last.

Lesson two: Proportions and relationships matter.

Some characters have more than fifteen lines, dots, boxes, swoops, and slashes (my own nonofficial descriptions). These elements relate to one another, and you can't have a dot that looks like a slash or a box that is too big when it should be only one-third in size next to a line. The second character in my name, 美 měi, has specific horizontal lines that must be in proportion to one another. Getting it right takes practice. Our weekly homework assignments consisted of writing characters a certain number of times in a row, composing original sentences using newly learned vocabulary, or copying paragraphs verbatim from the workbook. We wrote our homework on sheets with square grids for the characters that had a narrower vertical space on the right for the zhù yīn "alphabet." Having the zhù yīn next to each character helped reinforce the way to pronounce the words, because intonation is everything. (I could go on, but this is an essay, not a textbook.)

Lesson three: A word can contain multitudes.

A single character can have one meaning, and when paired with one or more characters, it becomes an entirely different word. 美 měi means "beautiful," and when paired with 國 guó, the character for *country*, it becomes 美國 měiguó, referring to the United States. The third character of my name, 華 huá, refers to China, and when paired with the word for *emigrant* or *expatriate*, 僑 qiáo, becomes the term for Chinese diaspora, 華僑 huá qiáo. The variations are endless.

Writing characters in my rudimentary way is one thing, but as calligraphy it's a fucking art. One year, Uncle Paul (Ellen and Simon's dad) gave a calligraphy demonstration, and it was a sight to see. The circular grinding of ink on stone, the posture and position of his hand, wrist, and arm with the brush poised at a ninety-degree angle. The deliberateness, speed, and care for each stroke. His breathing timed to each movement. Words are more than meaning and a set of strokes. Words are art.

A photo featuring, in front, my sister Emily (*left*) and me and, in back, (*from left*) Mom, Dad, and my paternal grandmother. We are gathered by a work of calligraphy of the Chinese word for *prosperity* or *blessing*, 福 fú.

My dad and my paternal grandfather also practiced calligraphy. We used to have a large framed piece of calligraphy by my grandfather of 福 fú, the character for *prosperity* (or *blessing, fortune, luck*), brushed in thick black strokes several inches wide with elegant curves and edges created with a turn of the wrist on red paper flecked with gold. I am not sure what happened to that piece, which hung in the front hallway of our home in Indianapolis, but currently a larger work of calligraphy by my grandfather hangs in one room of our home in San Francisco. It displays a hundred variations for 福 fú, showing how the ideogram evolved over thousands of years. Wildly different looking, same meaning. When I stare at them on the wall, these rows of characters remind me of my Chinese school homework and the revelation that *prosperity and blessings may not look the same to each person.* That's some deep shit.

Following tradition (a.k.a. the Patriarchy), my grandfather named my sisters and me. As the first Wong born in the United States, my name is literal and symbolic: 王美華, "a Chinese Wong in America," based on my probably inaccurate Chinese American interpretation. Is my name as generic and boring as 王大中 Wáng Dà Zhōng's? I wish I had a more expressive name, such as "Brilliant Spring" or "Ferocious Tiger," but maybe this was his way of reaching across the Pacific, inscribing his hopes and dreams in these three characters that evolved over thousands of years, trying to connect me to a past I can never fully know or understand. Or maybe that's just wishful thinking on my part. At this point in my life, I accept my given name and delight in reimagining it: "King of the Chinese Americans."

Prosperity
Fú

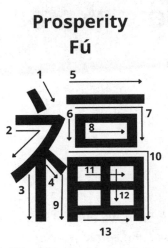

The Chinese character for *prosperity* (or *blessing*), 福 fú, with thirteen arrows indicating the order in which to write the word.

Chinese Homework

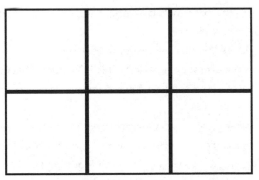

福

Prosperity, Fú
Due: Next Sunday

A grid for Chinese homework with six squares for practice, which is due promptly on Sunday.

Troublemakers

An interview with Ellen Wu (June 4, 2015). This conversation has been condensed and edited for clarity.

ALICE WONG: My name is Alice Wong. I'm forty-one years old. Today is June 4, 2015. I'm at the StoryCorps recording booth in the San Francisco Public Library to be interviewed by one of my oldest, bestest friends, Ellen Wu.

ELLEN WU: I'm Ellen Wu. I am also forty-one years old, oh my god. Today is June 4, 2015. I'm here at the San Francisco Public Library, and I am here to interview Alice Wong, one of my lifelong besties and, I would say, coconspirators.

ALICE: Yes, we are troublemakers in the best sense of the word.

ELLEN: Okay, Alice, first things first. This is location-specific: How do you make or take your coffee? I figured this was a critical question for a San Franciscan.

ALICE: For coffee lovers everywhere! Everyone has their own way. I do like to use the single cone drip. We would grind the beans fresh, put in the filter, and let it drip slowly. Three to four minutes. Then I used to add two and a half spoonfuls of sugar.

ELLEN: You did?

ALICE: I know. I don't know what happened, but I just started tapering down. I'm down to under a spoonful. I'm very proud of myself. I feel like you can really taste the coffee more. I don't miss it at all. Less than a spoonful of sugar and quite a bit of half-and-half. I'm from the school of full-fat milk.

ELLEN: Milky and sweet.

ALICE: None of that soy (not that there's anything wrong with soy or almond).

ELLEN: No, I totally agree with you.

ALICE: Give me the real thing.

ELLEN: I was thinking about whenever people ask how you and I know each other. I'm always willing to say that you're my very oldest friend, in that we were born three weeks apart. That we've known each other literally since the day you were born, three weeks after me.

ALICE: That's right.

ELLEN: One of the big things that we share in common, of course, is our upbringing in Indiana as daughters of Chinese immigrants in the 1970s and '80s. I'd like to ask you to tell me about your most vivid memories of this time. Perhaps some of the best, some of the worst, maybe some of the middle. Highs and lows, and that kind of thing.

ALICE: I feel like we really dealt with a very unique experience. The Midwestern Asian American experience. People always assume that Asian Americans live on the two coasts. It's so funny—when I moved out here, people had no idea that I was a Midwesterner. It's fun to be proud of that identity as well. Another minority identity in the Bay Area. I'm a Midwesterner, I'm from Indiana, and, yes, I was born and raised there.

ELLEN: I will not be shunned.

ALICE: Yes, exactly. And you were the one to coin the term *Hoosier Chino*, which is something I love. I think some of my central memories revolve around our very small Chinese community. We were so lucky, I think. A cohort of kids that were born around the same time. We had this Chinese community church. We all lived kind of close to each other. We went to different schools, but our cultural life centered around our church community. Things like Chinese school.

A bunch of Chinese American kids from our church with me (*front row, far left*) and Ellen (*front row, second from right*), who's wearing pigtails. The top photo features two rows of kids—five girls sitting in the front and five boys standing in the back—with everyone smiling. The bottom photo shows us all making funny faces. I am pulling my eyes open as far as I can to look like a monster, and the other kids are in various silly poses. There is one girl (*far right*) with her arms crossed; she's not one bit amused.

I remember I was the worst student. So *slackery*. You and Simon [Ellen's brother] and Emily and Grace [Alice's sisters]—you guys all advanced. I don't know what happened to me, but I just sort of, like . . .

ELLEN: Checked out?

ALICE: Yeah, I checked out. I was so over it, maybe around twelve or thirteen [years old]. I just stopped going. Things like that are funny. And our moms, they were involved in these ladies' groups. Those summers [when] the moms would get together and make something, and all of us in the house having fun, playing games at each other's homes, going to Friday-night Bible study, Saturday gatherings, and Chinese school that took place after church. Those are really some of the most cherished memories of mine. The sense of community. It was really small, actually, among kids. Maybe ten people that were part of our group of friends who were close in age. From Monday through Friday we went to our respective schools, and there really weren't that many other Asians. There were some, but it wasn't a bunch. I think it's always something really special. Something I'm really glad that we had in terms of support.

ELLEN: I think that's right. I remember you got really mad at me once because I said, "I'm really glad we don't go to the same school." I didn't mean it like "I don't want to be associated with you." I felt like we had our . . .

ALICE: Separate lives.

ELLEN: Yes. School lives, and on the weekend we found ourselves in this totally different world where it wasn't weird if, I don't know—what's a good example?—I don't know, to have your parents yell at you in Chinese or something.

ALICE: Or not getting some of the social conventions of a typical schoolkid who needs certain things. I do remember that in junior high

My ninth birthday party at ShowBiz Pizza Place, a family fun center with games, creepy animatronic singing animals, and very loud noises. Ellen is on the left, and I am on the right holding a gift from Ellen: three books from the Trixie Belden mystery series by Julie Campbell Tatham and Kathryn Kenny.

and high school, when you and our friends could start driving. That's what was great about being in different schools, that we would go to each other's events.

I remember you were really involved in theater, and in high school we would go to North Central High School and we would see you in musicals. I remember you were in the chorus of *Fiddler on the Roof*.

ELLEN: Right.

ALICE: It was really cool to support each other. That's what's nice, even though I am embarrassed that I got mad at you over such a trivial thing.

ELLEN: It sounds offensive.

ALICE: But it's embedded in your mind, and that's what's embarrassing, the thought that I . . .

ELLEN: I've done much worse by you. No worries.

ALICE: If someone asked me to describe you as a kid, I would say, "Ellen was super creative, super organized, and just multitalented in the arts, sciences. She could do everything." To me, I was always very like, "Wow, Ellen's a high achiever and super talented."

I remember you would do these . . . You had your own little library at home. You'd set up these little library cards so when I came over you'd allow me to check out a book.

ELLEN: I feel so very coercive, actually.

ALICE: No, it was really cool. You wanted visitors to check out books with the actual cards. You also wrote your own newspaper called the *Jelly Donut Press* and created a comic book character called Super Pickle. I was very impressed.

ELLEN: Precursor to the zine, I guess.

ALICE: Yeah. Absolutely.

ELLEN: I think for me, looking back, I would say you were ahead of your time in many ways. People today talk about foodies, but you were totally a foodie since we were little. I have a lot of great memories revolving around eating and drinking. We were probably eight or nine when your aunt and uncle came from Hong Kong, and they fixed us a typical Hong Kong treat, which is hot Coca-Cola with ginger or lemon. Most people and Americans will think that

that's totally disgusting. I always try to get Jason [Ellen's husband] to try it.

ALICE: It's good!

ELLEN: It is good. One of the best things I remember is— Well, I want to hear your take on this. We were probably in twelfth or eleventh grade when your parents kindly— Well, you orchestrated a field trip up to Chicago.

ALICE: Yes. So fun!

ELLEN: You tell the story.

ALICE: I guess I really was into the arts—not as an actual participant, more as an admirer. I think the Art Institute in the early '90s had a visiting Claude Monet exhibit. You could buy tickets ahead of time, and I thought, *Road trip!* We, as a family, and [like] a lot of Chinese families, would often just take a day trip to Chicago specifically for dim sum and grocery shopping.

ELLEN: It's like a three-hour ride to have lunch and buy groceries.

ALICE: That's what you do as Chinese Americans who have no decent groceries or dim sum in Indiana in the 1990s.

ELLEN: Sheer desperation would drive you.

ALICE: I'm sure now it's better, but folks these [days] didn't suffer like we did. The distance made you appreciate it so much more. The effort it took to enjoy that food. I thought, while we're out there, we can go to the museum, and why not have you and Simon join us? It was a ragtag van full of us with Emily and Grace. We definitely ate something before or afterwards.

ELLEN: I think we went to Giordano's stuffed-crust pizza [in the Chicago area].

ALICE: Mmmmmm. Giordano's.

ELLEN: You blew my tiny mind. That's really the first time I can remember going to a serious art museum. There was a huge collection of Monet paintings.

ALICE: They were really awesome. I remember this huge oil painting of peaches, and I got a magnet as a souvenir.

ELLEN: This was the thing. You always knew. For my birthdays you would give me literary books for gifts. One year it was *Angels in*

America. Another year it was a book about coffee. You planted the coffee snob seed in my head. I don't know how you knew about this stuff. Once you forced us to watch a David Lynch thing.

ALICE: That's the nerdy weirdo in me.

ELLEN: There was a lot of that, glimpses of that, at a pretty early age. I think it definitely shows your creative side. I even remember going to the Olive Garden and us asking for iced coffee. It [was] probably, like, in 1989 in Indiana, and they looked at us like we were from a different planet.

ALICE: Pre-Starbucks.

ELLEN: I think about that very proudly now.

ALICE: I do think we definitely influenced each other. I remember at your house for one of my birthdays, you threw me a gourmet pizza-making party. You prepared dough, and everybody could make their own pizza with gourmet toppings . . . *like asparagus*! [*laughs*] That was really ahead of our time, I think.

ELLEN: I think there was a story about Wolfgang Puck in *Seventeen* magazine.

ALICE: And you took me, for the first time . . . when we were in the Broad Ripple neighborhood and went to Bazbeaux Pizza, where they served all the cool, unique pizzas . . .

ELLEN: Blew your tiny little mind.

ALICE: Yes. Quattro formaggio. I never had four-cheese pizza before then. That was really fun. We had this mutual creative dynamic.

ELLEN: A yearning almost. A yearning to push out of [the] worlds that we were in, that we were circumscribed in some ways.

ALICE: This interest and curiosity. Even if [we'd] stayed in Indiana, I think we would be the kind of people that would want to try new things and bring in new experiences.

ELLEN: You can do that wherever. I think this segues into my next question. In contrast to the upbringing that you had in the Midwest, you spent most of your adult life in San Francisco. I wanted to ask you: What made you decide to move here? What did you imagine your life would be like here before you got here, and have things turned out as you originally imagined?

ALICE: I think we have a really idealized version of San Francisco. I think I definitely watched *The Real World: San Francisco* and thought, *Oh my god, is that what San Francisco's like? Every apartment is decorated in such amazing, funky Ikea decorations?* I thought, *This is so exotic.*

I moved out here for a lot of different reasons. This is getting back to disability-related stuff. Really, in Indiana, I did not have as much access to services. That's actually the reason I could not continue going to my dream school as an undergraduate, which was at Earlham College, which is a private Quaker liberal arts college in Richmond, Indiana. During my first months of college there, it was really difficult to find people to help me with my daily tasks. Not only was I moving out for the first time, but I was working with an agency to schedule people.

It is really difficult, but the difficulty was being on Medicaid. In Indiana, at that time, they gave me a few hours a day of services. I had to be very careful, and it definitely wasn't enough.

ELLEN: What did you do if you needed something and you ran out of hours?

ALICE: I had to rely on other roommates or ask for help from others in my dorm. It was not easy, especially being new. Just so uncomfortable with learning how to rely on people for help. Especially people you didn't know very well and being in such a new environment. It was really daunting while wanting to blend in. I actually think I was their [only] wheelchair-using student.

ELLEN: Ever?

ALICE: I think so? This is what I had to do early in my junior or senior year of high school (1991 to '92): I gave them a year's advance notice. I said, "I'm very interested in going to your school, and"—if I was accepted—"these are the things I [will] need assistance with." They had to create an accessible bathroom in the one dorm that didn't have steps for me within a year because they didn't have one. As a private school, they could get away with that. With only one dorm to be accessible, I couldn't visit . . .

ELLEN: Other friends.

ALICE: Yeah. Most of the bathrooms were not accessible. So basically there was a single bathroom in the entire campus that I could use, based on my memory. Can you believe it? They had certain buildings that were inaccessible, so they were very conscious about putting me in classrooms in different locations. I was definitely one of their disabled guinea pigs. It's not unusual for me to go somewhere and become the first one to test their services. That's happened to me quite a bit. This took place around 1992, basically two years after the A.D.A. [Americans with Disabilities Act]. So most public schools were also scrambling to make their buildings accessible, but private schools had a lot more flexibility as I understood it.

I do feel like I was one of the first, if not the first. Long story short, I got sick during my first term of school. Had to go home, take a year off. When I was ready to go back, there were cuts in Medicaid to my services, because that's what happens sometimes. States make cutbacks, and with the reduction of hours, there was no way I could live independently on campus. Thinking about the cost of my parents paying private tuition, it didn't make sense to pay for assistance out of pocket. That would have been ridiculous and unfair. I made a logical yet really depressing decision to stay at home and commute to a school nearby, Indiana University at Indianapolis [I.U.].

I was in a real funk for about a year when I recovered from respiratory failure. I was still not well, so I took correspondence courses through I.U. at home. The main thing was feeling incredibly jealous of my friends who were living a traditional campus life. It turned out well, in the sense that it gave me time to recoup and to think. During my undergrad years, that is when I really understood more about policies and programs and different opportunities. I read about California and how there were a lot more opportunities and availability of services.

During undergrad I wondered, *How am I going to get to San Francisco or the Bay Area? Okay, well, I'll try applying to graduate school. No problem, right?* With a lot of support and hard work, I got into U.C. San Francisco and never looked back. Again, it was a struggle with that school as well. I also reached out to them over a year ahead to find out what accommodations they could provide.

They were very honest with me. They were like, "[We've] had other wheelchair-using students, but we [haven't] had one that needed to live on campus." They actually had to also build me a temporary little room out of a garage. They owned a house for visiting faculty and made renovations in a very short period of time. It was actually pretty impressive that they were willing to do this. They built me this little one-room unit that was in the basement, or the garage level, of a home the school owned that was accessible, so I could move in during the fall semester.

ELLEN: Did it have windows?

ALICE: I don't think so.

ELLEN: Running water?

ALICE: Yes. The most important thing there was a bathroom, and it had no steps. That was another part of the process. I don't think I'm a pioneer, but it's often about educating people and advocating, not only for yourself but hopefully for other students. In the future, other students with disabilities will not have it as rough as I did.

I do know they built wheelchair-accessible housing in their larger units shortly afterward, but they didn't have any at the time I was coming in.

ELLEN: I appreciate that, because I think recently you had published an essay in *Amerasia Journal* sort of reflecting on growing up with a disability as an Asian American as well. What really struck me, as long as we've known each other, I didn't realize . . .

ALICE: The anger?

ELLEN: The anger and the depth. Again, I think it goes back to the original things that we were talking about. Just the ordinary things that we mostly take for granted as able-bodied people. Just how [disabled people] have to think out so many things so far in advance. They don't always work out, but also the emotional consequences of that, the psychological effect. The consequences of those challenges.

It makes me think of another question I had for you. Going back to living with disabilities, you have muscular dystrophy, and you were born with it. I know it's a big part of your life. I wanted to ask you to reflect on how it's shaped your views on living, on dying and your own mortality in particular.

ALICE: I'm so glad you asked me this, and I do want to thank you. You were the one who shared the call for submissions to *Amerasia* because they . . . I think it was their very first special issue on illness and disability. It was so exciting to see a journal about Asian American studies take this subject on.

When I saw the call for submissions, I said to you, "I don't know, what should I do? I don't have anything scholarly, but maybe they'll publish an essay." It was a wonderful chance to put my story out there. It's one of the first [of] my own personal stories really being out there. I want to thank you for encouraging me to do that.

I'm very in touch with my body and the changes with my body. I think people with disabilities who have similar conditions, we all realize that what is normal is on a continuum, and so is my functioning and my independence. It means it's very fluid. People think independence means being able to do everything yourself, by yourself. That's one way to look at it. Another way is to say, "As long as I can direct my own services and direct my own care, I am still independent."

ELLEN: Sort of an autonomy or decision-making power.

ALICE: That to me is the essence of what it means to be independent—a person that is exercising their autonomy to make their choices and take risks. People with disabilities are in a world that is still hostile, I think, to disability. We have to defend our autonomy and our personhood every day in these microaggressions. Like you said about only navigating through the physical environment, there's really the social environments where kids make fun of you.

I remember [when] people were just not being very nice. In second grade, a kid pushed me down in the playground because I was very wobbly and unbalanced. She pushed me, and I hit my head and had to go home. Things like that happened, and . . . it made you grow up really, really fast. It helped me become a sociologist, because I learned about power, about different groups, about shared meanings. Sociology gave me this framework to think about disability as more than just an individual, biological difference. That really helped me channel my anger in a lot of ways, too. To become more of an advocate and to use that individual anger to help other people.

I joke about being an angry disabled Asian girl, but it is something I'm proud of. It's formative.

ELLEN: A productive anger.

ALICE: It is. I embrace it. I think that's something that I really am thankful for—this emotion. It does provoke me. In turn, I try to provoke others. Some people I provoke more bluntly than others. I remember a few times [when] I did defend myself and I made people cry. I made my roommate at Earlham cry after I called her out on some really shitty behavior. She started crying. I was like, "Oh god, now I have to say I'm sorry."

ELLEN: You're just very persuasive.

ALICE: Now I have to say, "I'm sorry I made you cry, but I don't regret anything I said."

ELLEN: Sorry not sorry.

Ellen (*right*) and me, outdoors and momentarily close together, in summer 2021. I took my face shield off briefly to pose for this photo.

Excerpt from:

First-Person Political

MUSINGS FROM AN ANGRY
ASIAN AMERICAN DISABLED GIRL

Amerasia Journal (2013)

A friend recently emailed me a photo of my sisters and me at a birthday party in 1983. I recognized myself immediately in the photo: the chubby girl sitting in a chair wearing overalls sewn by her mom to accommodate her expanding girth. You can tell that girl enjoyed a good bowl of noodles. What struck me about the photo was the expression on my face, a look of quiet resignation with a touch of disgruntlement.

I can say I had a happy childhood with lots of friends and family support. However, when I look at old photos or reminisce with my sisters, I remember numerous moments of anger and frustration. In large part, having a disability from birth that progressively became more severe impacted my

A bunch of kids I mention in the chapter "Lessons from a Chinese School Dropout" (page 7). I am sitting in a chair wearing a turtleneck and overalls with two sets of buttons. Grace, my youngest sister, is in front, hamming it up with a big grin. Behind me are (*from left*) my younger sister Emily and childhood friends Amy and Ellen.

childhood experiences profoundly. Changes in my mobility radically affected my relationships with people and the built environment. At different stages those changes separated me from others. Sharing some of my memories in this essay is a way for me to reflect on and trace my evolution from an extremely angry girl to an extremely angry disabled woman.

My parents emigrated from Hong Kong to Indianapolis, Indiana, in 1972. I was born in 1974, the oldest of three daughters. The first sign that something was different about me was when my mom's friend noticed I couldn't lift my head up when I was around one and a half years old. My neck was too weak to support my head while crawling, so I transitioned from sitting to walking when I was a toddler. A neurologist diagnosed me with a form of muscular dystrophy when I was about two.

At the time of my diagnosis, there was limited understanding of the prognosis of the disease. The doctor told my parents that I would not live past eighteen years old. My parents told me they cried when they first heard the news of my diagnosis. Mom cried at home while washing the dishes, and Dad cried at the office—they were in a new country, speaking a new language, and starting a family all at the same time. My parents had little contact or interaction with people with disabilities, so they did not know what to expect. This turned out to be an advantage, because they raised me as best as they knew how, relying on their intuition and common sense. I am thankful to have been born first, since they basically practiced their parenting skills on me and expected me to lead my sisters by example, regardless of my disability. Heavy is the crown of the 老大 lǎodà, the bossy eldest sibling.

My mobility evolved over time, ranging from walking as a young child, to using a walker and manual wheelchair at age seven, to switching to an electric wheelchair at age eight, in addition to other supports that I currently use. As a toddler, I had hip dysplasia that was treated with surgery. After the surgery, I had to wear a metal-and-fiberglass brace at night that held my legs apart. I could not fall asleep easily, always begging my parents to leave their bedroom light on. Their lamp shone through the hallway into my door, a reassuring beacon in the dark. My mind would wander, trying to forget the soreness of my hip muscles that felt like rubber bands about to snap. In my first Houdini act, I slowly scrunched my body and learned how to reach and loosen the Velcro straps that secured my legs for some relief.

With the hip dysplasia slightly improved after surgery, I walked like a duck, waddling and leaning to one side at a time since one leg was longer than the other. This type of walking was uneven and unsteady. I fell and scraped my right kneecap so often I developed scar tissue the size of a coin. By the time I reached age seven, it was exhausting to walk. I huffed and puffed and could not keep up with my peers. I was afraid I would fall and grasped at chairs and handrails for support. Danger constantly swirled around me on the playground; kids at recess frightened me. I stayed near the classroom during recess, afraid to go into the nebulous gravel pits where all the cool kids gathered. I buried myself in books such as *The Incredible Journey* by Sheila Burnford and *The Mouse and the Motorcycle* by Beverly Cleary, and I couldn't wait to go back inside to the safety and stability of my classroom desk when the bell rang.

One day I ventured onto the black asphalt to join my classmates during recess. Three big girls approached me. I'll call these girls Piper, Phoebe, and Paige. Piper was the ringleader of this trio. She had a large mass of curly hair to match her towering figure. They were curious about my sudden appearance on the asphalt, their turf. One thing led to another, and *bam!* Piper pushed me down onto the sticky, hot asphalt. I injured my ankle when I fell, and later that evening my teacher called me at home. She asked who pushed me, and without thinking I said Piper. Piper got in trouble and went to the principal's office. This did not bode well for me. The next year, in third grade, there were rumors swirling through the playground grapevine that Piper was out to get me. Nothing like this happened to me again, but it is a memory seared into my mind since it was one of several encounters with violence because of my disability.

Even though my teachers knew about my disability, the concept of accommodations was not commonplace among my parents and teachers, much less me, in the 1980s. One day in second grade, I fell behind when my class lined up and walked to the library room. I couldn't keep up and struggled to carry my library books, which were due that day. I shuffled back and forth, holding three heavy books, until my arms gave way and the books crashed to the floor. It was already the middle of the class period and there wasn't a soul in the hallway. Sweating and panting, I made it to the library sans books, another indelible memory. This was normal for me, and I never thought of telling my parents about my problems. I did not know how to ask for help or say no until I was older. No one suggested I needed assistance going from room to room in school.

During this same time period, I had well-meaning friends who would encourage me to walk more. They would cajole me to walk a few laps around a room, thinking it would strengthen my muscles. Physical therapists would also emphasize walking and the need to stay bipedal for as long as possible. Not wanting to try harder meant I was giving up. I went through all those activities because I didn't want to be labeled a whiner and a bad patient. Most people probably think it is important to preserve mobility as long as possible. However, the cost of bipedal mobility was exhaustion, pain, and anger. No one asked me if I wanted to pay this price.

Eventually, I became weaker and could not stand or walk unaided. The physical therapist gave me a walker and expected me to use this device to get around in school. At this point, my legs strained and quivered as I pushed this metal frame with wheels step by freaking step. I walked like Frankenstein's monster, trudging slowly with this contraption. *Squeak, squeak, squeak. Here comes Alice!* I wish my adult self could have said this to my parents and doctors: "I am so fucking tired, guys. Please, I tried my best to humor and please you all. This walking shit ain't worth it." It is no wonder I looked so pissed off and miserable in some of my childhood photos.

By the time I was seven, my body rebelled and basically said, "Okay, the jig is up. I'm pooped and need some relief. Walking is so 1981." I graduated from a walker to a manual wheelchair. The manual wheelchair was easy to transport in and out of the house. At that time, our home had steps in the front entrance like most ranch-style suburban homes. It quickly became apparent that I did not have enough upper-body strength to push myself, and I soon transitioned into my first electric wheelchair.

The clouds parted, the disabled angels sang, and I took my rightful place on my motorized throne. It was total liberation: I was in a comfortable position and, most important, in control. I didn't need my parents or other people to move me around—a push of the joystick and I zipped around at dan-

My first day riding a school bus with a lift! Mom is on the left. It was my first experience with accessible transportation.

gerously fast speeds. I could express myself through movement for the first time. It may seem ghastly to most nondisabled people to rejoice in the usage of a wheelchair, but I consider it part of my natural development as an autonomous human being.

As my body changed, I had to adapt to the built and social environment and, in the same instance, those environments had to adapt to me. My parents built makeshift wooden ramps so I could enter and exit our home in my wheelchair. Eventually, my parents bought a converted van with a lift that would allow me to travel to places in my electric wheelchair with the family. Years later my parents were able to afford to have a home built with ramps and wider doorways. Clearly, socioeconomic status played a huge role in providing greater access, inclusion, and freedom.

There were clear benefits to using an electric wheelchair. I zoomed around the house and on the streets of my neighborhood, never on the sidewalk (sidewalks are for suckers). With this freedom of movement, this new mode of mobility presented a set of different challenges. I couldn't "pass" anymore by sitting on a couch or leaning against a wall. The new identity as a wheelchair user placed a stark spotlight on me in public spaces. I quickly learned that walking is the normative mode of mobility—anything that deviates from this mode is different and unfortunate. I felt like a second-class citizen often as I encountered physical barriers such as a restaurant with steps or a public building with a separate "handicap" entrance in the back. Of course, I do not suggest that these struggles are centered on the individual, but are systemic in a society hostile to difference.

I was never able to melt into the background during my childhood. This visibility made me acutely aware of the need to carefully negotiate the social landscape at school and in public. At most, there was a handful of Asian Americans (no more than five) in my classes all the way through high school.

My kindergarten class with my teacher Mrs. Fisher (*back right*). My legs are lying on the grass sideways since I could not sit cross-legged.

In most cases, I was the only Asian American, and almost always I was the only student with a physical disability. Always the only one or one of a few.

In elementary school, I was the only kid in a wheelchair mainstreamed in my local public school. I did not ride the school bus with my classmates. I took the "short bus," and it took me to school forty-five minutes early because its main destination was the district special education school. The bus dropped me off in darkness before most teachers would arrive. I would sometimes sit in the cafeteria as quiet as a mouse, waiting for the sun to rise and watching my classmates come in the "normal-sized" yellow buses. Other days I would enter the classroom as if I were a cat burglar at midnight. Sometimes I would peek inside my classmates' desks. Hey, what can you expect? I was bored as hell.

I think many people with disabilities would say they could deal with the difficulties of a health condition, a disability, or an inaccessible environment. What can be truly perplexing and infuriating are the reactions and attitudes of others. There are the general comments, stares, and whispers that occasionally happen when I am in public. Other times people ignore me or ask if I am with someone, as if I am incapable of being by myself. Here are some typical comments that I remember receiving as a child and young adult:

"How did you get like this? Were you in a car accident?"

"Don't you wish you could play sports?"

"Oh, God bless you! I'll be praying for you . . . Jesus loves you!"

"Do you know you can be healed if you accept Jesus Christ as your personal savior?"

Depending on my mood, I would sometimes respond politely and excuse their ignorance. Other times, I would engage and challenge their misconceptions. Sometimes people would act surprised or bemused when I would verbally defend myself. It was as if the idea of responding with a counterargument was absurd, which made my blood boil.

One of the most bewildering experiences I had related to faith and disability was when I went to an Evangelical revival with Mom and her friend. For my mom in particular, the church community sustained her and gave her a sense of belonging. I wasn't really involved in this decision to attend the revival, since I was about eight or nine years old and easily induced by a pack of bubble gum. It was cherry-flavored Bubble Yum bubble gum, and I got to have the entire pack, not just a single piece. I didn't have to share this with my sisters. Score!

There was a lot of singing, swaying, and preaching at the revival. People closed their eyes, fervently praying with their hands raised, speaking in tongues. Near the end of the service came the big finale: the preacher called for audience members who wanted a blessing and a chance to be healed by the power and spirit of the Almighty. Mom took me down to the front of the stage. When it was my turn, the preacher put his hand on my head, praying. Someone swung open the footrests on my wheelchair. He held my hand, and I stood up and took a few steps. The crowd went wild. *She . . . has . . . risen!* I was Ronald Reagan, Jesus's long-lost baby sister, and the American flag all wrapped in one.

If I had the chance to address the ecstatic audience, I would say, "Attention! I use a wheelchair but can still take a step if someone helps me. Just because I use a wheelchair, it does not mean I am paralyzed. What you are witnessing is not a miracle. The show is over." I never believed in miracles, at least when it concerned healing or curing me. My brief experiences with "trying really hard" and "hoping to get better" never materialized for me. I can't say I was angered by this memory, but rather puzzled by the whole spectacle.

What I think goes unsaid within some Asian American communities is the cultural tendency toward exclusion of people with disabilities and shame about disability in general. Among the Chinese Americans in our small Indianapolis church community, some people would ask my parents why they took me out in public with the whole family. After church services one Sunday, an auntie from China said to me, "Do you know how lucky you are?" She said it in regard to living in the United States and having a wheelchair and a supportive family. What bothered me so much about this question was the presumption that I should be grateful for merely existing. *Geez, Mom and Dad, thanks so much for not aborting me, especially if you knew what a burden I would have become.* Conversely, I have seen many Asian American families dedicated to and supportive of a family member with a disability. My parents and sisters were never ashamed of me—all our major activities included me to the fullest extent possible.

A major turning point in my politicization as a disabled person happened during my sophomore year at Carmel High School. I took an elective, Drama One. To take Drama Two the following year you needed a passing grade. I got a B and didn't think twice about signing up for the class. When I met with my guidance counselor, she looked uncomfortable and asked me to speak to my teacher. Ms. Tudor explained to me that I could not take Drama Two because there was a required physical component: pantomime. Students had to act out a story in detail using physical gestures and movements. I asked her why I couldn't do the same within my abilities, such as a pantomime of a person doing something like sitting down eating a meal. She refused, saying it was not "physical enough." The idea of a reasonable accommodation never entered her mind, and my guidance counselor agreed. I tried to advocate for myself and failed.

It was a slap in the face—pure discrimination. She did not see me the way I saw myself: a person with limitless potential. She looked at me and saw only the functional limitations of my body. I felt so disillusioned and disappointed by my teacher's response. I always thought educators and counselors would encourage students and advocate for them. This was one of several instances of blatant discrimination I experienced when I was in high school. The immediate consequence was the social distance from not advancing with my cohort of drama nerds. I remained active in the drama club, but it was not the same. I regret not fighting back harder and taking the issue to school administrators. After this singular experience, I swore to myself that I would never let anyone do that to me again.

Full of teenage angst, I found refuge in places I felt comfortable and unhindered. I went to the school library during lunch period to avoid the crowd. During these hours at the library, I learned about the disability culture hub known as Berkeley, California. Reading about the independent living movement opened my eyes to another world. I realized disability was part of my social, political, and cultural identity as much as being Chinese American and female. I occupied a place within this larger context, and this awareness helped me make sense of my experiences and emotions.

I went to college in 1992 and discovered disability studies and the sociology of disability. I felt such a kinship with the historians, philosophers, sociologists, and other writers who critically looked at disability. Paul Longmore, Irving K. Zola,

Jenny Morris, Michael Oliver, Susan Wendell, and others were the first to blow my mind. They provided various conceptual frameworks that reflected some of the tensions and social processes involved in my everyday life. The fact that some of these scholars were disabled people just like me encouraged me even more, knowing that my ambitions were possible. I channeled the anger and frustration that I could not articulate and understand as a child into writing and research about the disability experience as an adult. It was the beginning of my odyssey in disability research and activism.

Dear reader, this trip down memory lane has come to an end. To that nine-year-old girl with apple-round cheeks in the photo: I know you're tired and there are times when life sucks a lot. You may not believe it, but when you grow up, you're going to have so much fun and do many exciting things. The world is going to open up for you. Laws like the Americans with Disabilities Act and programs like Medicaid personal care services are going to help you live your life in the way you want. Most important, you will be in control and will have numerous choices. You are going to live in the greatest city in the world, San Francisco, and become a coffee fiend. You are going to become a notorious night owl. Just hang in there, keep reading, and stay angry.

Rest in Peace, Meowmee

Our family cat, Meowmee. He was a white domestic shorthair. This photo was taken by my sister Grace for a high school photography assignment in the 1990s.

I never had another cat after Meowmee because my entire family is allergic. I got Meowmee in seventh grade from a friend, and he was one weirdo kindred cat—not very affectionate, never wanted to sit on my lap, and scared to death of the vacuum. On special occasions we gave him canned tuna (with the tuna juice, which he loved), and on Thanksgiving Mom would give him the liver from the roast duck or turkey. I am still a cat person, but I worship them from afar. R.I.P., Meowmee, you were a real one!

The Americans with Disabilities Act

An interview with Rochelle Kwan (July 26, 2020). This conversation has been condensed and edited for clarity.

ROCHELLE KWAN: One of the reasons I'm really excited to have this conversation with you is because this year is the thirtieth anniversary of the Americans with Disabilities Act, the A.D.A.

ALICE WONG: Yeah. And I love how you are younger than the A.D.A.!

ROCHELLE: [*laughs*] I know!

ALICE: Oh, I love that because this is so funny. 'Cause I think—I don't know if we would call this an intergenerational conversation, but I guess it is, right? I think it is. So it's really a delight to also talk to you about this. So, I was sixteen, a sophomore in high school, when the A.D.A. passed. And to be totally honest, I don't really remember that much about it. I mean, I think at that time in my life, I was not really all that connected with any sort of consciousness about having a disabled identity other than my own kind of diagnosis. And I know that I was disabled, but I never said the word *disabled*, you know. And I think that was just the time I grew up in and you know . . . I struggled. I think I felt already, just being a teenager, no matter what decade you're in—it's a lot! I was uncomfortable in my own skin. I felt ashamed of myself. Like, I was embarrassed. I was like, just, you know, I really wish, as a wheelchair user, I would just melt in with the background, but I never could. I just really wanted to be invisible sometimes because I felt so hypervisible, you know.

I didn't have any role models. I did not have any adult in my life that also had disabilities, that ever said, like, "Hey, I've been where you've been. It's going to get better." And I also wonder, if I had that, would I have accepted it? Because I was in such a place where I was just uncomfortable. I was, to be honest, embarrassed to be around other disabled kids; sometimes I didn't wanna hang out with them because I so wanted to just be like everybody else.

ROCHELLE: Yeah. It sounds like you weren't connected with not only the disability community, but you weren't connected to the identity of being disabled. Before you came into that identity, did you think of it as just, like, *This [is] something that I have to deal with on my own?*

ALICE: Yeah, I think I definitely started after the A.D.A. was passed and just being a little bit older, as a teenager and reading and learning more. I just realized, *Oh my gosh. There are things going on in this world that are beyond my little world.* And I think one of the first things I read was in *Time* magazine, there was an article about accessible transportation. And it's right around the time that the A.D.A. came out. And at the moment I read that, I was just so floored by the idea of an accessible bus. And this is like, you know, you gotta imagine this: back then, it was just really rare. And I thought, *Wow, what would it be like to live in a community where I could leave my house and take a bus or a train all by myself?* I mean, at that point in time, I lived in the suburbs. My parents drove me everywhere. I did not have a driver's license and of course a van modification would be costly, so I didn't go through the typical rites of passage that all my friends did. I just felt very stymied. And reading about other places like Berkeley, California, which, really, it was an epicenter for disability rights and just accessibility in terms of California as a state, that really also planted a seed that, hey, there are disabled people living right now in a world that's much better and a world that's much more accessible. And then one day, maybe I could have that, too. Back then, it was a dream.

You know, I actually wrote a letter to the editor, and it was published in *Time* magazine. And I think that really was, when I was still in high school—that might've been the start of being on that journey of identifying and also being kind of engaged with the world. It was an awakening as I got older, graduated from high school, and definitely when I went to college and really learned a lot more about disability studies. And I kind of realized all this stuff that I did for myself isn't gonna help other people and isn't gonna make a difference. So it's really about systemic change. And I think that was a real switch for me as I became a college student and then went to grad school. I realized I could find so much to get something better for myself, for my accommodations as a student, but until we actually change policies, the next year, another student's gonna have to do it all over again. And that got me angry. I think that's what really drove me to think, *How can we do this? How can we make a difference? How can we work with others?* Because it's not just about what I care about. It's not just about what I need, but what all kinds of people need.

ROCHELLE: And I guess when the A.D.A. started, did you imagine the A.D.A. as that alternative world, that better world for the disabled community?

ALICE: I think people have a lot of misconceptions about the A.D.A. I think there's a lotta expectations, but it did not, let's say, solve everything, you know. Things didn't just magically become better overnight, especially in 1990, when it passed. I think it took a lot of years after it passed for all of us to see the changes, right? Like curb cuts, elevators, just some of the very basic things that we take for granted. All of the things have to still be fought for even today. But I will say that what the A.D.A. did was [give] us a law that we could call our own. It was the law that was for us, and it was the law that's enshrined in our legal protections. There were other laws before that, but the A.D.A. really was the one we could use as a tool. And I think it's a tool. It's just the beginning of creating change. And the law can only really do so much. I think sometimes we put too much stock into laws, because it's really about the spirit behind the law. What does it really mean when we say that you belong in the public like everybody else? And how do we get our culture to that place where everybody believes that? And I don't think we're—you know, it's sad to say, but thirty years later, we're not at that place yet. We're nowhere close to it. Change does not happen easily, and there's a lot of people who are afraid of change, especially those in power. And there's a lot of people that know the value of inclusion, especially with disabled people who've had a history of being segregated and institutionalized.

ROCHELLE: That is one thing that I have been thinking about a lot recently, is this, as we're in the middle of a pandemic and everybody is at home. Folks are tapping into these methods and organizing strategies that the disability community has been using forever, you know! And have built their communities from. And are people giving credit to the disability community?

ALICE: Yeah, real talk. I mean, it is ironic and a little bit bittersweet that there were conferences years ago that I couldn't attend because I would need to participate via videoconference. But my goodness! Look how quickly so many conferences are now virtual.

ROCHELLE: Yeah.

ALICE: So many people, disabled people, would get turned down for jobs when they asked to work remotely. And now many people are working remotely. And I think that's a very painful sticking point, because there's still major disparities in terms of the employment rate. So, every law is imperfect, right? So one thing about the A.D.A. is that there's really no way to enforce it. There's no A.D.A. enforcement to check on businesses, right? So, basically, for a large part, when disabled people make accommodation or access requests, and if they're thought of as reasonable requests, an employer still might treat it like a burden. And I think that still is a reason why so many people are afraid to even ask for them. I think that's one of many reasons why so many people aren't in the workforce. And there's a lot of reasons why people don't even disclose that they have a disability in the workplace. Because they don't wanna be seen as different. And I don't think anybody enjoys filing a complaint or lawsuit, but that's one option.

[*Rochelle chuckles*]

ALICE: Most of the time it's trying to rectify an unjust situation.

ROCHELLE: Mm-hmm.

ALICE: If there's any message I could share with people who are not disabled, [it] is the fact that access is so much more than just compliance with the A.D.A. Access is something that we all have capacity, in some way or another, to give to one another. So whether it's . . . hey, you know, if I say, "Oh, hey, Rochelle, can we talk later tonight instead of tomorrow morning? I had a bad day, or I'm just tired," you could say, "Hey, yeah. No problem." That's a form of access, right?

ROCHELLE: Do you have any last words about the D.V.P. [Disability Visibility Project] as a celebration of the A.D.A. and also a push to continue to better the present and future?

ALICE: Yep. You know, I think as we think about thirty years with the A.D.A., there's a lot to be thankful for. And I'm really just looking forward to the future and thinking about and dreaming big about what's possible. There's so much work to be done. The struggle continues. There's so much to critique and to be mindful of. But there's also so much hope. And I think with younger people—it just makes me so happy to see kids who are growing up with a community [that's] ready and welcoming them. That, to me, is just magical, to be part of this older group who is welcoming the next generation and future generations. And I know, I just know, things are gonna get better. And things are better now than we had thirty years ago. The possibilities are endless.

Letter to
Time Magazine

July 2, 1990

I am a sixteen-year-old disabled person. My friends can drive, and I'm relieved to know that soon disabled people will be able to travel more independently. Perhaps with this new law, employers will see that it is not the disabled who are handicapped; it is the people with closed minds.

Alice Wong
Carmel, Indiana

Content notes: surgery, hospitalization, medical trauma, blood, pain, scars

Untitled High School Poem

All responses to the world take place within our bodies.

—GLORIA ANZALDÚA

In putting together this book and making selections from past work, I desperately wanted to include a poem from my high school literary magazine to give readers a glimpse of my inner emo goth self. I emailed a librarian at Carmel High School in 2020, asking if they kept any digital or hard copies of the student literary magazine *The Prerogative* from 1991 or 1992. Unfortunately this was *too* far back in ancient history (yikes), and reaching out to a teacher who was at C.H.S. during those years didn't produce any results, either. Womp, womp.

However, three lines from the poem remained etched in my memory. Here are the words from my fractured, untitled, morbid poem:

I have a tube that feeds me
I have a tube that breathes me
Beeeeeep!

Referring to the flatline from a heart monitor, I ended the poem with death. How terribly melancholic and full of adolescent ennui. I cringe now at the thought of my hair, fashion choices, and writing at the time but truly marvel at the prescience of this poem as someone who has since talked and written about disabled people as cyborgs and oracles.

There were actually two poems published in *The Prerogative*, and they both almost didn't make it in. The second poem was about bitterness and candy; no specific lines or other details come to mind except the word *sucking*. Like I said, *cringey*. A student who worked on it told me when I saw her that year at Steak 'n Shake (an excellent place for thin smash burgers and super-thin fries) that the editor thought my content was "too dark." Luckily this student and others who worked on the magazine inserted it back in the final proofs. Thank you, fellow creative comrades! Nice to know I remain on brand to this day.

The more I think about the first poem foretelling my cyborg future, I understand it now to be rooted in a critical period of my evolutionary embodiment. I already was a cyborg teenager before acquiring the consciousness of being one.

By the time I was fourteen I had severe scoliosis, which put pressure on my lungs and shifted additional weight of my torso to the right side. I leaned in before white feminists made it a thing. When I could walk as a young child, I was wobbly and moved in slow, tentative movements. Using a wheelchair, I was still unbalanced, with this progressive curvature of the spine due to my back muscles unable to support my upper body. A back brace was just a temporary stopgap, providing better posture in exchange for sweaty, miserable discomfort. There were other signs of how the curve in my spine showed up in the rest of my body. When sitting and looking at my thighs, I could compare my unevenly aligned kneecaps. Time and biology shaped my body into a gnarled, knotty driftwood sculpture, marked by the elements and forces of nature into an abstract masterpiece. Joints contracted, muscles atrophied, sinews snipped and stretched to the brink. Great art comes at a great price.

Doctors advised me to get spinal fusion surgery when I was around twelve, but I was too freaked out by the thought of it because it was a serious-ass procedure. By eighth grade my parents told me I was near the final window for this surgery, which could improve my breathing and alleviate the deep fatigue I experienced every day. I relented—with no idea how it would turn me into a cyborg inside out.

Riley Hospital for Children in downtown Indianapolis was a beautiful space in the late 1980s and '90s. My pediatric muscular dystrophy clinic was at Riley, and I had my surgery there as well. Huge stuffed animals were perched on every floor that could be seen from the main atrium. Glass elevators in the center of the hospital made kids feel like they were at a hotel instead of a place for scary medical appointments. There were automatic doors and accessible spaces. Color everywhere. Soft-serve ice cream in the cafeteria! For all the unpleasantness that can come from the medical-industrial complex, hospitals, especially children's hospitals, were a place where I felt like I belonged in a very weird way. No one batted an eye at a wheelchair user or someone who looked different or who needed help eating or using the bathroom.

I spent six weeks in the hospital in the middle of a scorching summer, mostly in the intensive care unit, which was atypical. My delaying the surgery, which involved the insertion and fusion of Luque rods and wires to each affected segment of vertebrae in the spine, undoubtedly increased the complications and the recovery period. According to my parents, the surgery took much longer than expected. They figured it must have been touch-and-go but don't remember the specifics. Being under anesthesia for a prolonged period of time with my neuromuscular disability, I was on a mechanical ventilator and went through a succession of extubation and reintubation post-surgery when I could not breathe without assistance. Eventually, pediatric pulmonologists took over my case and slowly weaned me off the ventilator rather than a drastic withdrawal, which could cause a crash in blood oxygen levels. Shout-out to Dr. Kling, my orthopedic surgeon; Dr. Eigen, my pulmonologist, who actually had a post-surgery critical care plan that worked; and the amazing I.C.U. nurses who cared for me and performed the bulk of the labor during that time.

To say this was a period of incredible pain is an understatement. Fluid would build up in my lungs from being on mechanical ventilation. I couldn't communicate, but I buzzed for a nurse whenever I heard the crackles and gurgles grow louder and louder. Through eye contact and nods, the nurse knew what I needed and would trickle some saline down my breathing tube to break up the secretions, then thread a narrow cannula into my lungs and start suctioning. I could feel the cannula poking around as the nurse vacuumed my trachea. Having clear lungs felt wonderful afterward, but repeated suctioning caused some minor bleeding, and I saw spots of red in the sucked-up secretions once in a while. I had a gastric tube inserted through my nose for nutrition when it was clear my complications would require weeks of care. I had to swallow the tube as a resident stuck it forcefully up my nose so that it would go down into my stomach. I experienced internal bleeding and had to be rushed back to the operating room for examination. The air-conditioning didn't work for a few days on my I.C.U. floor, and the humid Midwestern heat made my small room feel even more oppressive on top of having a body lit on fire with a fresh, long incision along my back trying to heal. And I still got my period *and*, for shits and giggles, got a yeast infection due to all the medications I was on! Needless to say, I had a lot of things inserted into every orifice. These were the sights, smells, sensations, and sounds from my summer vacation, since my parents didn't want me to miss any school from the hospital stay (of course). Good times.

My sisters, Emily and Grace, had to fend for themselves as my parents took turns staying with me, driving from our home in suburban Carmel to downtown Indianapolis. Families from our church would bring food and take them out, but for the most part they spent their summer days camped out on the pull-out couch in the living room watching T.V. and being good little bunnies, like Flopsy, Mopsy, and Cotton-tail from Beatrix Potter's *The Tale of Peter Rabbit*. Emily and Grace didn't have a great summer, either.

Mom and Dad had it rough, but they never complained or showed worry. They were 100 percent there for me and that was their way. Mom spent a majority of the time by my side in a reclining chair for the brief periods she could rest, helping the nurses who came in and out of my room at all hours of the day. Mom was the first to notice I was disoriented when a respiratory therapist left my oxygen on too high or low. The privilege of having a constant parental presence sent a clear message to the hospital staff: "We are watching. We are here." I am sure this contributed to the quality of my care. Once in a while, Mom would try to sleep in the parents' lounge, but her wallet was stolen (along with other parents' wallets) in the middle of the night. I hope that person really needed the money, because who could be so cruel as to steal from exhausted, sleep-deprived parents of sick kids? I mean, really?! The shit was too real for all of us that summer.

Near the end of my hospital stay, as I prepared to go home, I found out that almost dying from this surgery and its complications had weakened my diaphragm to a point where I required respiratory therapy at home with intermittent positive pressure breathing (I.P.P.B.) treatments that temporarily expanded the lungs and provided medication such as albuterol through a nebulizer. When the doctor said this therapy was indefinite, not a temporary part of my recovery, I burst into tears because it was another major change in my disabled life, after I stopped walking and started using a wheelchair full-time. I also had to wear a nasal cannula with a low level of oxygen every night. This was before I started using a BiPap at eighteen years old, after another cyborg turning point brought about by respiratory failure.

I had to adapt or die. There was metal inside the core frame of my spine and additional attachments to my external humanoid shell at age fourteen. I had to figure shit out. And there would be more difficult shit to figure out in my twenties, thirties, and forties, as the driftwood became more weathered through pressure, fire, and rain, with craggy and bony bits damaged and torn away.

I do not regret waiting to have the surgery until it was almost too late. My parents respected the autonomy I had over my body, knowing the risks it might bring. What I did not realize was how there wouldn't be an end date for recovery, that it would be only one event in a cycle of writing and rewriting this operating system, each reboot preserving and accumulating memories. The long scar lining my back is less sensitive and spiky to the touch when it rains, a pain echo from the past. The lower left corner of my back where drainage tubes were left in after surgery remains numb and simultaneously itchy as hell because of nerve damage. My right inner wrist has two keloid scars that have grown over time from arterial lines placed to provide a convenient spigot instead of multiple blood draws during hospitalization. I was in the I.C.U. so long, one had to be replaced, and on both occasions, I was stabbed multiple times by residents attempting to insert the line into the radial artery, adjacent to the radial nerve. These two reddish-brown scars in particular are raised and have spread as I age. Even now, if I accidentally scratch or brush my wrist against a surface, I flinch at the overwhelming painful sensations. I look at the surface of the scar with its dry, cracked skin and cannot resist the impulse to pick it off, as if to remind myself of the past. Each new sensory input is another data point to be analyzed on what a body can endure and has endured. I may be an old cyborg model, but my programming is extremely sophisticated.

The poems I wrote in high school were my first attempts at

verbalizing and processing the violence my body experienced only a few years earlier. It was telegraphing messages of what's to come and the need to listen carefully. Nora Shen, a family friend, was recently cleaning out some old boxes and sent me two issues of *The Fine Print*, a college literary magazine from my years at Indiana University; she was unaware of this memoir, nor that I was in the middle of writing this very essay. Boom! Somehow the universe heard my cry and delivered more angsty crip technoscience* poetry. The connections have always been and continue to be there. Even bad poetry has the power of prophecy.

. . .

Hooked Up Online
(1995)

I have a tube that pees me
I have a tube that feeds me
I have a tube that breathes me

fluids dripping while others
swim in a raging torrent
urgently delivering goods
importing necessities
exporting wastes along these
worn down roads
no orifice left
un plugged
all functions hygienically
maintained

---

*For more about crip technoscience, check out the April 2019 special issue on crip technoscience, edited by Kelly Fritsch et al., in *Catalyst: Feminism, Theory, and Technoscience* (vol. 5, no. 1, D.O.I.: https://doi.org/10.28968/cftt.v5i1).

plastic wrapping
hermetically sealed
plastic straws
stick
   rub
      itch

the skin
sweat and dirt builds up around
the point of insertion
with a mound of ragged stained bandages
gauze and tape securing
the connections down
despite the incessant mosquito bite itch

tube upon tube,
intricate byways that laugh at nature
interconnecting, overlapping
the interstate of my body

                . . .

Time Restrained
(1996)

a fiberglass corset
a hull with
foam padding
the brace was constructed to slow the curvature
   of the bones

pressure on the structure
weakens the stature
like the one for that lady in new york

hers was made of iron and steel
to hold up her bulk

even she had problems with posture

old men surrounding her in
her underwear
applying plaster and
creating a mold of a girl aged nine

now you won't waddle like a duck
they said
when the orthotist presented her with this
new appliance

now you'll need to wear this every day
so it can hold you up
and give you balance
it'll be part of your normal routine in no time

in no time
encased in this insulated shell
is a soft mass of flesh
atrophied and decaying with
pockets of larvae wriggling for space
yearning to breathe
as the girl goes to school and sits
under the hot sun during recess

Did You Enjoy High School?

An interview with Anna Sale for the Death, Sex & Money *podcast (October 21, 2020). This conversation has been condensed and edited for clarity.*

ANNA SALE: Did you enjoy high school?

ALICE WONG: Oh gosh! Well, do you want the truth?

ANNA: Yes!

[*laughter*]

ALICE: Do you want the truth? Okay, hang on. I am so glad you asked me this question, because now I can just honestly call out my high school. I was so eager to leave Carmel High School. Like, I was one of those kids who had senioritis like way before I was a senior.

[*Anna laughs*]

ALICE: Like, I knew life was going to be so much better once I got into college. You know, I gotta tell you, I got in touch with my—my rage at an early age, and it served me well, I will just say that.

ANNA: I love that. [*laughs*] I love that. You can thank—you can thank your high school experience for tapping into your rage. [*laughs*] I wanna understand, just so—so I get what was—was, um, the feeling at the time. Did you have an experience of . . . were people directly cruel to you and bullied you? Or was it more the feeling of just being invisible and not seen?

ALICE: Uh-huh. You know, it's very ironic because I was invisible and yet so painfully visible at the same time. I was one of the few wheelchair users at that school, you know, so my locker was a desk in the nurse's office because all the lockers were inaccessible, they just didn't even think about, *Oh! Maybe we shouldn't segregate her this way.* Uh, and then I think my bus had to drop me off at my high school about thirty or forty minutes before school started—

ANNA: Oh!

ALICE: —because that was a bus that took other disabled students to another school. And, um, I would get to school and it would be pitch dark, and I would just sit alone and just wait for the students to arrive. I would go to the gym where they had a soda machine and buy a can of Mountain Dew, which was fifty cents, and I'd chug it down. That was how I stayed awake for classes. Like, that was my high school experience. I also had a teacher that refused to advance me to the next level of a drama class I was taking, so, um—which crushed my dreams, so, if you have time for this story, I'll tell you.

ANNA: Yeah, I wanna hear it. I love high school stories. [*laughs*]

ALICE: I did not realize we were gonna go in this direction, but I'm here for this.

[*Anna laughs*]

ALICE: You're just giving me a gift. A super-salty gift. Okay so, as a sophomore, one of the things that I loved as an elective was drama. So I took Drama I, [which] was taught by Ms. Tudor. At the end of the year, I had a B, and I signed up for Drama Two for the next year, and she called me after class and said, "Um, I need you to speak to your guidance counselor." She didn't have the guts to be ableist to my face. I went to my guidance counselor, Mrs. Sue Collier, and she said Ms. Tudor was not going to advance me to Drama Two because she had concerns whether I [could] "fulfill" the requirements. And let me tell you the passing requirements. There was a session on pantomime. Pantomime! And because I'm a wheelchair user, she just presumed I can't do pantomime from a freaking chair? And I was like, "Are you sure?" [Mrs. Collier] said yes. So I went back to Ms. Tudor and I asked her to reconsider, and she just shook her head and said, "I'm sorry, I don't think so." You know this class was one of the few things that I enjoyed, I had a passing grade, and she said I couldn't

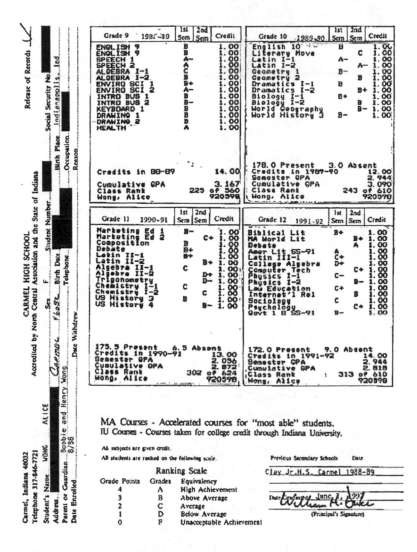

My transcript from Carmel High School showing what a mediocre student I was. Yikes, I totally forgot how my grade point average was around 2.9 or 3.0 during my years at that hellhole. Note: the grades for my two sophomore semesters of drama classes were a B and a B+.

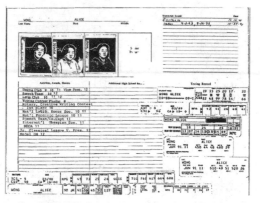

A scan of my Carmel High School transcript showing my dismal standardized test scores, my extracurriculars—such as Drama Club, Speech Team, and Latin Club—and a first place in the Rotary Club Creative Writing Contest. A note in the upper-right corner says the transcript was sent to the two colleges I attended: Earlham College and Indiana University at Indianapolis.

continue on because of my disability. She had no imagination or even willingness to be flexible, and for an adult, especially an educator who is supposed to bring up young people and get the best out of them, she drew the best rage out of me.

ANNA: I'm curious. So you felt rage. Did you—did you, as a teenager, tell people what happened and what had been withheld from you?

ALICE: You know, I told my friends, and they all felt horrible. But we didn't protest, we didn't create a ruckus. And you know, the forty-six-year-old me would have done some serious stuff. But at that time, I think I was already so self-conscious, and, frankly, because of the counselor and the teacher, I didn't think anybody else in the administration honestly would have my back. I also didn't really share this with my parents because—and I regret that now—but, um, I honestly [thought] they wouldn't consider it a priority compared to all the other things going on in my life, because it's just an elective. And I can understand that. I placed the responsibility of advocating for myself [on myself] and that's, you know, how I learned—

ANNA: How to make a ruckus.

ALICE: Later on, yeah.

[*Anna laughs*]

ALICE: Look at me now. Look at me now.

ACTIVISM

So much of the work of oppression is about
policing the imagination.

—SAIDIYA HARTMAN

You have to act as if it were possible to radically
transform the world. And you have to do it all the time.

—ANGELA Y. DAVIS

My Medicaid, My Life

The New York Times (May 3, 2017)

I am a Medicaid moocher. When Republicans talk about safety net programs like Medicaid, Social Security, and food stamps, they evoke images of people like me gabbing on their smartphones, eating steak, and watching T.V. from the comfort of home. Political rhetoric and media coverage paint us as unmotivated and undeserving individuals, passive consumers of taxpayer dollars who are out to "game the system," taking resources away from hardworking people.

The reality of being a disabled person on Medicaid is far more complex and nuanced. Many people do not even know the difference between Medicaid and Medicare and simply consider them "entitlement programs," as if tax breaks and corporate subsidies aren't entitlements by another name. Medicaid is more than a health care program. It is a life-giving program.

Like the thousands of people sharing their stories at town halls about how the Affordable Care Act saved their lives, I am sharing my Medicaid story to illustrate its value and the potential consequences of "reform."

I am an Asian American woman with a disability and I'm a daughter of immigrants. When I turned eighteen, my dad told me that I needed to make an appointment at the county office and apply for Medicaid. Living in an affluent suburb north of Indianapolis, I was indignant. Medicaid was for "those people," the "indigent." I learned that my parents paid exorbitant monthly premiums for my health care. Only one company in our state would cover me because of my preexisting condition, a type of muscular dystrophy. I had no idea of the financial pressure placed on our family for basic health insurance because of my disability.

I graduated from high school in 1992, two years after the Americans with Disabilities Act was passed. Learning about disability history and realizing I was a member of a protected class encouraged me to imagine and create the life that I want. Once I got over myself and realized I had a right to Medicaid, it made a difference immediately.

I began to receive several hours a week of services to help me with personal care. When I went away to college, I was able to hire attendants and live independently for the first time. It was an exhilarating taste of freedom that showed me a glimpse of what was possible. Before Medicaid, my family members, including my siblings, provided all my care, including bathing, dressing, and toileting. Now I had some choices and the basic human right of self-determination.

Unfortunately, Indiana made cuts to Medicaid the following year that resulted in fewer hours of services. My family couldn't manage both tuition and private pay for personal care, so I made the heartbreaking decision to leave the school I loved and move back home.

As I commuted to a school nearby, I learned about the activism by disabled people that led to expanded accessibility and services across the country, California in particular. Moving to San Francisco for graduate school in the late 1990s afforded me the privilege of being in a state with a program that allows me to direct my own personal care services, including hiring and training my attendants. This program, In-Home Supportive Services (I.H.S.S.), is funded by a combination of local, state, and federal funds. Without it, I wouldn't have been able to go to school, work, or volunteer.

By no means is it fun or easy receiving Medicaid. I follow strict eligibility rules and guidelines. I've been able to work as a researcher thanks to a state Medicaid Working Disabled Program, where I can maintain eligibility by paying monthly premiums. Over time, my disability progressed, and I needed substantial care that would normally take place in an institution if I didn't have any help. I became eligible for additional hours of service through a Medicaid waiver so that I could remain in the community and stay out of a nursing home, at a considerable cost savings for the entire system.

When you are disabled and rely on public services and programs, you face vulnerability every day. This vulnerability is felt in my bones and in my relationship with the state. Fluctuations in the economy and politics determine whether my attendants will receive a living wage and whether I'll have enough services to subsist rather than thrive. The fragility and weakness of my body I can handle. The fragility of the safety net is something I fear and worry about constantly.

Although the American Health Care Act—the Republican attempt to replace the Obama administration's Affordable Care Act—failed, the assault on poor, disabled, sick, and older people continues in other forms. The Centers for Med-

Me protesting cuts to Medi-Cal, California's Medicaid program, near San Francisco's City Hall in the aughts, I think.

icaid and Medicare Services can weaken regulations, place limits on the services states provide without legislation, and add new work requirements. States can request block grants and changes to eligibility and regulations from the federal government directly. Block grants and per capita limits force states to reduce or eliminate services to make up the difference from the federal government, affecting millions of people.

"Program flexibility" is code for the decimation of Medicaid that will put lives like mine at risk. Some people with disabilities may have to live in nursing homes if community-based services wither away under this flexibility and reform. We cannot disappear again after a history of segregation and institutionalization. When Republicans talk about freedom and choice, they don't realize that Medicaid gives those very things to people with disabilities.

This past March marked my twenty-fifth year of being a recipient of Medicaid. When I was young, I felt shame and embarrassment at being one of "those people" on benefits. Today I am unapologetically disabled and a fully engaged member of society. None of that would be possible without Medicaid.

Every day I resist forces that label me as the Other or a scapegoat for society's problems. With the disability community, I share our stories and speak out against threats to our future by using my privilege and tools such as social media. I hope my story will continue for decades to come.

The Politics of Change

2019 AUTISTIC SELF-ADVOCACY NETWORK ANNUAL GALA

Change is a calling & creative practice

DOES THIS BABY LOOK LIKE AN ACTIVIST? HELLS NO! WE ALL START FROM SOMEWHERE & WE ALL HAVE THE CAPACITY TO TAKE ACTION IN A VARIETY OF WAYS. AS A DISABLED BABY BORN INTO A NONDISABLED WORLD, I HAD TO ADVOCATE FOR MYSELF JUST TO SURVIVE & IT WASN'T UNTIL I WAS A YOUNG ADULT THAT I REALIZED SYSTEMIC & CULTURAL CHANGE IS MY ULTIMATE GOAL.

IT TOOK ME A LONG TIME TO IDENTIFY AS AN ACTIVIST BECAUSE THERE ARE SO MANY ABLEIST B.S. IDEAS OF WHAT ACTIVISM LOOKS LIKE.

I want change for us & by us

MENTORSHIP   COLLABORATION   BOUNDARIES

CIVIC PARTICIPATION   EXPERIMENTATION   SOCIAL MEDIA   PRACTICE

Embracing difference generates progress & beauty

HERE ARE A FEW QUESTIONS I WRESTLE WITH:

HOW DO WE LIFT UP EVERYONE?

HOW DO WE BRING IN FOLKS WHO ARE PART OF OUR COMMUNITIES & HAVE YET TO IDENTIFY OR DO NOT FEEL WELCOME?

HOW DO WE STOP EXPLOITING PEOPLE'S TIME & LABOR IN THE NAME OF ACTIVISM?

HOW DO WE WORK ACROSS MOVEMENTS & TRULY SHOW UP FOR OTHERS IN SOLIDARITY?

HOW DO WE EXPAND THE IDEAS OF WHO GETS TO BE AN ACTIVIST & WHAT ACTIVISM LOOKS LIKE?

ARTWORK BY LIZARTISTRY

SNACK MANIFESTO

Snacking is good.

Snacking often is better.

Sharing snacks is a love language.

Snacks fuel activism.

Snacks aren't inherently unhealthy; eat whatever makes you feel good!

Revel in being a picky cat about your faves.

Rest, like snacks, isn't a luxury or a guilty pleasure; it sustains life.

Stock up when you can for the rough times (and there will be rough times).

Excerpt from:

The *Olmstead* Decision and Me

Disability Visibility Project blog (June 27, 2019)

Before I start, I want to acknowledge the people who lived and died in institutions—we'll never know their stories or their names. I want to acknowledge the people currently in institutions against their will, who are at risk of abuse and neglect, and the people struggling to live in the community who have unmet needs, who are on waiting lists for Long Term Services and Supports and housing.

I also want to be up front about myself. I have never been institutionalized, but I am a person at risk of institutionalization. On paper I am someone with "severe" disabilities who has high care needs. Every day I rely on someone to get me out of bed and dressed, to help me in almost every aspect of my daily activities. The 1999 *Olmstead* decision has had a direct impact on my life because I am on two programs: a Medicaid Home and Community-Based Services (H.C.B.S.) waiver and In-Home Supportive Services (I.H.S.S.), a state program that provides personal assistance services. These programs provide the hours of care and services I need to remain in the community and out of institutions.

I am so thankful for what the disability community has achieved in the last twenty-nine years with the A.D.A. and twenty years with the *Olmstead* decision. I owe a lot to Lois Curtis and Elaine Wilson, the plaintiffs in *Olmstead v. L.C.*, 527 U.S. 581, and everyone who came before and after. But I

As of ▮▮▮▮▮▮▮▮▮, the services you can get and/or the amount of time you can get for services has changed.
Here's Why:
Total Hours:Minutes of IHSS you can get each month is now: 283:00 . This is a/an increase/decrease of 00:00 .

You will now get the services shown below for amount of time shown in the column "Final Amount of Service You Can Get." That column shows the hours/minutes you got before, the hours/minutes you will get from now on, and the difference. If you are getting less time for a service, the reason(s) is shown on the next page.
1) If there is a zero in the "Authorized Amount of Service You Can Get" column or the amount is less than the "Total Amount of Service Needed" column, the reason is explained on the next page(s).
2) "Not Needed" means that your social worker found that you do not require assistance with this task. (MPP 30-756.11)
3) "Pending" means the county is waiting for more information to see if you need that service. See the next page(s) for more information.

SERVICES NOTE: See the back of the next page for a short description of each service.	TOTAL AMOUNT OF SERVICE NEEDED HOURS:MINUTES	ADJUSTMENT FOR OTHERS WHO SHARE THE HOME (PRORATION)	AMOUNT OF SERVICE YOU NEED HOURS:MINUTES	SERVICES YOU REFUSED OR YOU GET FROM OTHERS	AUTHORIZED AMOUNT OF SERVICE YOU CAN GET HOURS:MINUTES		
					NOW	WAS	+/-
DOMESTIC SERVICES (per MONTH):	03:26	00:00	03:26	00:00	03:26	03:26	00:00
RELATED SERVICES (per WEEK):							
Prepare Meals	09:20	00:00	09:20	00:00	09:20	09:20	00:00
Meal Clean-up	03:30	02:20	01:10	00:00	01:10	01:10	00:00
Routine Laundry	02:00	00:00	02:00	00:00	02:00	02:00	00:00
Shopping for Food	01:00	00:00	01:00	00:00	01:00	01:00	00:00
Other Shopping/Errands	01:00	00:00	01:00	00:00	01:00	01:00	00:00
NON-MEDICAL PERSONAL SERVICES (per WEEK):							
Respiration Assistance (Help with Breathing)	00:00		00:00	00:00	00:00	00:00	00:00
Bowel, Bladder Care	10:20		10:20	00:00	10:20	10:20	00:00
Feeding	03:05		03:05	00:00	03:05	03:05	00:00
Routine Bed Bath	00:00		00:00	00:00	00:00	00:00	00:00
Dressing	04:05		04:05	00:00	04:05	04:05	00:00
Menstrual Care	00:48		00:48	00:00	00:48	00:48	00:00
Ambulation (Help with Walking, including Getting In/Out of Vehicles)	01:45		01:45	00:00	01:45	01:45	00:00
Transferring (Help Moving In/Out of Bed, On/Off Seats, etc.)	04:40		04:40	00:00	04:40	04:40	00:00
Bathing, Oral Hygiene, Grooming	07:00		07:00	00:00	07:00	07:00	00:00
Rubbing Skin, Repositioning	05:50		05:50	00.00	05:50	05:50	00:00
Help with Prosthesis (Artificial Limb, Visual/ Hearing Aid) and/or Setting up Medications	05:15		05:15	00:00	05:15	05:15	00:00
ACCOMPANIMENT (per WEEK):							
To/From Medical Appointments	00:16		00:16	00:00	00:16	00:16	00:00
To/From Places You Get Services in Place of IHSS	00:00		00:00	00:00	00:00	00:00	00:00
PROTECTIVE SUPERVISION (per WEEK):	00:00		00:00	00:00	00:00	00:00	00:00
PARAMEDICAL SERVICES (per WEEK):	07:00		07:00	00:00	07:00	07:00	00:00
TOTAL WEEKLY HOURS:MINUTES OF SERVICE YOU CAN GET:					64:34		
MULTIPLY BY 4.33 (average # of weeks per month) TO CONVERT TO MONTHLY HOURS:MINUTES:					x	4.33	=
SUBTOTAL MONTHLY HOURS:MINUTES OF SERVICE YOU CAN GET:					279:34		
ADD MONTHLY DOMESTIC HOURS:MINUTES OF SERVICE YOU CAN GET (from above):					03:26		
TOTAL HOURS:MINUTES OF SERVICE YOU CAN GET PER MONTH:					283:00		

TIME LIMITED SERVICES (per MONTH):						
Heavy Cleaning:	00:00	00:00	00:00	00:00	00:00	
Yard Hazard Abatement	00:00	00:00	00:00	00:00	00:00	
Remove Ice, Snow	00:00	00:00	00:00	00:00	00:00	
Teaching and Demonstration	00:00	00:00	00:00	00:00	00:00	
TOTAL HOURS:MINUTES OF TIME LIMITED SERVICES YOU CAN GET PER MONTH:					00:00	

Questions?: Please contact your IHSS social worker. See top of page for phone number.
State Hearing: If you think this action is wrong, you can ask for a hearing. The back of this page tells how.

An I.H.S.S. notice of action from many years ago. All participants are reassessed annually. The form includes a table containing categories of tasks I need help with. Columns list the time I need for each task, any adjustment from the previous year, and the final authorized amount broken down into hours and minutes. For many years, I received 283 hours of care per month—the maximum. When I worked as a staff research associate at the Center for Personal Assistance Services, I got to conduct qualitative research about disability and tried to ground some of our policy work in the lived experience, including my own. This assessment form is an example of the bureaucracy of care and what I call the work of disability, a concept that emerged out of my time as a researcher. Thank you, sociology!

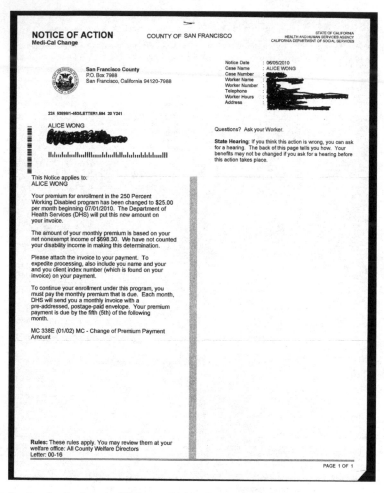

NOTICE OF ACTION
Medi-Cal Change

COUNTY OF SAN FRANCISCO

STATE OF CALIFORNIA
HEALTH AND HUMAN SERVICES AGENCY
CALIFORNIA DEPARTMENT OF SOCIAL SERVICES

San Francisco County
P.O. Box 7988
San Francisco, California 94120-7988

Notice Date : 06/05/2010
Case Name : ALICE WONG
Case Number :
Worker Name :
Worker Number :
Telephone :
Worker Hours :
Address :

224 53898/1-453/LETTER1.584 20 Y241

ALICE WONG

llılıılılılıllıılllllıılılıllılılılılılıllıılll

Questions? Ask your Worker.

State Hearing: If you think this action is wrong, you can ask
for a hearing. The back of this page tells you how. Your
benefits may not be changed if you ask for a hearing before
this action takes place.

This Notice applies to:
ALICE WONG

Your premium for enrollment in the 250 Percent
Working Disabled program has been changed to $25.00
per month beginning 07/01/2010. The Department of
Health Services (DHS) will put this new amount on
your invoice.

The amount of your monthly premium is based on your
net nonexempt income of $698.30. We have not counted
your disability income in making this determination.

Please attach the invoice to your payment. To
expedite processing, also include you name and your
and you client index number (which is found on your
invoice) on your payment.

To continue your enrollment under this program, you
must pay the monthly premium that is due. Each month,
DHS will send you a monthly invoice with a
pre-addressed, postage-paid envelope. Your premium
payment is due by the fifth (5th) of the following
month.

MC 338E (01/02) MC - Change of Premium Payment
Amount

Rules: These rules apply. You may review them at your
welfare office: All County Welfare Directors
Letter: 00-16

PAGE 1 OF 1

A notice of action from the 250 Percent Working Disabled program from 2010, which states a change to the monthly premium of twenty-five dollars I need to pay in order to remain on Medicaid, also known as Medi-Cal in California. I had to report changes to my income promptly in case it affected my premium. This is another example of structural ableism, where disabled people have to jump through inordinate hoops to work without risking access to critical services they need to live.

am also very salty and frustrated at the outright attempts to weaken regulations and programs that are vital to our civil and human rights. So I'm gonna get real with y'all.

While I have help that I need, it's still not easy. The struggle is *real* when it comes to surviving and remaining in the community. I feel very vulnerable and know that I'm one crisis or policy change away from institutionalization. This is the lived reality of a lot of disabled people like myself. This vulnerability extends to the systems and policies I'm enmeshed in.

- **Bureaucracy and labor involved in participation in programs.** I have to check in with a social worker every six months for a plan of treatment as required by my waiver and an annual redetermination for Medi-Cal, which is Medicaid in California. There's always a need to verify and document my needs for these services.
- **Poverty trap (Medicaid) asset/income limitations.** Did you know I can have only two thousand dollars combined in my checking and savings as of 2020? I'm in the community, but am I really in the community? Do I have opportunities to grow like other nondisabled people? Nope.

All these realities are anxiety producing, especially when there's a mix-up or a delay. I've also had years when the state required additional paperwork and requested my medical records after a redetermination. It is hard to describe how on edge and frantic I feel when gathering, printing, scanning, and mailing this information. The work of disability never ends.

There's a long way to go to truly fulfill the spirit of the *Olmstead* decision. Aside from my experiences, here are a few broader examples of challenges many disabled people currently face in the United States:

- **Freedom to move from state to state.** Many disabled people like me have to think twice before moving because of the variation in Medicaid L.T.S.S. services by state.
- **Institutional bias.** States that receive funding from Medicaid are required to provide institutional care, but H.C.B.S. is optional.
- **Subminimum wages.** Did you know that the Fair Labor

Standards Act allows some employers to hire disabled workers and pay them below minimum wage, sometimes one or two dollars an hour?

- **Cuts by states.** Anna Landre is a student at Georgetown who almost had to drop out of college because the State of New Jersey cut her daily hours of personal assistance from sixteen to ten. The difference of six fewer hours of care is significant. She had to fight really hard, using social media, to get this resolved, but it was an extraordinary effort. And there are many people like Anna who face these types of barriers and who just want to live their lives and pursue their dreams like everyone else.

These are all systemic barriers rooted in ableism, the idea that disabled people are incapable of making their own decisions or living independently with support, or that they don't deserve the same freedoms and rights as other people, such as opportunities for marriage, employment, and education.

This leads to another aspect of community living that's not talked about enough, and that's civic and political participation. There are still significant barriers disabled people face in civic and political participation: for example, voter turnout of disabled people is lower than nondisabled people. But this goes beyond voting and its embedded physical and social barriers—it's about being welcomed and valued, being able to show up, being involved with your local government and community organizations; it's about advocating for what you care about. In fact, a report by the Miami Lighthouse for the Blind and Visually Impaired discovered that every website for the candidates running for president in 2020 was inaccessible for blind people. Yeah, that's right. How basic can you get?

People sometimes say, "Oh, Alice, you're so amazing," and I'm like, "Yeah, yeah, yeah, whatevs . . ." (eye roll). But you know what? I want people to expect me to be in the same spaces as them, but the expectations are so low. People still find it exceptional or surprising that disabled people have children, or careers, or amazing talents, or wild adventures. This is both a cultural and political problem. And this is why visibility and representation are so important to me.

What does community living look like for me? If I want to eat ice cream for dinner, I will. If I want to stay up until 4:00 a.m. (which I often do) and watch Netflix nonstop, I'm gonna do that, because this is my life, damn it! This is what community living means to me. Until every disabled person can live the life they truly want, the fight isn't over by a long shot.

ARTWORK BY LIZARTISTRY

#CripTheVote

THEN AND NOW

Discussions with guests Andrew Pulrang and Gregg Beratan on the Disability Visibility *podcast, episodes 1 and 99 (September 13, 2017, and March 21, 2021). These conversations have been condensed and edited for clarity.*

ALICE WONG: Hey there. Welcome to the very first episode of the *Disability Visibility* podcast, conversations on disability politics, culture, and media. My name is Alice Wong, and I am honored to be your host.

With a gazillion podcasts out there, you might wonder, *Why this one? Why now?* The short answer is I don't see shows about disability culture and politics by N.P.R. or other major media organizations, and there are not that many around. The revolution is here. One podcast, one transcript, one tweet at a time.

Today's guests are Andrew Pulrang and Gregg Beratan. The three of us are copartners in #CripTheVote, an online movement encouraging the political participation of disabled people.

This episode was recorded in July, days after the Republican health care bill died in the Senate. We look back on the attempts to repeal and replace the A.C.A. [Affordable Care Act], what Medicaid means to disabled people, and the activism that took place all year long in opposition of the bill.

So let's talk a little bit about disability activism this year, especially about the G.O.P. health care bill that was in the House, that's known as the A.H.C.A. [American Health Care Act]. Then it became the B.C.R.A. [Better Care Reconciliation Act], and then it mutated into this O.R.R.A. [Obamacare Repeal Reconciliation Act]. We are talking today on July 29, 2017, and just two days ago, the bill was killed in the Senate. How are you two feeling about the political roller-coaster ride, what you observed, and what you experienced?

GREGG BERATAN: Can we just start by saying let's hope it sticks this time?

ALICE: Yeah!

[*Gregg laughs*]

ANDREW PULRANG: I agree. I was gonna say that's one of my reflections, is that I think that this is probably gonna be something we're gonna have to deal with in some way for at least another couple years, probably, off and on. It feels like we've reached a threshold or a certain turning point, but that doesn't mean it won't come up again.

ALICE: And also, we have to keep in mind that legislation isn't the only way to dismantle Medicaid or other safety net programs. There's a lot of decisions that can happen from C.M.S. [Centers for Medicare and Medicaid Services] and other departments. So we all gotta be vigilant on that. I definitely think that what we've seen in terms of people sharing their Medicaid stories, that it'll still really be needed throughout the entire four years . . . hopefully just four years. But yeah, I think that it's been really a great awakening in the sense that finally, nondisabled people have a little sense of what Medicaid is, what it does, and just how many people it touches.

ANDREW: Yeah, no, I agree. Six months ago, I would not have said that there would be as much support for Medicaid as there is right now. And not just with the disability community, but overall. I think what you just said is correct that people have woken up to realize that Medicaid is a thing, and it's a thing that people actually like and appreciate. It's not some sort of crappy, expensive entitlement that nobody really likes. People actually appreciate it. And of course, we have things that we wanna change about it, but [there was a perception that people on Medicaid despised it] and wanted to get off it as soon as they could kind of thing. That's just not really the case.

Surveys show that people who are on Medicaid are overwhelmingly happy with it. And that half the reason that people don't like the marketplace exchanges is because they'd rather be on Medicaid, you know, than pay through the nose for a sort of half-hearted private plan.

ALICE: Mm-hmm. And I think it also speaks to one of the reasons why people are satisfied or happy for Medicaid, is because they know so many people that aren't insured or [are] discriminated against because of their preexisting condition. And that we still live in a country where health care is not guaranteed for every single person. So of course we're gonna be very thankful and reliant on Medicaid, because we're still not at that point where everybody's covered. I really appreciated these stories about how Medicaid really supported people in education, in public schools. People did not realize the reach of Medicaid beyond poor and disabled people.

ANDREW: Right.

ALICE: I think that's another thing that, "Oh, my parents might be in a nursing home!" Like that might be a risk. Or these kids who need services at school. It's like, oh! Kind of broadening the base of the reality of Medicaid, which I think, in a way, was good. It was good in terms of getting nondisabled people engaged and aware that it's important to everyone.

GREGG: Yeah. I think one of the heartening things has been seeing people realize what value Medicaid adds to our society, that people are able to work and live and raise their families, go to school, give birth to healthy kids, because of what Medicaid provides. And I think in that way, Andrew, you're right: it helped Medicaid reclaim its good name. I mean, as you said, no one has been more critical of Medicaid's flaws than the disability community. But we were never advocating doing away with it but fixing it.

ANDREW: The Republicans, I think, have made a mistake in thinking that complaints about a system mean they have a license to just tear it up, and I just think they're finding out that they kinda don't. [*chuckles*] Hopefully.

ALICE: Well, right, in the sense that they wanna tear it up and not really even have a plan for something that's similar or comparable or better. I mean, that was a huge, huge, huge red flag, and I think clearly, people saw through that.

GREGG: I think they put their dreams of serving a certain constituency ahead of serving their whole constituency. That's never a good recipe.

ALICE: Well, yeah. I mean, look at Senator [Mitch] McConnell and Kentucky. Kentucky has so many people that need health care.

GREGG: Yes.

ANDREW: Well, that's the hard, hard kernel that we may never fully crack, which is there are people who fundamentally need these things. But for a variety of reasons, they sort of, on a level, despise them. So you get lots of people in places like Kentucky who gripe and moan about the fact that their neighbors get Medicaid and they don't, or this person gets Medicaid and shouldn't. And they complain on that moral plane about freeloaders and all that stuff. And then the politicians take that and say, "Okay. So clearly my people don't like Medicaid." It's not quite that simple. Even if people make these sort of really disgusting comparisons and criticisms, that doesn't mean that they don't need it. If they could get their heads around it in a different way, they would probably support it.

ALICE: Well, it's also funny that there are those folks all over the country—not just in the middle of the country, not just in the South, but everywhere. They don't realize that the plan that they're on is funded by the A.C.A.

GREGG: The interesting thing for me, Alice, you mentioned people not realizing they're on A.C.A.-funded plans. I think part of what we've seen is people start to realize that they are and that people they know depend on Medicaid across the country. And that's why we've seen so many people come out. I mean, there were protests in thirty different cities.

ANDREW: That's fantastic.

GREGG: Isn't it?

ALICE: Yeah, and also the whole idea, the aspect of the resistance, is that all three of us are on Twitter. We've seen just so many different ableist comments about Trump and the way they're talking about the issues. And that in itself is problematic and just goes to show how far we need to go. And the fact that most of what we see in terms of disability activism is just very substantive. It's got the bigger picture versus this cult of personality.

GREGG: And we've gotten to see that close up. I mean, the fact is #CripTheVote could've easily degenerated into "I like this politician and I like that politician," but it never did. I mean, to the community's credit, everyone, almost without exception, kept it on the issues, whether it was during debates or whether it was one of the chats we had on a particular topic. It never devolved into partisan crap, or it was always about how this will affect our community.

ALICE: Yeah, I mean, we've been at this now for—talking July 2017, so it's about . . . we've been in existence for over a year and a half. Originally, we were gonna wrap it up after Election Day last November. I'm so glad that we decided not to, that no, that there's still a huge need for it, and it's only gonna continue onward. It's much more than just about voting; it's about political participation. It's about having a voice. And it's also about just having a space for conversations.

For the listeners who don't know about #CripTheVote, most of our activities are on Twitter, and we have about once a month, roughly about once a month, a Twitter chat about some sort of disability issue.

So just what were some of the highlights that you both wanna recall from our last four chats?

ANDREW: I think, more than any particular chat, what sticks in my mind is that we're continuing with these topics that some of them aren't really on the front burner otherwise. With our chats, we would take a little time each month to look at a topic that's important but maybe has fallen off the radar. And I think that's really important going forward, because there's all kinds of issues that matter to our community that aren't necessarily burning right at the moment, but they could be at any time.

GREGG: I mean, the one on the media, I think, was kind of amazing for me, just seeing the outpouring we got. People were—there was a lot of frustration that people seemed to finally be able to give voice to.

ALICE: I agree. I feel that way about the death penalty chat, because, I mean, similar to Talila A. Lewis, who also guest-hosted our chat last year on mass incarceration, I feel like I am still really shocked that the death penalty issues are not a priority within the disability rights community.

ANDREW: And that's an evolving process for a lot of people, evolving from thinking of disability as a fairly simple and narrow range of issues to being something that relates to a huge tent of issues.

ALICE: And there's so many different issues in terms of race, class, and disability. And I think that's another thing that we could do: point in

Voter access is a THING! Me holding an absentee ballot from the November 2020 U.S. election.

the direction of these issues that may not seem [like] our issues, but to say that yes, they are our issues.

ALICE: Welcome, Andrew and Gregg. It's wild that we're talking again in 2021, in my next-to-last podcast episode! Since we started #CripTheVote in 2016, what are some of the major shifts you've seen by candidates compared from then to now in 2020 that you've noticed in the way they engage and talk about disability?

GREGG: I think the way I would characterize it when we started, disability was a tick box for most politicians. It was something they had to acknowledge or cover to an extent, but not something they needed to go in depth for. It was not a community that they recognized in any way as a constituency. It was more something used to signal their own goodness in the way we see so often in inspiration porn.

It was used to say, "Look, I'm such a good candidate, I care about the disabled." You could start to see the shift in the 2018 midterms a little. But 2020 started to see, particularly with the presidential candidates, people taking the disability community very seriously, and the policies were well thought out. They weren't just, you know, a quick page slapped together on a website. It was detailed, well thought out, to the point where they're getting into the nitty-gritty of policies like LEAD-K, which is Language Equality and Acquisition for Deaf Kids, which is a very small bill that's traveling across the country, but one that's very important to the community and growing in popularity. But I think the fact that we're seeing them get into that level of detail is something that's amazing. I don't know that we could've expected that four years ago, but I think it definitely was a gradual shift that we saw happening.

I think in the 2018 midterms, we saw people pressuring politicians on particular issues to get answers, to see where they stood. I mean, there are specific issues that politicians got pressed on in those midterms in ways that they probably hadn't been before. And I think the thing we saw in 2020 was that people came out with these really well-thought-out plans. And we talked about this when it came out, that the Biden team came out with their plan a bit later than everyone else. And it was sort of disappointing to the community, even though in 2016, that would've probably been the best plan we'd seen. And so, I like seeing how the Overton window [the range of politically and societally acceptable policies], the idea of what is needed, has shifted in that time.

ALICE: Yeah, and I think one thing that's really notable, at least to me, it's that there's more disabled people working on campaigns and having a really active role in the formation of these platforms and policies. I mean, we have Molly Doris-Pierce, who originally was on Senator Warren's campaign, who's now on the Biden campaign. We have Emily Voorde, who was on the Buttigieg campaign. We have a lotta other disabled people who've been really involved in giving input, sharing their expertise. And I also wanna emphasize that disabled people have been involved behind the scenes and front and center for decades. It's just now, it's a culmination of a lotta things that people have built over time. Andrew, what's your take on then and now?

ANDREW: It's hard to know for sure the effect that we had and the role that we played. And I agree, Alice, I definitely believe that we weren't the cause of all the progress. I think that we maybe were an avenue that nobody had really planned for. And one of the things I'll say about the better platforms and stuff put out by candidates is there was a lotta love going around about the policies from various candidates, but also criticism from the community and even within the community over what should and shouldn't have been in them, what bits were good, what bits were bad. Often, it was a mix. Candidates who put out policies—and you could tell that they thought they were just gonna get nothing but praise because they put out a detailed platform—were kinda taken aback to get pushback on stuff. That's a good sign, too, because it means the fact that we have disagreements, you can't really have disagreements over empty policy. You can't have disagreements over "I support the disabled."

ALICE: What are some issues that you both are keenly interested in under this new Biden administration?

ANDREW: Yeah, I have four main things. Their personnel: as in, who do you hire to take care of disability issues in the administration?

COVID: getting through that in a way that tries to cut back on some of the particular injustices [directed at] disabled people. Undoing bad policies: you know, it's specific things that've been done in the last four or so years that've been bad for the disability community. Where it's possible to undo them relatively easily, maybe, with executive orders and things. And then trying to get a start on some of the bigger, [what] I call the bread-and-butter, disability issues—I don't know if that's a perfect term—but the ones where if you do make a change, that the vast majority of people with disabilities will materially notice it.

And I think of things like Social Security and S.S.I. [Supplemental Security Income] and S.S.D.I. [Social Security Disability Insurance] and its relationship to Medicare and Medicaid and working. Like, if they could make it so that more of us could work while still collecting benefits, that's something that millions of disabled people have been complaining about forever and literally have never had hope of that ever changing, right? All we hope for is being able to tiptoe through the working incentive system with expert help, which is great when you can get it. But we never—people barely ever talk about changing it. And now, again, finally in candidate policies, we're talking about actually changing it: more benefits, you can have them for longer, you can earn more without losing them.

And again, that may take a long time to do, 'cause messing with Social Security is really, really hard to do, even if it's done in a good way. But, yeah, that. And, of course, these ongoing issues with access to home- and community-based services so that people don't have to go into congregate care because they need help every day just to live. That's another bread-and-butter issue that has had much more activity over the years but still isn't finished.

GREGG: All of those things are probably on my list. I think the home- and community-based services is near the top. The pandemic has highlighted the problems in congregate care. And the disability community's always known about this. We've always talked about this. And yet we still have to fight case by case to get people into the community. *Olmstead* is litigated literally one person at a time.

We have not got a system for ensuring that anyone who wants community service, home- and community-based services, gets them. You have to litigate on a case-by-case basis. And this is problematic. I mean, people have a right to live in the community. There is no one that cannot be better served in the community than in a nursing facility. No one. And I'd love to see a politician recognize it.

I'd love to see the move on health care. I think I don't see it happening, 'cause Biden's committed to mainly expanding Obamacare. But, for example, in New York, we've got a bill, New York Health, that has a chance of passing this year that I'd love to see passed. It's a Medicare for All bill that builds in long-term care in the most elegant of ways, and it will expand who gets access to home- and community-based services [H.C.B.S.]. It will prioritize H.C.B.S. over institutional settings. I'd love to see more of that from politicians. I'd love to see it in this administration. I don't know.

I'm fairly skeptical about this administration moving on disability issues. I think, throughout the campaign, we weren't their priority. They put out a disability policy after we hounded them. They did a good job of it. I mean, it's a decent policy. I'm not trying to attack the policy. I just don't see the commitment from them on actually prioritizing the community. An administration gets only so many priorities to carry out in its first term, but I don't see much of what's in their disability policy as something they're gonna prioritize. And I hope I'm wrong, and I hope we hold their feet to the fire and push them on these things.

ALICE: So, on that note, I wanna thank both of you as copartners in this project for the last four years, but also your friendship. Thank you, Gregg. Thank you, Andrew.

GREGG: Thank you, Alice, and it's been a pleasure.

ANDREW: It's been a highlight of my life, too, I'll tell you that. Certainly the last several years for sure. And one of these days, we need to actually meet in person.

ALICE: Yeah! If not 2021, 2022.

ANDREW: There you go.

Inclusive Politics & the Disability Community

I GOTTA SAY, I'M SALTY A.F. BECAUSE THE MAJORITY OF CONVERSATIONS AROUND INCLUSIVE POLITICS ARE PERFORMATIVE IN MY OPINION.

Dear Progressives,

make your shit accessible

PLAIN LANGUAGE

TRANSCRIPTS

LIVE CAPTION

IMAGE DESCRIPTIONS

disability is diversity

WE WANT MEANINGUL ENGAGEMENT

IF YOU DON'T KNOW, HIRE DISABLED PEOPLE

build & collaborate with us

BE ACCOUNTABLE, NOT DEFENSIVE

every issue is a disability issue

Unlearn your ableism

& now for some hot disabled sparkles

WE HAVE AN INTIMATE KNOWLEDGE OF MULTIPLE INSTITUTIONS

WE ARE CREATIVE & INNOVATIVE AS HELL BECAUSE THIS WORLD WAS NEVER BUILT FOR US

ACCESS IS A COLLECTIVE RESPONSIBILITY

WE UNDERSTAND INTERDEPENDENCE AS A STRENGTH

WE KNOW EVERYONE HAS INHERENT VALUE REGARDLESS OF THEIR PRODUCTIVITY

ARTWORK BY LIZARTISTRY

Content notes: filicide, suffocation, murder, death, ableism, eugenics

Bay Area Day of Mourning

On Sunday, March 1, 2015, the Bay Area disability community gathered at the Ed Roberts Campus to remember and mourn the deaths of disabled people at the hands of their parents, caregivers, or care providers or by law enforcement and other authorities. This event, the Day of Mourning, is taking place in cities across the United States and internationally. Here are my prepared remarks for the vigil.

Hi, my name is Alice Wong, and I am the founder of the Disability Visibility Project. One of the aims of our project is to record the stories of people with disabilities by people with disabilities . . . in their own words and on their own terms.

Why is this important? Related to this day, it's because our lives are so easily forgotten, ignored, and excluded. When we are alive, we have to fight for recognition, and in death, our lives are cast in stereotypes and clichés that rob us of our innate humanity.

I'd like to say a few words and remember the lives of Ben, Max, and Olivia Clarence, three disabled children murdered by their mother, Tania Clarence, on April 22, 2014, in London.

With her husband and nondisabled daughter out of town,

Tania Clarence suffocated her three children and then tried to kill herself. She said she could "see no hope for the future" of her children and felt that their quality of life was more important than the length of their lives.

While Tania Clarence admitted to killing Ben, Max, and Olivia at home, she denied murdering them. The charges of murder were dropped in exchange for a guilty plea to manslaughter on the grounds of diminished responsibility.

In the words of the prosecutor: "It is clear on the evidence Mrs. Clarence killed her three children because she wanted to end their suffering and at the time she committed the act she could not see any alternative or any other way out of their joint suffering."

When I learned about this case, it hit me hard in the gut. You see, I have a similar disability as Ben, Max, and Olivia. The press on this case described spinal muscular atrophy as a "muscle-wasting" disease. In the media, words like *abnormalities*, *suffering*, *deformities*, and *life-limiting* are used to describe this condition that is my lived experience while failing to mention the impact of social support, adequate services, and disability pride.

In another world, in another set of conditions, with another set of parents, that could have easily been me. If I could speak to Ben, Max, and Olivia, I would say something like this:

Yes, you needed total help with your personal care.

Yes, your muscles were going to continually become weaker over time.

Yes, most people considered you vulnerable and "wasting away."

But you know what? I bet you also knew how to have fun, enjoy life, and dream big.

I wish that people didn't think that you were trapped in your body, powerless and filled with suffering.

I wish that the three of you lived until you were old enough to use a computer so we could connect.

I wish my disabled friends and I could have welcomed you to this funky crip universe and mentored you in whatever ways you wanted.

As a fellow disabled kindred spirit, please know this:

Even in death,

you are not alone.

You are valued.

You are remembered.

You are loved.

Ben, Max, and Olivia will never have a chance to write their own futures, to make their decisions, and to become their actualized selves, whether they lived to fifteen, forty-five, or eighty years old. Their mother robbed them of that choice because of her evaluation of their quality of life and societal worth. Tania Clarence got a plea bargain for what I believe is a hate crime and genocide.

And it is because of the murder of Ben, Max, Olivia, and countless other children and adults with disabilities at the hands of their parents, guardians, or care providers that I'm here at this vigil to honor the dead and fight like hell for the living.

I'd like to imagine a time when disabled people do not have to prove their humanity and defend their right to exist. So much work remains, and it is up to all of us to claw and lash out at our ableist oppressors, in all of ableism's insidious forms. We are here. We will not forget.

Just Say NOPE

These are just a few paraphrased examples of the kinds of ridiculous requests I get. I wish I could share all the bizarre responses from entitled people who don't seem to understand or respect my decisions.

Activist Wisdom

Good shit takes time. Extend time, bend time, crip time.

Prioritize your shit and let everything else flow from that.

If you can, back up your shit (external hard drive, cloud storage, etc.).

Make your shit as accessible as possible from the outset and keep refining your practices as you learn and grow.

Don't shit on other people's joy and celebration (this is what private group chats are for).

Compliments aren't everything.

Punch up, not down.

Keeping things under wraps until they're ready. > Oversharing.

There will be things that fall by the wayside or things you will forget. It's inevitable and do not beat yourself up over it.

Credit and shout-out people as often as possible. Be enthusiastic and loud about the people you love and those who are *doing the work*!

Be generous with your time and energy with the people you care about.

Don't use words or concepts you don't fully understand.

Your opinion or hot take isn't always needed or important. Ask yourself if you are really the right person for an opportunity, recommend others, and do not expect praise for "passing the mic."

Have the foresight to end certain things on a high note. Don't ever feel obligated to continue something unless you really want to do it.

Collaborate with people you trust, and if things don't work out, let it be a lesson for the future.

Fuck me over once, I'll learn from it. Fuck me over twice, you are dead to me.

Keep a folder or a spreadsheet to remember all the fuckers who are dead to you, with any screenshots or receipts for reference if needed.

Relationship building. > Empire building.

Embrace being selective and saying no.

Being a "very busy person" is not all that. Don't believe the capitalist hype.

One way to create boundaries and preempt any unrealistic expectations and requests is to set up an autoreply to your email accounts. Here's mine from 2022:

> **PLEASE NOTE** I am unable to reply to all requests for professional or personal advice. For speaking requests ONLY, please contact Emily Hartman at [redacted]. **DO NOT** send me unsolicited manuscripts or other work. This is for your protection! The Disability Visibility Project is **not** a disability rights organization, and it does **not** provide advocacy, referral, or social services. The D.V.P. is a one-person operation that creates media and offers consultation services. Thank you for understanding.

Build joy, pleasure, and care into your everyday life.

Access

Access for the sake of access or inclusion is not necessarily liberatory, but access done in the service of love, justice, connection, and community *is* liberatory and has the power to transform.

—MIA MINGUS

One of Those Aha Moments

An interview with Eric Koenig, former director of the Office of Student Life at the University of California, San Francisco (U.C.S.F.), at StoryCorps San Francisco (October 25, 2014). This conversation has been condensed and edited for clarity.

In 1987, there were two students with disabilities at U.C.S.F. By 2013, there were more than one hundred fifty students with disabilities. As a new student to U.C.S.F. in the late 1990s, Eric was one of the first people from the school whom I met.

ALICE WONG: I was a prospective student thinking about going to U.C.S.F., and I distinctly recall being very apprehensive, especially being from the Midwest and contemplating a move and the idea of going to graduate school plus having a visible disability, worrying about housing—you know, just basic how-to-live questions.

And I made a cold call through the directory, found your name, and you called me back. And I remember it was like in the evening in Indiana, and you were just so open and willing to talk about, you know, the challenges and what U.C.S.F. could realistically offer me, and I think, to me, that was just a revelation, because it was such a generous and wonderful gesture to have this conversation, and it really gave me some sense that there was a possibility that I should pursue this. So that led to a trip out to U.C.S.F., where I met with you, and I think we talked a lot about what if, what kind of plans would need to be made if I was accepted. We're not assuming I was accepted, but if I was, what were the plans in place that we would have to make.

ERIC KOENIG: I remember we had a number of conversations, and I guess I had been waiting to meet you before you contacted me. And I didn't know who would actually call, and you were the caller that I was expecting for a few years previous to your call. In some ways our timing was very good, because there were accessibility issues at the university, and you were asking about some very specific issues that needed to be resolved, housing in particular. And I think we both quickly understood one another [so] that there was a very collaborative style to begin with in our conversation, and as you articulated some of your concerns, I was able to articulate either how we could accommodate you or at least an attitude and a willingness to accommodate.

ALICE: Mm-hmm.

ERIC: And so I think, you know, our main issue was really about the lack of accessible housing; there really wasn't any appropriate accessible housing.

A photo taken by Yosmay del Mazo at Storycorps San Francisco in 2014. At the time I did not need to use my BiPap during the day. On the right is Eric Koenig.

ALICE: As I recall, it was right around that time the Aldea San Miguel student housing was still being built, and I think that would have been the accessible housing, but it was not available yet. So I think, you know, the main message that you communicated to me was that U.C.S.F. is somewhat small and unique and the sense that, you know, we can definitely try to figure things out together.

ERIC: Right.

ALICE: And I feel like U.C.S.F., at that time when I applied, was at a really interesting moment when I was able to get customized, individualized assistance, and that's really unique. Once I was accepted, many processes were put into motion. You connected me with the director of housing, and they did some renovations to faculty housing on Fifth Avenue, which is only a block away from the main campus. Within several months, I believe, the Housing Department was able to retrofit a bathroom, and that apartment was already on a garage ground floor. But it was really getting an accessible bathroom—that was a major thing to do, because that takes a long time to fund and plan any sort of change or renovation, and the fact that U.C.S.F. was committed to having this done before I arrived really meant a lot to me as a student because, you know, I already felt so [*laughs*], you know, really, like, singular in a lot of ways.

I am certainly not the first student with a physical disability at U.C.S.F., but I feel like [one of the few]. There have been others, right, to your knowledge?

ERIC: Yeah. The campus was an interesting mix of being kind of behind the curve in terms of being accessible, but also, we did really well in responding when students were coming with whatever needs that they may have that we were not equipped to deal with. And so I think what I was trying to communicate to you in our phone calls was, if you're willing to be a pioneer and be the first one and understand that change will need to occur, I believed that the change would occur. And so we weren't accessible, or we weren't properly accessible [*laughs*], I should say, but by being present and by being willing to accept some temporary accommodations that you and your family were very gracious about, you understood that by coming to campus, the campus would then make the changes that were, you know, appropriate and accessible.

I just wanna comment on your ability to connect with people and to educate and advocate and to assess an institutional environment. Your instincts around how to prompt change are just superb. And you're also extremely adaptive [at] figuring out, you know, who the allies are and how to connect with steering committees, advisory groups, and so those are really important attributes. It's not always easy for people with disabilities who are in environments [that are] not as accommodating as they would like [them] to be. It really represented a really positive model of change: how to connect with the members of the community and to help them understand some of the challenges and really effect change that improves the environment for everyone, not just people with disabilities.

ALICE: Well, I really do feel like we were equal partners in this. And that's what most people wouldn't imagine between a student and an administrator, you know, having this kind of power dynamic, but I really feel like we both worked so well together at these broader aims. And there was this opening, but I think part of it, too, is the institutional culture at U.C.S.F. When I arrived in '97, there were still a lot of issues and, you know, that was all laid out clearly for me, and I accepted it, and I thought, *I think I can work with these people on campus to make it a better place.*

ERIC: The style and attitude with which I used to approach my job, or at least my area of services for students with disabilities, was really that the students were the experts, and I needed to know from each student what their needs were, especially in cases when, you know, we hadn't served a student with a particular disability or requiring a certain kind of accommodation or facing a certain set of challenges. I was always interested in knowing what worked for the student before. I got a lot of guidance from students, and I got a lot from you.

It was fun to see how the A.D.A. started to change things. There was a large committee [of] all the different stakeholders that were affected by changes in accessibility requirements: parking and transportation and facilities design, the architects and designers and so forth on the campus. And so there was a large group that was formed and certain changes were prioritized right away. [But] because of budget, not everything was done, and you know, later on when you arrived, you pointed out the elevator buttons were vertical, and some people who use chairs couldn't reach the higher buttons to get to the higher floors.

ALICE: 'Cause there's, like, so many floors and there's, like, several rows of vertical buttons. There's absolutely no way to [reach them all from a sitting position,] and I remember we met with one of the people in facilities management or an architect, and I proposed adding an additional panel, a horizontal panel, and he's like, "Oh, we can do that!" And now there are horizontal panels on these elevators that are used by visitors, patients, staff, students, and whenever I see it, it makes me smile, because I know that it started with my individual need, but these simple accommodations really make a difference in everybody's lives.

ERIC: It's the universal design.

ALICE: And I notice in elevators able-bodied people who—let's say that the elevator is full—they'll use the side buttons because they are by the side of the elevator door. They can't get to the front where all the buttons are, so I see how everybody is using them and that makes me so happy.

ERIC: The elevator-button story is, I think, one of the greatest ones that we worked on [while] on campus, and I, too, whenever I walk

Horizontal and vertical elevator buttons inside an elevator at the U.C.S.F. Ambulatory Care Center, 400 Parnassus Avenue, San Francisco.

in an elevator on that campus, I actually think of you. [It] is a really beautiful story about how change occurs, because what happened was, if I'm recalling this correctly, the Muni stop [at Arguello Boulevard and Irving Street] was made accessible, which gave you much better options for traveling independently on public transportation. The bad news was the stop was near an elevator in the dark corner of a basement of a building. [And] one evening at ten thirty or eleven at night, you were waiting [by yourself because you couldn't reach the buttons inside] the elevator. And that's a safety problem, and I immediately thought, okay, one, this change should occur. But two, you know, a member of our campus community or a patient or visitor could be compromised in a position, you know, of safety. And so we used that and got together with key people. And I think we actually went to an elevator . . .

ALICE: I think I had [to demonstrate it,] and I think having a real person who uses it really sealed the deal for these engineers. And they were like, "Oh, yeah, we can do that." They saw and they got it.

ERIC: Right. It was one of those aha moments where people who are in design positions and maintenance positions never—it never occurred to them.

I really love this story, because the campus has a lot of elevators, and at first, the folks we were dealing with, you know, looked at it and the wheels were turning, going, "Yeah, we should do something," and then the dollar signs were starting to turn over. And so the approach that we took was, well, what are your paths of travel?

They were managing the budget issues [and] wanted you to be accommodated, but they then made a commitment, and every time an elevator was gonna be renovated a horizontal pattern would be included. I thought it was just a beautiful example of an institutional change, recognizing that a member of the campus community could not freely and independently move around the campus, so they let you provide a list and say, "Here's where I go."

ALICE: Yeah.

ERIC: And they did it. Ultimately, they didn't even wait to renovate the elevators. They just started putting them everywhere. Again, you were in a position to point out a need and did so in a very gracious, certainly assertive [manner], and you engaged the right people.

ALICE: And this is where [this] partnership works, where you connect me with your [colleagues], and you were with me in these conversations and meetings and that added a lot of weight. It wasn't just this student coming to see this engineer or architect. It's this idea that offices that serve students with disabilities really should be the advocates and allies of the student.

Why Disabled People Drop Out

A TWITTER THREAD

Alice Wong 王美華 ✔ @SFdirewolf · Apr 24, 2019
Really appreciating everyone's powerful stories with the
#WhyDisabledPeopleDropout tag.

Here's my not-so-brief story.

I loved sociology ever since high school and knew the humanities & social sciences was my jam. [thread]

💬 7   🔁 163   ♡ 348   ⬆   ılı   W

Alice Wong 王美華 ✔ @SFdirewolf · Apr 24, 2019
Replying to @SFdirewolf
I experienced a major healthcare crisis in my first year of college that forced me to take time off. When I was ready to return, there were cuts to Medicaid in my state that decreased my hours of home health aides.

💬 1   🔁 10   ♡ 75   ⬆   ılı   W

Alice Wong 王美華 ✔ @SFdirewolf · Apr 24, 2019   ⋯
Paying college tuition on top of attendant care was exorbitant and unrealistic. I decided to stay home & commute to my local university. I would then plot and claw my way out of Indiana. While it was rough, I found some great friends & teachers during my undergrad years.

💬 1   🔁 9   ♡ 78   ⬆   ılı   W

Alice Wong 王美華 ✔ @SFdirewolf · Apr 24, 2019   ⋯
I wanted to be like my professors: writing, researching, teaching. Creating knowledge. Disabled scholars like Irving K Zola & Barbara Waxman Fiduccia were the few out there who gave me hope. The same for the historian Paul Longmore.

💬 1   🔁 12   ♡ 86   ⬆   ılı   W

Alice Wong 王美華 ✅ @SFdirewolf · Apr 24, 2019   ···

I was strategic in applying for PhD programs in California and was thrilled to be accepted in a medical sociology program where I wanted to focus on the sociology of disability & qualitative research

💬 1   🔁 9   ♡ 90   ⬆   ıl| W

Alice Wong 王美華 ✅ @SFdirewolf · Apr 24, 2019   ···

Hooo whee, I felt like such a suburban bumpkin when I arrived. There were about 7 in my cohort and everyone was so sophisticated & smart, some with already established careers & multiple degrees.

💬 1   🔁 8   ♡ 63   ⬆   ıl| W

Alice Wong 王美華 ✅ @SFdirewolf · Apr 24, 2019   ···

I was one of the few physically disabled grad students at this health sciences campus and was a guinea pig of sorts on accessibility & other services for students w/ disabilities (late 1990s)

💬 1   🔁 11   ♡ 86   ⬆   ıl| W

Alice Wong 王美華 ✅ @SFdirewolf · Apr 24, 2019   ···

2 things immediately became clear in my first few years of grad school: I struggled academically and felt completely out of depth. I also hit a wall of sorts, I didn't realize how hard I've been pushing my bodymind ever since junior high. I was spent and could not keep up.

💬 2   🔁 9   ♡ 100   ⬆   ıl| W

Alice Wong 王美華 ✅ @SFdirewolf · Apr 24, 2019   ···

I ended up taking incompletes and kept renewing them. It was awful because I felt guilty and the longer it took the more stuck I felt. It got to the point where my advisor met with me and gave me an ultimatum to finish my coursework and complete my qualifying exams

💬 2   🔁 9   ♡ 85   ⬆   ıl| W

Alice Wong 王美華 ✅ @SFdirewolf · Apr 24, 2019   ···

And dear reader, I stuck to the agreed upon schedule and finished the work. The question was whether to advance and start the dissertation phase. It seemed impossible to complete a PhD based on me barely getting by the first 2 years. I felt like a failure.

💬 1   🔁 11   ♡ 95   ⬆   ıl| W

Alice Wong 王美華 ✔ @SFdirewolf · Apr 24, 2019   ···
Internalized ableism made me think that having a PhD would give me more cultural capital and opportunities. It became clear to me that my heath & wellness was more important. I also realized I could still be involved in research but as a staff member, not faculty

💬 2   ↻ 20   ♡ 126   ⬆   ⅼⅼⅼ   W

Alice Wong 王美華 ✔ @SFdirewolf · Apr 24, 2019   ···
So I ended up with what the school called a terminal Masters because the program didn't really offer a Masters. I just completed enough to leave with something. It still felt like an asterisk on my achievements and something that was short of what I expected from myself

💬 1   ↻ 10   ♡ 88   ⬆   ⅼⅼⅼ   W

Alice Wong 王美華 ✔ @SFdirewolf · Apr 24, 2019   ···
Years later one professor from my program came up & apologized to me. He said he wished the department did more to support me. They weren't ready for me and I didn't listen to or care enough for my bodymind. The rigor & relentless pace was impossible to sustain

💬 1   ↻ 21   ♡ 134   ⬆   ⅼⅼⅼ   W

Alice Wong 王美華 ✔ @SFdirewolf · Apr 24, 2019   ···
I ended up working 10+ years as a staff research associate at that very school and had a rewarding time. I was able to work on projects & grow as a scholar. I also ended up becoming more involved with activism & community scholarship

💬 1   ↻ 14   ♡ 116   ⬆   ⅼⅼⅼ   W

Alice Wong 王美華 ✔ @SFdirewolf · Apr 24, 2019   ···
I don't regret my decision to drop out. It was an act of liberation and led me to where I am today which is exactly what I was meant to be.

But my memories of the pain, the loneliness, the insecurity, the anxiety, and lack of support still haunts me.

💬 4   ↻ 24   ♡ 188   ⬆   ⅼⅼⅼ   W

Alice Wong 王美華 ✔ @SFdirewolf · Apr 24, 2019   ···
Every once in a while I wonder what I could have offered to the academy, what my contributions would have been to the fields of disability studies & medical sociology. It would have been epic, but that's their loss and we'll never know.

So ends my #WhyDisabledPeopleDropout story

Excerpt from:

My Day as a Robot

Ability Tools blog (May 1, 2018)

Resistance to assistive technology is futile. As a sci-fi nerd, I have to make a *Star Trek* reference whenever I talk about technology and disabled people. The disability community is living in the darkest timeline right now—at least, that's what it feels like under the Trump administration in the United States; yet at the same time we are living in an age of the internet, social media, and technology, which have revolutionized the way we connect, communicate, and participate in social life.

While activists continue to fight for disability rights and against attacks on the safety net and multiple marginalized communities, it's important to take time and reflect on the amazing, fun things that happen to all of us. This is one of my stories.

In 2015, I was invited to the White House for a celebration of the twenty-fifth anniversary of the Americans with Disabilities Act. At the time, I served as a member of the National Council on Disability and had launched the Disability Visibility Project the year before. I don't travel anymore by plane for a number of reasons and did not plan to attend. This is a fact of life, and it took some time for me to adjust and reconcile. It's a major bummer to miss meetings, opportunities, and social events because of my disability (and larger systemic factors), but I've reached a place where I try to focus on ways I can participate remotely or behind the scenes. FOMO (fear of missing out) is a form of internalized ableism! I came to this conclusion after decades of being sad about missing events because of lack of access.

Maria Town, who served as senior associate director for the White House's Office of Public Engagement, followed up with me and told me that I could attend the event thanks to arrangements they made allowing me to use a Beam Pro telepresence robot. I had presumed I simply couldn't attend and didn't even think an online accommodation was possible. I was incredibly touched and thankful to Maria and everyone involved with the event who made this possible and hope to see this more widespread at the White House.

A telepresence robot looks like a computer screen attached to legs with a base and wheels. Using my laptop at home, I could see everything with its webcam, and everyone could see and hear me as well. I could independently move around physical spaces by navigating using the arrows on my keyboard. It was very simple to use.

A screenshot taken from my laptop as I operated a telepresence robot in the White House. The image shows three file windows: First, a view from the robot's perspective of the Blue Room, where a marine in white dress uniform is introducing me to President Barack Obama, who is looking right at me. Second, a smaller file window below the first that shows the wheels of the robot so I don't encounter any obstacles. And third, a file window on the right side of the screenshot that shows my laptop camera's view, which is the image people see when they look at the robot. In the image, I am smiling with my mouth wide open in delight from my bedroom.

Of course, I started live-tweeting my experiences, capturing screenshots of what I saw during the event. This was a major adventure and I had to document it! I got to "walk" around the Blue Room and Green Room while waiting in a queue to meet President Obama. This was something I did not expect—I was already excited just to attend the celebration.

My memory is a bit blurry on what I said to President Obama; our meeting couldn't have been more than five minutes, but he was definitely interested in my presence as a robot. I got a chance to demonstrate how I could move around, and near the end we posed for a photo. A copy of that photo is now framed and in my living room. It's a priceless memento of an unforgettable experience.

Many disabled people right now are using assistive technology that allows them to participate fully in society. I wrestle and think about the privileges I have when it comes to access to technology: I can afford a smartphone, a laptop, and broadband internet service. I don't face accessibility barriers when using YouTube, Twitter, or Facebook. I am able to access and process online content with relative ease.

I wish all disabled people had what they need in order to live the lives they want. The realities of poverty, ableism, the digital divide, and many other factors keep assistive technologies, services, and devices away from the people who could benefit from them the most. In an ideal world, I'd buy a Beam Pro for myself, but that is way out of my budget. Even if I had one, I'd need to make arrangements to ship it to the location and have someone on-site set it up, charge it, and ship it back. For people who use it as part of their work or education, I hope this is considered a reasonable accommodation if requested. Outside of work or education, there are so many other uses for a telepresence robot: meeting up with friends, traveling, enjoying life outdoors.

All technology is assistive technology—the term itself may be outmoded someday. So many products that exist now were never developed specifically for disabled people yet are used as such. I love the blurring of these boundaries and look forward to a post-robot world.

An official White House photo by Pete Souza showing President Barack Obama greeting me in the Blue Room on July 20, 2015, in the form of a telepresence robot.

An official White House photo by Pete Souza showing President Barack Obama standing next to me, in the form of a telepresence robot, on July 20, 2015.

Excerpt from:

Net Neutrality, Accessibility, and the Disability Community

MediaJustice blog (November 22, 2017)

Let's face it, social media can be a troll-infested, fetid dumpster fire. There are days when I don't want to be online. Though I try to practice self-care, I invariably return to the internet because it is my second home, my playground, and my workshop.

Net neutrality is important to me because the internet and social media are essential tools in my activism and social participation. I'm the founder of the Disability Visibility Project, an online community dedicated to creating, sharing, and amplifying disability media and culture. With the D.V.P., I've been able to build a community and amplify our media to the public with Twitter chats, a podcast, and blog posts. As a copartner in #CripTheVote, I've seen firsthand the power of hashtags that create a space for action and conversation. Without net neutrality, I wouldn't have the same reach, platform, or voice.

The internet is also where I go to find support, solidarity, and friendship across time and space. Some disabled people like me encounter barriers while being out or are isolated socially and geographically. There are disabled people who cannot leave their beds and are badass activists with incredible social media presence because of the internet. It is a literal lifeline for many, including myself. For me, net neutrality is a civil right.

Pre-internet, I felt socially isolated and rarely saw myself reflected in media. I didn't realize I was part of an incredibly powerful and vibrant community until I found my people online, especially other disabled people of color. Since it's difficult for me to attend protests or large events in person, social media is my main mode of civic and political engagement. I use the internet as a tool to create community, share our stories, and push back at the predominant narratives about disability. And on a self-serving note, my blog posts and podcast episodes can't reach people without an open internet, so without it, folks are gonna miss out on all my glorious knowledge.

Even with a free and open internet, there are major issues that prevent us from fully engaging and harnessing our power. According to a 2016 Pew Research Center survey, people with disabilities consistently have lower rates of broadband service usage and ownership of smartphones, computers, or tablets, compared with people without disabilities. The digital divide is real and wide for the disability community. Economic reasons are one part of the equation, but another major problem is the resistance of individuals, corporations, and institutions to follow web accessibility standards and other regulations.

Imagine if you could access only a small percentage of YouTube videos or podcasts. This is the current media landscape that Deaf and disabled people experience: videos without captions, radio without text transcripts, images without alt text, or apps that don't work with one's assistive technology. Imagine not being able to apply for jobs or access services through online portals because of your disability. Imagine trying to take the same online courses with your classmates at universities that refuse to comply with the Americans with Disabilities Act.

Here's my public service announcement to everyone: Stop creating inaccessible media and tech. Stop discriminating against disabled people who have the right to the same information, services, and content as everyone else.

To quote from *Hamilton*, "I wanna be in the room where

it happens." A free and open internet allows me to be in every boardroom, classroom, homeroom, back room, playroom, and beyond. A free and open internet allows me to take up and hold space unapologetically. A free and open internet allows me to be me. We all deserve to be in the room where it happens.

Internet access is power. This power belongs to everyone, not a handful of corporations.

The Last Straw

Eater (July 19, 2018)

I live in the Mission District of San Francisco, where delicious taquerias, bakeries, cafés, and bars are everywhere. And as a disabled person who uses a wheelchair to get around and a ventilator to breathe, the pleasure of eating and drinking is mediated by a number of factors. When I leave my home for a latte or burrito, a number of calculations go through my head: Will the place have its door propped open so I can enter? If the door is closed, will someone exiting or entering open it for me? Is the counter low enough for the server to see me? Can they hear and understand me with the mask over my nose if it's incredibly noisy inside? Will I be able to sign my name on the touchscreen or receipt, depending on the counter height?

At one of my favorite neighborhood places, Sightglass Coffee, when I make my order I feel comfortable asking for and receiving assistance. I'll ask the barista to bring my drink to my table since I cannot reach the high counters or carry a full cup. I'll even ask for help adding sugar when I'm feeling indulgent, because a glass dispenser is too heavy for me to lift. When I'm at any café, two items I always ask for with my drinks are a lid and a plastic straw, emphasis on plastic. Lids prevent spillage when I'm navigating bumpy sidewalks and curb cuts; straws are necessary because I do not have the hand and arm strength to lift a drink and tip it into my mouth. Plastic straws are the best when I drink hot liquids; compostable ones tend to melt or break apart.

It's not easy or pleasant asking for help in public spaces like restaurants, because you never know what attitudes you'll encounter: indifference, pity, or outright rejection. I don't see these types of help as special treatment or inspirational for someone to surreptitiously post on social media as feel-good clickbait; they're simply examples of excellent hospitality.

Plastic is seen as cheap, "anti-luxury," wasteful, and harmful to the environment. All true. Plastic is also an essential part of my health and wellness. With my neuromuscular disability, plastic straws are necessary tools for my hydration and nutrition. Currently, plastic single-use straws are the latest target by environmentalists in the move toward zero waste. Major restaurant groups such as Union Square Hospitality Group and companies such as Starbucks and others in the travel industry announced plans to phase out single-use plastics.

Starbucks's announcement—and the news that Vancouver and Seattle recently banned plastic straws, with other cities, like New York and San Francisco, contemplating proposals—struck a raw nerve with me for several reasons (and I won't even get into the problems of recyclable plastics and greenwashing):

1. Plastic straws are considered unnecessary items used by environmentalists as a "gateway plastic" to engage the public in a larger conversation about waste. According to Dune Ives, executive director of the Lonely Whale Foundation, "Plastic straws are social tools and props, the perfect conversation starter." But one person's social prop is another person's conduit for nutrition. It's as if people who rely on straws—older adults, children, and disabled people—don't matter and our needs are less important than the environment. I feel erased by these attitudes.

2. Plastic straws are ubiquitous, whether we like it or not. Once you have something that provides access, it is difficult and harmful to take it away from a marginalized community that depends on it. I live in a world that was never built for me, and every little bit of access is treasured and hard-won. Bans on plastic straws are regressive, not progressive.

The plastic straw ban is symptomatic of larger systemic issues when it comes to the continual struggle for disability rights and justice. The Americans with Disabilities Act turns twenty-eight next week, on July 26, and yet people with disabilities continue to face barriers at eating establishments. The A.D.A. is considered by many small businesses (and the National Restaurant Association) as a source of frivolous lawsuits brought by greedy lawyers and clients. Ableist attitudes that cast disabled people as "fakers" or "complainers" obscure the very real and painful experiences of not being able to eat and drink freely.

As demand increases for alternatives to plastic, so do the voices from the disability community sharing their concerns about how these bans will create additional labor, hurdles, and difficulties. On social media, many disabled people have been sharing their stories and keeping it 100 percent real. I observed and experienced all sorts of microaggressions and outright dismissal of what disabled people are saying online.

People have told me that I still have access to biodegradable straws at Starbucks, despite my reasons for using plastic ones. People have told me to bring my own reusable straws without thinking about the extra work that entails. Why should a disabled customer have to bring something in order to drink while nondisabled people have the convenience and ability to use what is provided for free? This is not just, equitable, or hospitable.

This is the experience of living in a world that was never built for you: having to explain and defend yourself while providing infinite amounts of labor at the demand of people who do not recognize their nondisabled privilege. There are days when I want to put this on repeat: "Believe disabled people. Period." I refuse to apologize or feel shame about the way my body works and how I navigate the world. Everyone consumes goods and creates waste. We all do what we can to reduce, reuse, and recycle. We should recognize that different needs require different solutions. I'm not a monster for using plastic straws or other plastic items that allow me to live, such as oxygen tubes.

Restaurants are theater; they are also highly politicized, contested spaces. There are times when I go out and the waiter asks my companion for my order instead of me. I've gone through creepy, dirty side entrances just to get into a restaurant. I've been called "the wheelchair" by front-of-house staff when they commiserate on which table to place me, since I apparently take up too much space. I also love the places where I feel welcomed and respected. As they provide thoughtful and authentic hospitality, I respond by being a loyal customer who appreciates the little touches that make a visit enjoyable.

The ban in Seattle comes with an exemption for people with disabilities, where restaurants can provide plastic straws upon request for medical reasons. This is optional for restaurants, so they may choose not to make any available. What people don't understand with bans like this is that having to ask for a plastic straw puts an unfair burden and scrutiny on people with disabilities. They should not have to prove a medical need or even disclose their disability status when having a fun night out with friends. This is not hospitality.

So where do we go from here? How can we cultivate accessible and hospitable environments while reducing waste? Until someone invents a compostable straw with the functionality of a plastic one, I have a modest proposal for establishments that have banned plastic straws and those that are considering it:

- If you are an establishment with straws at a counter, provide both types, clearly labeled, for people to choose from. If a café or restaurant wants to provide straws by request, have the servers offer plastic and biodegradable versions, just as they would give any customer a choice of still or sparkling water, so as to avoid alienating an entire group. Customers can choose what is best for them.
- Reexamine the kinds of plastic you use in your establishment (e.g., plastic wrap, containers) and find additional ways to reduce your consumption.
- Expand your ideas about hospitality and accessibility; they are one and the same.
- Think about the intentional and unintentional barriers your establishment sets that may keep people from visiting your place. Listen and learn from your customers' critiques, including disabled customers. Don't wait for protests or boycotts before engaging with the disability community (I see you, Starbucks).

   If cafés can offer four types of milk for espresso drinks and restaurants fifty types of wine and beer, small businesses and large corporations can manage offering two types of straws. The key is to have the same level of access for all items. You can accommodate all your customers while reducing waste at the same time. Customers respond to choice and flexibility.
   Because in the end, isn't it all about welcoming everyone into your space with authentic and inclusive hospitality?

. . .

Submitted to the clerk of the board of supervisors, the assistant clerk for the Land Use and Transportation Committee, and the board of supervisors of the City and County of San Francisco

July 31, 2018

Hello, President Cohen and Supervisors Brown, Fewer, Kim, Mandelman, Peskin, Ronen, Safai, Stefani, Tang, and Yee,

My name is Alice Wong. I am a resident of District 9 and a disabled person who uses plastic straws for various drinks when outside of the home. I humbly ask you to vote no on item #29 in today's agenda.

I may be one of the few people in the city not in favor of the Food Service Waste Reduction Ordinance and I would like to explain why.

The current exemption for people with disabilities in the ordinance is unclear and inadequate: "Strict compliance with this Chapter 16 is not required in instances where it would interfere with accommodating for any person's medical needs" (page 11, lines 6–7).

What does "strict compliance" mean to businesses? What is the difference between "compliance" and "strict compliance"? Won't most businesses find this confusing?

The exemption needs additional language requiring businesses to keep plastic straws in stock and available upon request. Without explicitly including this in the ordinance, businesses will have no obligation to provide this option to individuals. Having this language in the implementation plan is not the same.

Regarding the usage of "medical needs" in the ordinance, you are suggesting customers must disclose, explain, or identify their needs in pathological terms? This sets up an expectation by businesses that customers like me must look a certain way or mention a diagnosis of some sort to obtain a plastic straw. Some needs are not apparent. Ideally, any person should receive a plastic straw if requested without scrutiny or skepticism. This is the weakness of an exemption that places hurdles in front of customers that didn't exist before.

I applaud Supervisor Tang and others who use reusable straws for their favorite drinks. However, there are other people in our community for whom biodegradable and reusable options are hazardous and unhygienic. This is an issue of privilege and equity. Not everyone has a caregiver or dishwasher machine to sanitize these reusable straws. People on limited incomes struggle to buy food and pay rent, let alone purchase an item that used to be widely available. Besides, why should people with disabilities have to bring their own utensils to drink if nondisabled people don't have to?

Sustainability and zero waste goals should be flexible enough that they don't come at a cost of excluding marginalized communities. The ordinance in its current form sends a message to older adults and people with disabilities that their access to drinking and nutrition doesn't matter and that they are *bleep* out of luck if their local café no longer carries plastic straws. My need is not medical, it is due to a lack of access. I urge you to take a step back and revise the ordinance in partnership with community stakeholders who will be adversely impacted if passed.

Sincerely,

Alice Wong
Founder and Director
Disability Visibility Project

. . .

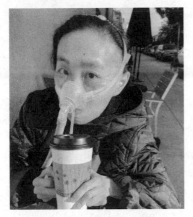

A photo taken by my friend Allie Cannington of me looking devilish with a coffee cup and a straw at an outdoor café.

August 27, 2018

TO: Supervisor Katy Tang
Ashley Summers, legislative aide to Supervisor Tang
Debbie Raphael, director, S.F. Environment
Nicole Bohn, director, Mayor's Office on Disability

FROM: Alice Wong
Disabled resident, District 9

RE: FOOD SERVICE WASTE REDUCTION ORDINANCE AMENDMENT

Hello! I enjoyed being on the phone during the disability community stakeholder meeting on August 23. I hope you got a sense of the lived experiences of disabled people and why our usage of plastic straws is tied to our ability to participate in society. At the end of the letter I included additional stories by people with disabilities. Please check them out if you have time.

Here are a few elements I would like to see in Supervisor Tang's amendment in a revised exemption:

1) All food service providers must be required to make plastic straws available upon request. Without this requirement,

providers can opt out and effectively exclude parts of the disability community.

2) Replace the words *medical needs* with *access needs* in the amendment and in any signage created by S.F. Environment for food service providers.

3) There must be parallel access to straws. The key is not to add a new hurdle for people with disabilities who need them. For example, if a café has compostable straws by request only, the same goes for plastic ones. If a café leaves a stack available at the counter, the same for plastic ones.

4) Clear signage by food service providers on the availability of plastic straws if they are by request only.

5) Include clear guidelines in the amendment to food service providers that people requesting plastic straws do not need to identify, disclose, or prove their disability. Just ask and they'll get one, no questions asked. This should be included in any signage, media campaign, or guidance by S.F. Environment.

As a next step, perhaps you could host another stakeholder meeting with more specifics about the amendment before the next Land Use Committee hearing on this issue? We need to have ample notice to prepare our public comments before any hearing. We deserve to see how much of our expertise and input appears in the proposed amendment.

After all, what is the point of participating in listening sessions if we cannot influence policy that directly impacts us?

Respectfully,

Alice Wong
Disabled activist, lover of coffee,
and Mission District resident

Excerpt from:

Ode to a Spit Cup

Body Talk: 37 Voices Explore Our Radical Anatomy
(edited by Kelly Jensen)

Spit. Drool. Saliva. Our bodies secrete this clear liquid every day, up to two liters a day. Depending on your hydration, diet, medication, and other factors, saliva can be watery, sticky, bubbly, and infused with whatever is in your mouth at the moment. Bodily fluids can be endlessly fascinating, and I developed a brand-new respect for saliva because of my increased difficulty with swallowing.

I consider my power chair an extension of my body. It is part of my personal space and sense of self. In the last few years, I gained another bodily extension: my spit cup.

What is a spit cup? Very simply, it's a cup I keep nearby so I can spit my saliva rather than swallowing it. I was born with a neuromuscular disability, meaning all my muscles progressively weaken. Over time, the direction of my body's trajectory has always headed downward, its pace unknown. I stopped walking around the age of seven and developed severe scoliosis that required a spinal fusion surgery at fourteen years old. Complications after this surgery added new concerns on top of lack of mobility. As my diaphragm muscles weakened, being able to sleep and breathe became a major issue. I had breathing treatments with a nebulizer and intermittent positive pressure breathing machine, used oxygen at night, and other interventions that kept me going until I developed respiratory failure at eighteen years old. With severe sleep apnea, I needed to sleep at night with a BiPap machine or else I could die from respiratory failure.

I can still swallow, but it's actually quite tiring over a single day. The spit cup provides a shortcut and a way to preempt possible aspiration in case things go down the wrong pipe. My spit cup has become my new friend, a brilliant adaptation, and a source of wonderment.

I'm now hyperaware of two interconnected bodily functions: my ability to breathe and swallow. Previously, breathing was the top priority. I continue to fear the tremendous toll getting sick with the flu took on my body as I tried to cough out my secretions. I still worry about the amount of battery life on my BiPap machine when I am out for a long time or during a power outage. Whenever I eat a full meal, I cannot talk or breathe comfortably. Through all these concerns and changes, I adapted. I reduced my exposure to crowds during flu seasons. When I needed my BiPap the entire day, I got the machine connected to my wheelchair battery for extended life. I changed my diet and focused on high-fat, high-protein meals to make the most out of every bite. I scheduled smaller meals and snacks to lessen the feeling of distension.

When I wear my BiPap, there is a set number of breaths that the machine produces per minute. These breaths are not initiated by me; my rhythm is dictated by the machine. When I talk there are "unnatural" pauses because of the incoming breaths. Swallowing becomes complicated when you're working on a machine's timetable. I can't just swallow my saliva or anything else whenever I want; I have to time it right after a breath. Sometimes a breath comes in while mid-swallow, which causes me to panic and choke. The BiPap has given me an incredible amount of respiratory support, and I know my life span and my ability to conserve my energy have increased because of it. But since I cannot separate it from my body, I have to work within this technical ecosystem as conditions evolve and shift.

Maintaining my ability to breathe is the undercurrent that drives my life's activities. Within the last five years, swallowing is the second major function that has reshaped the direction and orientation of my world. Imagine how many times humans swallow food, liquids, or saliva in a twenty-four-hour period. Think of the nerves and muscles involved in chewing, swallowing, and breathing that work almost effortlessly for most people.

As I grow weaker, I become more in tune with the constant rhythms of breathing-swallowing-eating-talking. I appreciate the sophistication of how each action is interlocked with the others and how fragile one can be when these functions are no longer set on autopilot. I used to choke on the simplest things: a drink, a tiny bit of saliva, laughing while eating. Aspirating creates a chain reaction that feels like a life-and-death situation. I frantically try to breathe, and no air can come in. My eyes suddenly bulge and tear up, and my face becomes flush as I struggle to cough, clawing and grasping at my mortality. Everything tenses up and then slowly eases as the trachea relaxes and opens up again. By then, my face is a wet, sticky mess, my breaths ragged and irregular, soggy tissues scattered everywhere, yet filled with relief to be alive.

Is saliva my enemy? I don't think so. It's always present and an important part of the digestion process. Aspiration shocks my system, reminding me of the frailty of life and of human vulnerability. Rather than hating and fighting it, taking medications to reduce it, or being depressed about the growing difficulties with yet another major bodily function, I started using a spit cup as a D.I.Y. hedge against frequent choking. It gave my esophagus muscles a break, however slight. The spit cup was a gift to myself, a literal life hack.

I learned how to present myself and move through spaces with this new accessory. Outside of the body, saliva is seen as gross and messy by our culture's standards. Spitting and drooling in public is gauche. It's also an act that is infantilized,

A clear plastic cup filled with tissues that are soaked with saliva and streaked with brown from something chocolatey.

making it easy to feel shame and internalized ableism. I had to work through my self-consciousness, holding the cup to the side, handling it carefully, discreetly spitting in a paper cup when out with friends. I worried about accidental spillage (and yes, it's happened a few times) and people staring or looking at the cup's contents. But the biggest thing I had to confront was my aversion to seeing my spit in significant quantities.

Every day, my spit looks different when it's in a cup. It can be kind of icky, but, like my body, it's ultimately a work of avant-garde art. It's swirled with food and stained with rainbow hues from liquids such as coffee and soup. I can produce spit that looks like soft dollops of cappuccino foam after talking animatedly with someone, or solid pieces of mucus from my nose that dripped back and came out from my mouth, or abstract formations and sculptures as the spit soaks into tissues that I stick inside the cup to prevent spillage. This is something that my body produces on the regular, and seeing it outside places it in an entirely different context. Maybe I can become the Yayoi Kusama of saliva art?!

Seeing my spit and being in contact with it every day demonstrates the amazing beauty and intimacy of the human body. Saliva serves me and I am also at its mercy. The spit cup is an indicator of my disability's progression. My spit cup is a public signifier that this bodymind is hella creative.

When we think of interdependence, we often think about relationships with people and with communities. As my body has changed, I have become more enmeshed with objects and see them as part of this complex web that provides the infrastructure for my survival. My cyborg body is tethered to orbiting satellites of objects. These bits of hardware, machines, and everyday objects may not live and breathe, but they are a part of me. They simultaneously ground me and liberate me. They center me and allow me to make the most out of my life.

Like breathing, swallowing saliva is an invisible taken-for-granted task most bodies perform all the time. My disability forces me to listen to my body and MacGyver the hell out of it. I am as grateful for my cyborg existence as I am grateful to my ever-trusty spit cup.

Getting to the Marrow

In my family I am infamous for being a 馋裴 chán pēi, a term my Shandongnese parents use to describe a person who craves food and is a bit of a rascal. Hard to translate, but I describe it as someone who thinks a lot about food, dreams up certain dishes, delights in eating, and has particular preferences for how, when, and what to eat. A picky connoisseur cat times a bajillion. In short, I can be a pain in the ass about food.

I like scones split in half, spread with butter, broiled until a golden crisp, and slathered with strawberry or peach preserves. I like eating only the skin and fat of soy braised pork belly and pig trotters or roast duck. I like the crispy bits of a muffin or cookie and will nibble around the edges like a snobby squirrel. I like twice-fried duck-fat french fries with aioli or ranch dressing (made with real herbs and buttermilk). I like thin crust pizza where the bottom has a cracker crunch and the toppings don't droop in a soggy-ass mess. Microwaving leftovers is fine, but reheating a dish in the oven or on the stove is better (even though that requires more work). Did I mention I can be a pain in the ass?

In our family I help out by finding recipes to try, ordering food online, and making grocery lists. The bossy cat in me keeps us organized and stocked up so we don't have to stare at the refrigerator wondering what to make for dinner since my parents need to eat healthy, low-carb meals while I am on the opposite end of the spectrum. When I get super hyped about my next treat—for example, Japanese-style Basque cheesecakes from Basuku Cheesecakes (they are legit stellar)—my parents say my eyes are too big for my stomach. The tragedy of having unbridled enthusiasm and limited space in my tumtum is what it means to be a 馋裴 chán pēi, too.

I center much of my day around eating, and being a 馋裴 chán pēi has kept me alive in more ways than one. When I was younger, I ate almost everything with gusto. Before I had spinal fusion surgery, I wore a fiberglass body brace that kept me upright and pushed my torso into a corseted vise. I would ask my parents to loosen the straps after eating a huge, delicious meal, and it was sweeeeeet relief! It might be a dinner of comfort food, such as barbecue ribs, mashed potatoes and gravy, corn, and apple pie from Gray Bros. Cafeteria in Mooresville, Indiana, or a corned beef on rye with mustard, a potato latke (grated, not shredded) with applesauce, and macaroni and cheese at Shapiro's Delicatessen in Indianapolis in the 1980s. The drive back home with a loosened brace allowed me to breathe easier and digest my full belly. It was the *best* feeling! I am so thankful that my parents never made me feel self-conscious about eating or being a "noncompliant" patient. Both of my parents knew hunger, having grown up in poverty. Because of those childhood experiences, they valued the importance of eating well.

Having a progressive neuromuscular disability meant several realities: strength would decrease over time, changes could be gradual or immediate, and the trajectory of my future might be unpredictable. This also meant I developed a continual appreciation of the power of adaptation and creativity.

In my late thirties and early forties, it became harder for me to breathe unassisted during the day. I already used a BiPap and oxygen at night, but I felt more tired when talking, eating, and swallowing. I also developed lower back pain that imperceptibly became worse. New to chronic pain, I didn't realize how it affected my energy and appetite, which in turn impacted my nutrition. The idea of choking on liquids and food also frightened me, which factored into a significant weight loss and low protein levels. Structural barriers contributed as well: accessible scales for wheelchair users at home are expensive as hell. Neither was it easy getting weighed regularly at my doctor's office, even though it had an accessible scale. Such is life in a world that was never built for you.

A referral to a nutritionist produced mixed results. I was clear about wanting to try noninvasive interventions before considering a feeding tube. The nutritionist made a hard sell on the benefits of a feeding tube (a.k.a. a G-tube or a gastronomy tube, a surgically placed device connected to the stomach) and scared me about my declining protein levels. I knew eating, hydration, and administering medications would be a lot easier with a G-tube. I also spoke with other disabled people with G-tubes who love having them and who can still eat and drink by mouth. A G-tube (or intravenous nutrition) may certainly be in my future, but I wanted a little more time before the next major change to my daily routine.

It's very easy for a health care provider to recommend a procedure, but they do not take into account the upkeep and additional support required. Do I have room in my closet for all the new G-tube supplies to be shoved in with my other medical equipment? Do I have the capacity to educate and train myself and my attendants on using and maintaining one? Even with its advantages, do I want to deal with the prospect of infection, skin irritation, and leakage of stomach fluids that come from having a G-tube? In the end, I advocated to improve my health on my own terms, prioritizing bodily autonomy and what quality of life means to me at the moment.

Food access is often framed as a lack of money, resources, or proximity to food. Food access is also framed as a policy or systemic issue. For me, food access is all those things and a challenge in order to eat safely, easily, and deliciously. Pleasure, flavor, and joy should be embedded in access, and that's what I tried to do when faced with this new serious situation. Listening to and respecting my evolving body has been a process of experimentation and adaptation. Here are a few things I've figured out:

- I started using the BiPap machine during the day, and it allowed me to conserve energy in between meals and snacks. I didn't have to worry about feeling short of breath after eating. Bonus: I drank more water, too.
- At a recent appointment with a new nutritionist, I learned of Very High Calorie Boost. The nutritionist was able to prescribe it, and it was covered by Medicaid! It is a game changer from the high-protein variety I used to drink.
- I plan smaller meals and snacks throughout the day instead of large amounts at once.
- I try to avoid talking or being distracted when eating to avoid potential accidents. Hipsters would call this "mindful eating." I call it "trying not to choke to death."
- Another method to prevent choking: I lean forward with my chin tucked downward as much as possible when swallowing.
- I have a spit cup nearby if I'm eating and realize there is a piece that might be difficult to swallow. At times I enjoy a juicy chunk of meat by chewing and spitting it out. Unfortunately, spills happen and you just gotta suck it up (ha).
- Soft, creamy, fatty, liquid-based foods are easier for me to swallow, so I find ways to modify favorites into those textures. I can still enjoy some crispy textures that aren't chewy, fibrous, or stringy (e.g., potato chips, fried chicken skin, tempura sweet potatoes). *Fat is flavor and a choking deterrent!*

I miss popcorn dearly, but aged white cheddar Pirate's Booty is a close-enough approximation. Instead of a lobster

A photo taken by my friend Mia Mingus when we met up at Sweet Adeline Bakeshop in Berkeley, California, in 2014. On the table are three desserts: two slices of chocolate cream pie heaped with luxurious whipped cream, and one slice of yellow cake with fresh strawberries. The chocolate cream was rich and not very custardy, so it plus the whipped cream really worked well. I actually think the whipped cream was the star of the show. I also enjoy topping a mug of coffee with whipped cream whenever I fancy. This is living!

roll, I can have lobster bisque. Beef or lamb is no longer an option, but I love me some unctuous, sexy, jiggly bone marrow on Parker House rolls with a glass of blanc de blancs from Schramsberg Vineyards or a piping-hot mug of bone broth that I sip with a glass straw. Barbecue ribs are no longer on my menu, but I can tuck into gooey slow-cooked baked beans flavored with burnt ends for some delectable smoky, meaty notes. And thank god for creamy peanut butter, yogurt, tofu, eggs, ice cream, cheese, jook, and pureed soups.

Many disabled and chronically ill people deal with loss and the sadness, anger, and misery that comes with it. Having a loving relationship with a radical body is not easy, but it generates an appreciation of what I have right now and what I had in the past. I can relish warm memories of excellent meals and the voracious appetite that allowed me to consume them, and I can look forward to new gastronomic adventures by getting to the marrow of my desires.

Feeling limited in what I can eat at this stage in my life has given me license to be a hardcore 馋裴 chán pēi. I'm going to hold on to my ability to nourish myself and feel good through food for as long as possible. I'm not going to fear the G-tube on the horizon. And I'm not going to hold back on the whipped cream or a second slice of pumpkin pie while I can still eat! Adaptation is care work. Adaptation is survival. Adaptation is a negotiation between the past and the present. Adaptation is a science and art. Adaptation pushes boundaries and creates new futures.

POTATO CHIPS
& CHAMPAGNE

SOONDUBU JJIGAE
WITH SEAFOOD

FOOD

O-TORO NIGIRI

生煎包
PAN-FRIED BUNS

韭菜鱼水饺
FISH & CHIVE DUMPLINGS

蛋撻
EGG CUSTARD TARTS

PEACHES & MANGOES

CHAWANMUSHI

HEAVEN

卤猪蹄
BRAISED PIG TROTTERS

FRENCH FRIES
WITH AIOLI

Excerpt from:

Let's Recognize Why #AccessIsLove

Rooted in Rights blog (February 14, 2019)

I spent much of my childhood and young adulthood finding myself and community. I didn't have the words or concepts such as *ableism* or *intersectionality* that helped shape me into who I am today. Disability pride and identity took a long time for me to develop, and the process accelerated once I started reaching out to other disabled people. They didn't have to look exactly like me or become my best friend, but I received a glimmer of recognition, the "yeah, I got you" understanding of our lived experiences that kept me going.

When I first moved to the San Francisco Bay Area twenty-two years ago, I felt like a Midwestern suburban mouse arriving at the epicenter of crip culture. Disabled women and disabled people of color in particular embraced me, sharing their lives, time, and culture with me. My self-education grew as I learned about disability justice and connected with people online beyond the Bay Area bubble.

As I began to embrace and accept myself, I had to acknowledge the messiness, shame, and internalized ableism that will always be a part of me. It is thanks to the love and generosity of disabled people that I have opened up to new ways of being, thinking, and moving in the world. Individual acts of love and kindness became part of a larger collective force holding everyone together with bonds of interdependence.

Every community, big or small, has conflict, drama, and a whole lot of dysfunction. Every community also has a reservoir of intergenerational wisdom, energy, and love that has the power to build, create, and mobilize for change. As a member of multiple communities, I love them all because they anchor me while providing freedom to splash around with joy unapologetically, to grow, and to carve out new spaces in collaboration with others.

Last fall, after years of friendship, I got to spend time in person with Mia Mingus and Sandy Ho. We talked about Mia's keynote address at the 2018 Disability and Intersectionality Summit (an event founded and co-organized by Sandy) called "*Disability Justice* Is Simply Another Term for Love." This quote from Mia resonated with me deeply:

I would argue that *disability justice—disability justice* the term—it's simply another term for love. And so is *solidarity, access,* and *access intimacy.* Those are just other ways of saying "love." I would argue that our work for liberation is in itself simply a practice of love, and it's one of the deepest and most profound practices of love there is. . . . And the creation of this space also is an act of love.

Three disabled Asian American friends. *From left:* Mia Mingus, me, and Sandy Ho.

Magic happens when you get brilliant disabled people together. During our conversation about how we can advance these ideas in a creative and fun way, a new project was born: Access Is Love. Started by Mia, Sandy, and myself, we launched the campaign with the following goals:

- Expand the idea of access beyond compliance and the disability rights framework.
- Encourage people to incorporate accessibility in their everyday practices and lives.
- Show solidarity and give support to activists across movements outside and within the disability community.

We created a list of resources on accessibility and disability justice and ten steps people can take to start thinking and acting intentionally about access. We also designed some merchandise to share these themes with others. With all this in mind, I invite you to think about these questions:

- Who do you love? Who are your people?
- How do you show love for your communities?
- What does it mean to show up for others?
- In what ways are access, solidarity, and disability justice forms of love?

Who we love and how we love are inherently political. We declare our kinship through our actions and words in both explicit and subtle ways. It's not easy or simple, but I hope everyone will find their people and ways to express love for their communities each and every day.

Pureed Spinach & Mushroom Soup

INGREDIENTS

1–2 teaspoons olive oil

6–8 cloves roasted garlic

3–4 large handfuls baby spinach

2 cups diced shiitake mushrooms (or any type)

1/2 onion, diced

1/2 pint (8 ounces) heavy whipping cream, or coconut milk

3–4 cups chicken or vegetable stock

salt (and pepper, if that's your thing) to taste

DIRECTIONS

1. Place a saucepot on the stove over medium-high heat. Add the olive oil.

2. When the oil is hot, add the spinach, mushrooms, and onion. Sauté for 5 minutes, then turn heat to medium and cover with a lid. Cook for 5 minutes or until the veggies soften.

3. Add the stock to the saucepot with the veggies. Cover and let cook over medium heat for 10–15 minutes.

4. Throw in the roasted garlic and turn off the heat.

5. When the soup is not too hot, use an immersion blender to puree everything to your preferred consistency. Turn heat to medium high. Add the heavy whipping cream. Stir gently and let warm until the soup is hot again, about 5–10 minutes. Add salt (and pepper) to taste.

6. Serve in a handled ceramic mug and with a glass straw if you are disabled! Makes 4-ish servings.

SUCK IT
IT,
ABLEISM

CULTURE

I *am* a mutant. And I want people to know who and
what I am. I tell people because, hey, if we're going
to have a problem with it . . . I'd like to know.

—KITTY PRYDE, *ALL-NEW X-MEN #13*

Without community there is no liberation.

—AUDRE LORDE

BABY TIGER CUB!

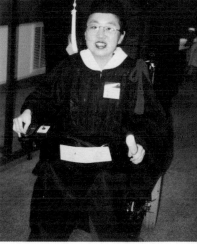

世界日報

王美華　殘障人照顧殘障人　獲明燈獎

輪椅人生活得精采

灣區群像

TELL YOUR STORY

StoryCorps
storycorps.org

Alice Wong

Our mission is to provide Americans of all backgrounds and beliefs with the opportunity to record, share, and preserve the stories of our lives.

Suck it Ableism

Access Bitch

#SuckYouPhilips

ASIANS FOR BLACK LIVES

18MR.ORG

Public Authority Governing Body President Alice Wong poses with her Beacon Award from the San Francisco Mayor's Disability Council.

National Honor for Alice Wong

Longtime San Francisco IHSS Public Authority Governing Body member and current President Alice Wong was appointed by President Barack Obama to the National Council on Disability (NCD) on January 31, 2013. The NCD is an independent federal agency that advises the President, Congress and other federal agencies regarding disability policy. "In close collaboration with the Administration, Congress and disability stakeholders, NCD has promoted policies which have advanced equal opportunity, economic self-sufficiency, independent living, inclusion and integration into all aspects of society for individuals with disabilities," noted incoming NCD Chairperson Jeff Rosen.

Alice Wong is a Staff Research Associate for the National Center for Personal Assistance Services at UCSF. She is also a board member of Asians and Pacific Islanders with Disabilities of California. Ms. Wong served as Vice Chair of the Chancellor's Advisory Committee on Disability Issues at UCSF from 2006 to 2009. She received the Mayor's Disability Council Beacon Award in 2010, the 2010 Chancellor's Disability Service Award and the 2007 Martin Luther King, Jr. Award at UCSF for leadership on behalf of the disability community. *Congratulations, Alice!*

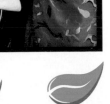

The 1 Percent Disabled Club

A discussion with W. Kamau Bell on the Denzel Washington Is the Greatest Actor of All Time Period *podcast, episode 63 (January 21, 2016). This conversation has been condensed and edited for clarity.*

W: KAMAU BELL: Welcome, Alice Wong, to *Denzel Washington Is the Greatest Actor of All Time Period*. Thank you for coming on.

ALICE WONG: Oh, thank you for having me. I'm utterly thrilled!

KAMAU: Well, yeah, thank you. Just to let people know about you, we met at a show that I did in Berkeley, *Home by 10*. You came to that show, and afterwards we talked and took a picture. And then recently, when we reviewed *The Bone Collector*, Kevin [Avery] and I did [it] originally. It was just the two of us, I think. And in the middle of the review, I was like, "I really don't know enough about disabled people to really know that part of this movie," which we should talk about, 'cause it's a major part of *The Bone Collector*. It's the, you know, it's essential to the plot that he's disabled. And so, Adam Hartzell [@FilmEssaying] reached out on Twitter and said that I should have you on. And I saw your picture, and I'm like, "Why does she look familiar?" And then you sent me the picture of us at *Home by 10* in Berkeley over the summer.

ALICE: As my proof.

KAMAU: Yeah, proof! [*laughs*]

W. Kamau Bell and me at his *Home by 10* comedy show in Berkeley, California, in 2015.

ALICE: I have to thank Adam for mentioning me. And I'm happy to give the point of view of the disabled people and how people view stuff.

KAMAU: Yeah. And yeah, and I really appreciate that. And just to let people know, on Twitter you're @SFdirewolf.

ALICE: Yep.

KAMAU: Which is a very— That's a lotta Twitter name. Direwolf. Sounds like a superhero or something.

ALICE: Well, it's a reference to *Game of Thrones*. I don't know if you watched it.

KAMAU: Oh! That's—I'm always out of the loop on *Game of Thrones* references.

ALICE: Ah!

KAMAU: That's what that is. I'm always—

ALICE: You gotta get into it!

KAMAU: I-I-I—I'm not wired that way, Alice! [*laughs*] I don't have— It's funny, 'cause my cousin is into N. K. Jemisin, who's an acclaimed fantasy author. Her books have been written—like, one of her books was in the *New York Times*'s top 100 [Notable Books] of 2015.

ALICE: Wow.

KAMAU: And I've never read any of them! So it's in my—

ALICE: You are a bad relative.

KAMAU: Yeah. She got the fantasy gene. I did not get the fantasy gene.

ALICE: You're not a blerd?

KAMAU: I'm a blerd, but I'm more of a blerd through the superhero side, not the full-on swords.

ALICE: And have you ever heard of Cyborg?

KAMAU: I have, yes, *Teen Titans*.

ALICE: Yeah.

KAMAU: See, I'm old-school, Alice. I know *Teen Titans*, yes.

ALICE: But not only is he Black, he's disabled!

KAMAU: Oh, that's so— It's funny to think that, 'cause Cyborg, for people who don't know, 'cause we're going to deep-cut nerdistry here—

ALICE: Yeah, yeah, yeah.

KAMAU: —he's basically like, he's a cyborg. [*laughs*] I guess it actually, it says on the tin. He's a cyborg. So he's a Black guy who is part machine. And that's, I mean— Al, this is why I'm glad to have you on. 'Cause you just kinda blew my mind 'cause I never thought of him as being disabled.

ALICE: Oh my god. Well, let me tell you that I think a lot of my friends and I use tech every day. Many of us have tech that's on our bodies, in our bodies, attached to our bodies. And, you know, I joke to my friends all the time, we are already cyborgs.

[*Kamau laughs*]

ALICE: And that we already are living the sci-fi/futuristic life. And we're just kinda already out there.

KAMAU: Yeah, we just— It just hasn't been fully incorporated into our skin, but that's coming. That's coming.

ALICE: Yeah!

KAMAU: So, now we're here to talk about the thing. Alice, how dare you. You made me watch *The Bone Collector* again. I'm not—

ALICE: I made you? You made me!

KAMAU: That's true. That is true. And just, it's a Denzel Washington movie that, last I looked at my rating, I gave it a "Led Astray," which is a two-star Denzel rating.

ALICE: Mm-hmm.

KAMAU: 'Cause this was early in the podcast, and it was a movie that

I had . . . I don't know if I'd consciously avoided it. I'm not interested in those procedurals, "We gotta find the killer of the blah, blah, blah." I mean, like everybody I went through a *Law & Order* phase like we all did.

ALICE: Yeah.

KAMAU: So, it's Jeffery Deaver who wrote the series of crime novels based on this series—this character, Lincoln Rhyme. And it stars Denzel Washington and a young Angelina Jolie, who plays the police officer he adopts and [who] helps him solve the cases 'cause she's got the eye that he has. And he plays a quadriplegic ex–police detective who helps, who is brought in to solve a murder case, a complicated series of murder cases by a serial killer. So that is what the movie is. Basically, it's a very sort of late-'90s procedural from the people who went to the movie *Seven* and thought we should make a movie like that.

ALICE: Right.

KAMAU: But you know? [*laughs*] It's pretty— It's a little bit slashery; it's a little bit gruesome. It's got that *Seven* thing where every scene, it's, like, where it's— You're supposed to blech. In every scene, somebody turns a corner and gets scared, but it's not anybody to be afraid of.

ALICE: Yeah.

KAMAU: Anyway, that's just the plot, and I've also judged it a little bit.

ALICE: Oh, go on.

KAMAU: So my question is, have you seen this movie before?

ALICE: Yes, I have.

KAMAU: And I mean, my mom talks about this, and I would be interested to find out how you feel, if you're in the same position. My mom said there was a point at which she saw every movie that Black people were in because there weren't that many. And she was just excited to see a Black person on-screen, whether or not she actually liked the movie or not.

ALICE: Uh-huh, uh-huh.

KAMAU: Now, this is different, 'cause Denzel Washington's clearly not a quadriplegic. But when you went to see this movie, was it because, well, he's playing a quadriplegic, and I should . . .

ALICE: I don't remember if that's the main reason why. But I think the main reason why I even remember it is that it does feature life as a disabled person. So you do see things that resonate with my own life: the equipment he uses, [the] camera's point of view from his bed, and just little things about the way people treat him. And it just takes in a perspective I think that was kinda so rare. You still don't see that many movies where the main character is the disabled person.

KAMAU: Yeah. And I think it certainly is a—as far as for Denzel as an actor, you know—it's a pretty big acting stretch, because he's known for being this sort of like . . . he's not an action hero necessarily, you know. He's known for his walk. We talked about it. And even in this movie, it's like the movie goes, "You're not gonna see him walk a lot." So they gave him "the walk." The very first scene is his sort of "the Denzel walk." And so he's a character where he's confined to the bed for the whole time until the very end—spoiler alert. I'm assuming that that was part of the reason he took the acting challenge on.

ALICE: Yeah. And I think, again, this is where some of my friends in the disability community, we get a little annoyed that nondisabled people get [roles like this]. It's Oscar bait.

KAMAU: Oh, yes.

ALICE: I mean, so many characters with disabilities who are featured in these end up being this really amazing stretch for these actors!

[*Kamau laughs*]

ALICE: [*sarcastically*] The talent. "What is it like to be quadriplegic?! And what is it like to have to not move your legs when you're acting?! How can you do that?"

[*Kamau laughs*]

ALICE: "How can you embody something so alien and so impossible to really be like?" I mean, that in itself, I think, is somewhat insulting, where all these nondisabled actors are just lauded for pushing themselves. Like *My Left Foot*. And a recent movie about Stephen Hawking, *The Theory of Everything*.

KAMAU: Oh, yes.

ALICE: There was a lot of discussion about [how] it's really to serve nondisabled people in their quest for a "challenge."

KAMAU: So basically, Alice, what you just did—and I just wanna highlight this—I said Denzel stretched by doing this movie, and then you called bullshit on that. Thank you, Alice. [*laughs*]

ALICE: Well, you know.

KAMAU: I appreciate that.

ALICE: And I'm sure as actors who wanna be different and creative— I mean, it's an interesting role choice for him and really different from what he's done before. So, you know, nothing wrong with that. But often I think there's this weird perception that somehow it's brave for these nondisabled actors to really imagine this horrific reality of being disabled while not even giving disabled actors a shot.

KAMAU: Yeah. That's— I mean, that's— Yeah. It's interesting to think that there's no other disabled characters in the movie.

ALICE: Nope, I don't think so. But again, this movie was about Lincoln Rhyme and his young Padawan.

KAMAU: [*laughs*] His young Padawan! But let's talk about it from the perspective of how do you think Denzel did playing a quadriplegic in the movie?

ALICE: Well, I'm not quadriplegic myself.

KAMAU: Okay.

ALICE: But I do use ventilation. So he uses this vent device, I think it's called a sip-and-puff ventilator. So you saw that little straw that is attached to his bed. So he sips on that for ventilation. And I think that was nice, because you don't often see that used anywhere in the movies that often. And that was nice.

KAMAU: Mm-hmm.

ALICE: I think you see his hospital bed, and later on in the movie, you see his wheelchair, him using a wheelchair. And I gotta give them props for that wheelchair look[ing] pretty accurate.

KAMAU: [*laughs*] Oh, they didn't get him a hoopty?

ALICE: No, they did not.

KAMAU: They got him a nice sedan.

ALICE: And I did appreciate how he used computers—

KAMAU: Mm-hmm.

ALICE: Voice-activated assistive technology—I think that was really somewhat ahead of its time in the '90s.

KAMAU: Well, yeah, we talked about that last time, how this movie really is pushing the technology side of it, and which led to one of our favorite things we recall on the show when we talk about it, is . . . I call him Al Bundy. But what's his name, the actor's name, plays Al Bundy?

ALICE: Ed O'Neill.

KAMAU: Ed O'Neill. Ed O'Neill. At one point when they're talking about "we need to scour everything to find what we need to find," he goes, "Check the internet," as if that's a thing. [*laughs*] So.

ALICE: I remember that chess game he was playing online.

KAMAU: Yes.

ALICE: It's so quaint now.

KAMAU: Yes, yes.

ALICE: It's like, aw.

[*Kamau laughs*]

ALICE: It's so old-timey. And it makes you wonder, shouldn't Lincoln Rhyme have been watching porn online?

KAMAU: [*laughs*] And the movie begins with him talking about how he basically— We didn't even talk about this in the last episode, how I think, watching it again, I did see it through different eyes, 'cause it's a pretty dark beginning. He's basically trying to set up—

ALICE: Yeah!

KAMAU: —he's setting up his assisted suicide. 'Cause he has nothing to live for.

ALICE: Yeah. And again, that's—I have my notes—that's under my problematic part.

[*Kamau laughs*]

ALICE: I have, like, notes under "problematic" and "nice."

KAMAU: This is two weeks in a row we've done problematic Denzel Washington movies. So you're saying—

ALICE: I think it should be the buzzword of your podcast.

KAMAU: Yes. And what do you mean? What was problematic about it? I mean, I guess, but . . .

ALICE: Well, you know. Again, it's like he— I guess this is really similar to a lot of people who are recently injured or recently disabled, where they really can't imagine a future, they don't wanna live life like this.

KAMAU: Mm-hmm.

ALICE: They feel like they're trapped in their bodies.

KAMAU: Mm-hmm.

ALICE: And they feel like, "I want dignity." And they feel this loss of control over their life.

KAMAU: Mm-hmm.

ALICE: And at the same time, Lincoln Rhyme has a lot of privilege—

KAMAU: Yeah.

ALICE: —and a lotta skills. I think the Ed O'Neill character talked about Lincoln to someone: "This guy's a genius. He's written books, and he's given talks." And I'm thinking he can still do those things.

KAMAU: Oh, yeah.

ALICE: Right?

KAMAU: Yeah.

ALICE: Nobody says you have to have two legs that are working to give expert testimony or to write a book—

KAMAU: [*chuckles*] Yeah.

ALICE: —or to give consultations. So, in a lotta ways, you know, it's sad that the character thought that his life wasn't worth living. And in a lotta ways that really does bring up the reality of how people really view disability.

KAMAU: Oh!

ALICE: "Oh my god, if I can't breathe unassisted, or if I can't move unassisted, life isn't worth it." And that's really from an able-bodied point of view. And I'll tell you myself, Kamau, I mean, people have told me, "Oh my god! I can't imagine what it's like to be in a wheelchair." I'm like, "Yeah." And you know—

KAMAU: *Whoa!* People have said that to you?

ALICE: Oh, this is so typical.

[*Kamau laughs*]

ALICE: People don't even think. They just assume that everybody wants to be nondisabled, right?

KAMAU: Yeah.

ALICE: And that people truly believe that everybody who's disabled should want to be nondisabled, and few have ever had to think what's wrong with that presumption.

KAMAU: Yeah, and I hear what you're saying. It's not about— They don't build the case for why he's depressed. It opens with him sort of, I guess, having a nightmare about how his accident happened.

ALICE: Yeah. He's been through some trauma for sure.

KAMAU: And they don't build a case for "he's got a bad life, so he wants to kill himself."

ALICE: Right. I mean, did you see his apartment?

KAMAU: Yeah. He's got a nice one! [*laughs*] He's living in one of those *Friends* apartments where it's like, where do you get all that space from in Manhattan?

ALICE: Oh my god. First of all, he has every piece of equipment that he possibly needs. He has this loyal and amazing twenty-four-hour nurse played by—

BOTH: Queen Latifah.

ALICE: That was one of my problematic parts. I'm like, "He's still on the job, and they mention he has great insurance."

KAMAU: [*laughs*] Cheer up!

ALICE: He has his nurse who never seems to take a shift off.

KAMAU: Yeah. There's never another nurse who replaces her. She is just there twenty-four hours a day. Yeah.

ALICE: Right. I mean, hello! That is, you know, like, the one-percenters of disabled people.

KAMAU: Yeah.

ALICE: And there aren't that many one-percenters out there.

KAMAU: Wow. I didn't even think about that, that like he's living it, he's— And I think this is the thing those of us able-bodied people, and I include myself in this, don't think about, like his life as a disabled person is better than most people's lives who are able-bodied. [*laughs*]

ALICE: Hell yeah. So he wants to kill himself because he's rich and he's smart and he has great support.

KAMAU: Yes.

ALICE: Wow! I feel so sorry for you, Lincoln Rhyme!

KAMAU: Lincoln Rhyme! [*laughs*]

ALICE: [*dramatically*] Lincoln Rhyme: He's not even on Medicaid! Lincoln Rhyme!

KAMAU: Yeah. It's not about a disabled person who's on Medicaid, who has— I mean, and I'm sure this happens a lot, where the act of being disabled—you incur a lot of medical bills.

ALICE: Absolutely. Yeah, and his house—I mean, his apartment. I mean, for anybody to get a place like that, accessible and—

KAMAU: Yeah, but his apartment doesn't have a water view. You didn't notice that, Alice. There's no water view. How can he be forced to stay in his loft apartment?

ALICE: But remember, he has a visiting falcon.

KAMAU: Oh, that's right. He does have a [*laughs*]—has a falcon!

ALICE: And that symbolism is so heavy, right?

KAMAU: Oh, the symbolism of the falcon who can fly! Oh, Alice!

ALICE: And in the end, he became the falcon.

[*Kamau gasps*]

ALICE: 'Cause he now has wings thanks to his able-bodied helpmate.

KAMAU: Oh. And he got a nicer wheelchair, yes. That's, I mean, the end of that movie is so . . . I kinda feel like this is another thing the movie cheats on, too, that the end of the movie is like him and Angelina Jolie. There's a little bit of flirting in it that could be construed as sexual harassment. But— [*laughs*]

ALICE: Oh, at the station? Yeah.

KAMAU: Yeah, where she's sort of helping him, trying to get something out of his lap. And he's sorta like, "Take your time." It's like, "Oh, slow down, President Clinton."

ALICE: Well, also, didn't it seem like a sudden shift [when], at the very beginning, he was making these arrangements to die and suddenly he started looking more well groomed and motivated to solve the case?

KAMAU: [*laughs*] Yes.

ALICE: Like it was even before he met the Angelina Jolie character.

KAMAU: Yeah, yeah.

ALICE: It's those photos of the crime scene. So, in a way, the serial killer saves Lincoln Rhyme.

KAMAU: [*laughs*] I think you— They need to—they should've hired you to write the poster tags, like the taglines, the log line, on the poster. But it is funny, because if I were depressed and then Angelina started coming into my house every day— I mean, I'm married now, so it'd be different. But if I were single and every day she started hanging out in my house asking me to tell her "what are we gonna do today," it'd turn things around for me.

ALICE: Yeah. And I think what's nice about it, under my "nice" category of notes: she doesn't give a shit about his attitude, you know. She doesn't seem to feel sorry for him.

KAMAU: Mm-hmm.

ALICE: She calls him out on his bullshit, and that's kinda nice. Some people are really, you know, they get really flustered or freaked out when they meet disabled people. And they often tend to be overly nice—

KAMAU: Mm-hmm.

ALICE: —or overly coddling or infantilizing, and she doesn't do that.

KAMAU: No.

ALICE: So I thought that was a nice touch. And it's pretty clear that they definitely, the two characters, had chemistry, both intellectually and physically.

KAMAU: Yeah.

ALICE: And there's a lotta that kinda intimacy going on: him talking to her through her earpiece.

KAMAU: Yeah, there is. There is an intimacy. And I mean, I don't know if I totally buy that by the end, they would be—

ALICE: Yeah!

KAMAU: Like the end of the movie implies that—

ALICE: Yeah, it does quite a bit.

KAMAU: Yeah. Yeah. Well, there was a time shift, so we don't know. Maybe it was five years in the future, but yeah, by the end, she's at his house for Christmas.

ALICE: Uh-huh.

KAMAU: And she has called his sister to come over, and she puts her hands over his hand, which implies, like, oh, they've been doing some things. I kinda feel like although that's the movie, I wanna see the movie about that relationship, [which] would be interesting. That's not the—you know, that's— Again, this could've been a franchise, but obviously it did not franchise out.

ALICE: Well, I would've preferred a *Devil in a Blue Dress* [franchise]— [*Kamau laughs*]

ALICE: —over *The Bone Collector*.

KAMAU: I think you're probably standing in a camp with everybody.

ALICE: Yeah.

KAMAU: I'm the only person to ever suggest there should be a *Bone Collector* sequel. Yes, there's definitely more [of a] chance that they will resuscitate the *Devil in a Blue Dress* franchise over the *Bone Collector* franchise, yeah.

ALICE: Mm-hmm, mm-hmm.

KAMAU: So, anything else in your problematic column?

ALICE: I think the wealth and privilege and the seemingly omnipresent, great nursing care.

KAMAU: Yes.

ALICE: That, to me, was like, yeah, okay. That's really inaccurate.

KAMAU: So basically you need the scene where he called Thelma, which is, first of all, just to take it to the Black side, one of the most classic Black names in the history of everything: Thelma. Thelma is the female version of Leroy. So you would like a scene where he's like, "Thelma!" And then the other health care provider comes in who's not Thelma, who's mean, doesn't care, and isn't attentive and doesn't care about his falcon. [*laughs*]

ALICE: Mm-hmm, yeah. The fact that she is not only a nurse, but she does a lotta other stuff. Did you notice how she does a lotta other duties that go beyond that role?

KAMAU: Yeah.

ALICE: So that's kinda another stretch, I think.

KAMAU: Yeah. That your health care worker, that your nurse, would also be like, "I'll also pick up your dry cleaning. I'll also—"

ALICE: She was teaching Angelina Jolie how to access online files.

KAMAU: Yes.

ALICE: You remember that part?

KAMAU: Yes, I do. "Get her up to speed on the computer."

ALICE: Yeah, okay. I went to nursing school for this?

KAMAU: Yeah.

ALICE: So there's that.

KAMAU: A highly specialized field. Also, I'm good with computers and police tracking software.

ALICE: Not to be nitpicky, but . . .

KAMAU: No, but that's what we're here for. And I mean, I think the important thing, the reason why I wanted to have you on and to have this conversation, is 'cause these are the things that blew past me.

ALICE: Mm-hmm.

KAMAU: Like I was just like, "Man, good for Denzel for stretching into this role."

ALICE: Mm-hmm.

KAMAU: "And his legs haven't moved the whole time. He's really a good actor." [*laughs*] I was just sorta like . . . and then I focused on the plot, which I think is sort of, as we said, is a little bit of—a little bit, you know, it's just kind of a slasher film and sort of procedural drama, which—

ALICE: Yeah, I mean, that almost was, like, not the least interesting part, right?

KAMAU: Yes.

ALICE: I mean, I think it did try to, kinda. It was in line [with] *Seven* and *Silence of the Lambs* in terms of how gross they can go. On the whole, the killer was really not that interesting.

KAMAU: Yeah, it's the thing where they sorta set you up. It's a classic movie where they set you up like it's gonna be one guy, which if you watch any movies, you know, well, it's clearly not gonna be that guy, 'cause they want me to think it's that guy. The mean, angry police detective, the other [one] who sorta works at the station. But it ends up being some other guy who you never knew, who there's no way you could've ever thought it was going to be him! [*laughs*]

ALICE: Yeah, and I was really sad that that guy who we reveal—I'm gonna spoil this—I think he's probably a respiratory therapist or somebody who had his equipment.

KAMAU: Oh, yeah.

ALICE: But, you know, he killed Thelma! No!

KAMAU: Yes. Yeah, no. That was the hard part of that movie. It's the death of Thelma. Yeah.

ALICE: Totally sad.

KAMAU: It should be *Bone Collector*, subtitled *The Death of Thelma*.

ALICE: Yeah.

KAMAU: But no, yeah. 'Cause you don't wanna see Queen Latifah die in a movie.

ALICE: I know!

KAMAU: And then the other thing is that they have the fight. Denzel falls out of bed. Denzel bites the guy on his neck in a real like, "Arrrr!"

ALICE: Yeah!

KAMAU: I don't know that I would ever—forget able-bodied/disabled—I don't know if I could bite some guy through the neck in a fight. I don't know that I have that in me. I'd be like, "I think you're just gonna beat me up, sir, if it comes to that." But then apparently in the book he bites the guy through the neck, and the guy bleeds out. But in the movie they have Angelina then come in as his helper.

ALICE: Yeah. You know, that, to me, was a disappointment. First of all, I give Lincoln Rhyme's character props for— You know, because it is scary. I use a hospital bed, and I'm tethered to these devices. And if there was a power outage or somebody pulled me down, that, to me . . . I sense that fear as well.

KAMAU: Mm-hmm.

ALICE: So that, to me, was really real.

KAMAU: Oh, wow.

ALICE: And I just loved—if you're really vulnerable already as a physically disabled person, but also depending on electricity to help you breathe. But that part, I just thought that was like a triumphant moment, when he's gonna play possum.

KAMAU: Mm-hmm.

ALICE: You know, he whispers and gets the guy closer to him. And he used the main physical ability that he had, his voice, his mouth. And he chomped!

[*Kamau laughs*]

ALICE: And I really wanted to see more blood spray, you know?

[*Kamau laughs*]

ALICE: Biting his carotid! There should've been more spray.

KAMAU: Yeah. 'Cause you just said it was gross earlier. Now, you're like, "But at that moment, I would like more blood spray."

ALICE: Just to give a little triumphant ending. Because, you know, it's just playing into this idea that oh, disabled people can't defend themselves.

KAMAU: Yeah.

ALICE: They're so helpless. They're so weak. And that was kind of nice to see Lincoln Rhyme chomping on him and, you know, playing with these assumptions.

KAMAU: Yeah. And also using that guy's assumption of him as being defenseless as a way to suck him in to take a bite through his carotid artery. [*laughs*] So he basically [thinks], *You think I'm helpless, so I'm gonna play on that.*

ALICE: And I think we're living in the *Walking Dead* era of copious blood.

KAMAU: Yes.

ALICE: But you know, I think there wasn't enough blood. And I was sad that Angelina got to shoot [the killer].

KAMAU: Yeah. So when they go back and redo the collector's edition, the redux of *Bone Collector*, the Alice Wong edit, you can dub in some more blood and some more crunching noises of the carotid artery and some more blood splatter. You can sort of have them put some more blood splatter. And can also edit out the part of Angelina shooting the guy. You can just make it all happen from Denzel biting him on the neck.

ALICE: Mm-hmm, mm-hmm. And then he develops . . . a taste for blood.

KAMAU: Oh! That's the sequel: *Bone Collector 2: Taste for Blood.*

ALICE: Yeah, and then he moves on to the marrow. Get it?

KAMAU: Ahhhh!

ALICE: Ahh!

KAMAU: Bone marrow! There we go! Good job. Wait. That was all—this whole review has been a setup for that bone marrow joke. [*chuckles*] Thank you, Alice! Thank you.

ALICE: I've done my job.

KAMAU: You've done your job. And I'm glad that we had you on here to talk about [this movie], 'cause it does give us a different perspective through which to view [it]. And we have a whole bunch of movies we can go check out. And maybe I'll start watching *Game of Thrones* now.

DISABILITY FIGHT CLUB

The time is

MEOW.

Ableism won't stand a chance.

Cat Life

Artwork by Sam Schäfer

I love cats. They delight and amaze me.

It is a truth universally acknowledged that cats know how to live.

Humans have a lot to learn from them.

Cats are loud and clear about what they like and don't like.

Cats spend most of the day resting, playing, and indulging: a model of self-love.

Cats take up space unapologetically. They belong everywhere.

Cats secretly strategize and conspire, fighting for what they want. Enemies beware.

Cats question authority and give side-eye to all things shady.

Cats are assholes when they want to be.

Cats have boundaries.

If you touch one without consent, it will let you know.

Cats give and receive affection freely but always on their own terms.

Cats are aware of their surroundings and sensit to weird vibes.

Body positivity and self-care have become toxic, hollow, and commodified concepts. I have struggled with both and found the fiercest role models, from the domestic *Felis catus* to the wild *Panthera tigris*, on how to truly savor each day and allow yourself all the good things. Curl your body under the sun, eat to your heart's content, hiss at your mortal nemeses. It takes practice to live the Cat Life, but I'll get there eventually.

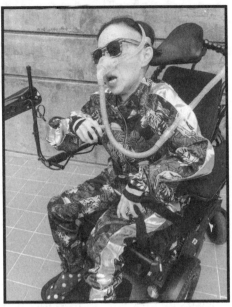

Me with my sharp claws out like a baller tiger in this magnificent tracksuit.

So even if you're not a cat person, unleash the ferocious feline in you!

How I Spend My Caturdays (and Nights) at Home

Get out of bed and sit on the toilet for a good twenty to thirty minutes

When I sleep with my BiPap on and my mouth open, my stomach tends to trap air. I end up feeling bloated and uncomfortable after getting up and immediately start what I call the "degassing process." No wonder babies are so cranky! Gas is a demon whether you have to burp or fart it out. Gas and constipation . . . Humans are such delicate creatures so easily made uncomfortable. Sitting on the toilet, taking my sweet old time, is the closest I get to meditation. My mind wanders, and I'll come up with a random line or title for an essay or new project idea. I would sit and let my imagination run a bit more, but eventually my neck becomes strained from supporting my head and my legs fall asleep. Those are good signals to get back in my wheelchair.

Wakey wakey

After getting dressed and ready, my first meal comprises three components, a holy trinity of fuel:

- One big-ass mug of coffee (dark or medium roast)
- One large heaping spoonful of creamy peanut butter
- One sweet treat: a cookie, a doughnut, a slice of cake, or some kind of pastry

Instead of yoga, I center myself when I drink coffee. The first three sips at peak temperature are when time stands still and I am one with the universe, ready for the rest of the day. Feeling the hot rivulets of coffee go down to my tum-tum is a caffeinated hug I give myself. *You got this, Alice. Let's fucking do it.* The rest of the coffee goes downhill within twenty minutes, although I have no issues with drinking it warm or at room temperature (I may be high-maintenance, but I'm not unreasonable). Meanwhile, I hold the spoon like a lollipop and give long cat licks to the peanut butter, which softens easily because of my superheated tongue (insert your supersexual thoughts here) thanks to the coffee. This facilitates my ability to swallow and eat this critical source of protein. The sweet treat counterbalances my coffee, which has only milk or whipped cream. I eat my meal in front of the T.V., where I watch the news and get caught up on what's happening in the world. And then it begins.

Tweets, Zooms, texts, and more

Since I am a late riser, I often have one or two online meetings back-to-back. Or I'll have one meeting and another one after dinner in the evening, depending on the person's flexibility. While waiting for a meeting to start on Zoom or Google Meet, I'll check my Twitter notifications, text messages, and WhatsApp chats. Occasionally I'll scroll through Facebook Messenger and Instagram. There are usually a few requests per day asking me to share something on social media. People will have to wait if they expect a reply, but on Twitter I can retweet something easily if they tag or direct message me in something that's of interest.

Post-meeting admin

After meetings, there is a shitload of things I need to do, either as a follow-up or an email or calendar item I need to send. I try to attend to these immediately; otherwise, things will just slip from my attention. I use the Stickies and Notes apps on my MacBook Pro and iPhone to remind myself in case I forget and constantly reorganize my to-do lists based on priority. I also add reminders to my Calendar app and Google Calendar to build in redundancies. And yet, I will still mix things up or forget something. C'est la frickin' vie.

It's a Chinese thing

A few hours after my first meal, I drink at least one piping-hot mug of water. I loooooove hot water and believe it's under-rated. As of this writing, it has not been colonized, and I hope this stays the case. One of the hazards of enjoying hot drinks is burning my tongue or throat. Once I drank a very hot mocha with a straw and I burned the inner part of my upper lip without realizing it. Later on I wondered why my upper lip felt puffy, and well . . . grrr. Still, warming my body through drinks is worth the risk, and I'm much more cautious now, taking little dainty kitten sips first.

Relaxation and procrastination

I will watch T.V. for several hours, switching back and forth between shows and fast-forwarding through some. I have to digest and relax after eating—I hate being rushed. I am that bitch who has basic cable, several premium cable channels, a D.V.R., and subscriptions to several streaming services. I can watch on my laptop, phone, T.V., whatever—but I am unapologetically a dinosaur when it comes to home entertainment and cannot cut the cord just yet. In addition to enjoying food delivery services, access to a whole range of T.V. shows and films is a luxury that adds pleasure to my daily life.

Inbox hell

There are days when I'll check my inbox earlier, especially if I am expecting an important reply, but I won't do a deep email dive until way after what is typically considered C.O.B., close of business, unless I am expecting something important or time sensitive. I used to take days off from checking my email, but my inbox ends up becoming a bloated corpse that repels me, which ruins the original intent of having less stress. I also delete or mark certain messages as spam and move various emails into folders. Good email hygiene keeps things manageable, although it can take me two to three hours per day. It creeps me out how much time I spend on emails every day. Here are some of the types of emails I receive:

INVITATION TO A CONFERENCE, TO SUBMIT AN ESSAY FOR A PUBLICATION, OR TO CONSULT ON A PROJECT

Range of replies: a polite "no thank you" with suggestions of other people who might be a better fit; a slight interest with a slew of questions regarding payment, access, timeline, and purpose before saying yes; an immediate yes if it's something that's in my wheelhouse where I feel like I have something to contribute.

I have a speaking agent: Emily Hartman of Steven Barclay Agency. She now manages all my talks, and hiring her was one of the best things to happen to me in 2021. It was too much work to become a vendor or to submit forms just to receive an honorarium for a one-time event from a university, a non-profit, or a company. Over these past few years, I could have written a book titled *The Unpaid Work of Getting Paid*, because it became an untenable energy suck. It may sound fancy or elitist to have a speaking agent, but it's no different than having an assistant or another form of support so I can spend less time on administrative tasks. May we all receive the help we need to make our lives a little more bearable.

RANDOM QUESTION OR REQUEST FOR INFORMATION OR ADVICE
Range of replies: depending on my energy level and mood, I'll do a quick search and offer some links or suggestions, or respond that this is out of my expertise and that they should find someone else; reply with information that they need from me for something I'm involved in, such as my availability or a document; gentle pushback that my opinion is less important than they think and that I have no specific advice I can give; no response and allow my autoreply to cover my boundaries and capacity. And people still don't read the autoreply!

INBOX AUTOPSY

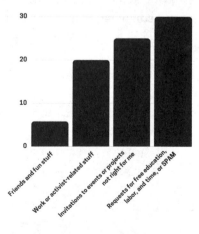

Email filters are a thing, I know. I still worry about missing an important message, so I scroll through each one quickly. Some days, my inbox is majority trash. It is so dreamy, marking emails as spam or blocking people. Try it!!

PERSONAL MESSAGES THAT I ACTUALLY ENJOY RECEIVING
Range of replies: setting up a date to catch up; checking in and delighting in talking with someone about something unrelated to work.

Second and third meals

For my second meal, I try to eat something that is semisoft or solid, easy to swallow, and high in calories. Days when I talk for too long during an event or a meeting result in a tired esophagus and a heightened risk of choking while eating. On those days I keep it to something liquid-based, like a soup. My go-to third meal is one bottle of high-protein Very High Calorie Boost, a nutritional drink that is an acquired taste. I have a sweet tooth, but this is not a delicious beverage. However, it has twenty-two grams of protein and 530 calories per serving. It gives me what my body needs. For someone who cannot chew or swallow fibrous vegetables and fruits or eat chewy and thick meats, this drink fills in the gaps and helps me maintain my weight, which has been a struggle for years with the progression of my neuromuscular disability. And *no*, I do not want any advice on nutrition.

More procrastination and admin

Throughout the day I scroll through Twitter, and that can lead me down lots of rabbit holes: a YouTube video, online shopping, books and articles I'll never get around to reading. Another intermittent activity is shit talking or trading hot goss in various group chats with my sisters and friends. Twitter and group chats are my main forms of socialization other than Zoom playdates.

No more messing around

Aside from the work of emailing, these are some examples of activities that require my attention:

- Answering interview questions or preparing notes for a talk or a presentation
- Sending interviewees questions for the Disability Visibility Project. When people ask me to feature them on my website or my podcast (which ended in April 2021), they think it's goddamn easy to throw together some questions, but it's not. I put a lot of time and care into crafting questions. Sometimes people flake out and never reply, even after a gentle reminder!
- Uploading a new guest essay for the D.V.P. and scheduling tweets about the essay using TweetDeck
- Uploading and scheduling posts to my Disability Visibility Substack newsletter, in which I arrange with various publishers to give away books by disabled writers
- Reviewing work and providing consultation as part of my side hustle
- Participating in boards, steering committees, and other work groups
- Creating graphics and image descriptions for social media and my website
- Other website maintenance, such as deleting caches. Damn the caches that keep my website from loading quickly!
- Scheduling meetings and sending email reminders
- Sharing and promoting other people's work
- Outlining and writing proposals, essays, or manuscripts for books *like this one for instance*
- Financial stuff, like paying bills, bookkeeping, and balancing checkbooks (eeeeks)

All these things are on top of what I call the "work of being disabled," which can entail numerous bureaucratic requirements, planning meals, ordering medical supplies, finding information, managing services and personal care, and interactions with the medical-industrial complex. And don't forget *emotional and intellectual labor*!

Late-night snack and relaxation

More hot water and a smaller snack, such as another large spoonful of peanut butter, a bowl of full-fat yogurt with a generous amount of peach preserves, a sliced banana, a pouch of applesauce, or a bowl of ice cream. I like to rotate between vanilla, chocolate, coffee, or peanut butter fudge ice cream. Variety is important. And more T.V. watching to reeeelax.

Sleepy time

Time to turn in. I floss, brush my teeth, spend quality time on the toilet for some deep thoughts. I double-check my calendar to make sure of when I need to wake up the next day and jot down any new items for my to-do list. Once I lie down in bed, with my electric blanket cranked all the way up, I am ready to appear in someone's nightmare.

Disabled Faces

A discussion with artist and author Riva Lehrer for the Disability Visibility Project *blog (December 9, 2020). This conversation has been condensed and edited for clarity.*

ALICE WONG: Hey, Riva, please introduce yourself and share a little bit about your background.

RIVA LEHRER: Okay. So, I'm sixty-two, I'm white, I'm Jewish, I'm short, I'm under five feet tall. I have spina bifida, so I have a curved spine and very large orthopedic shoes, which are a continuous theme in my life. And I have white hair that I streak with red. So [that's] a little bit of what I look like. And I talk in [*Golem Girl: A Memoir*] a lot about what I look like and how it gets me treated. So I'm describing myself for multiple reasons. I'm from Cincinnati, but I've lived in Chicago for over forty years. I'm a portraitist, so I go out and paint people, almost entirely people who deal with stigma. So whether that's because of an impairment or gender presentation or sexuality or anything that has gotten someone the kind of message that their body or their way of being in the world is unacceptable. This is the route to beauty for me.

And so, for almost more than twenty-five years, I've been doing portraits of people, a lot of people in the disability community. Because at the time, I was one of the only people doing this, and there still are not very many. I've seen at times that it's been used as a way to discuss the disabled experience from a different standpoint than the one that [is] usually sort of medical or sometimes political.

As with all disability culture, it's a road into our lives that gets to a different place.

ALICE: On October 6, 2020, your first book came out. *Golem Girl: A Memoir*. First, congratulations! What has it been like since the launch of your book, if you could share with me?

RIVA: Strange. The [publisher] apparently thought it was gonna be a bestseller; they came out with a pretty big printing. But the combination of Trump and the coronavirus; and right before the book came out, Ruth Bader Ginsburg died; and right as the book was coming out was the Amy Coney Barrett thing; and then the pandemic was shooting up. And, anyway, there's been a lot of complicated stuff. But basically it's been incredibly impossible to get attention from the national media. I've been getting more attention from the Jewish press, surprisingly, than anything else. And besides the disappointment and frustration there—this book is probably just gonna have a long, slow life, and hopefully I'll stick around for chunks of it.

But what's really enraged me is that we are in the middle of a fucking pandemic and, as you know, disability is still somehow not in the conversation! You know? I just can't . . . I can't wrap my mind around it. But my editor thought, "Your book is gonna be so important right now, because everyone's dealing with illness and embodiment and rights and the right to health care and all this stuff, and your book is really gonna help people talk." And instead it's been fairly roundly ignored . . . I've just been gobstruck [by] how hard it's been to be in the conversation.

ALICE: In addition to all the ups and downs of promotion and the book launch, what has been the response from disabled people? Because clearly, this is also something for us, by us.

RIVA: It's for us, by us, yes.

ALICE: So what have you heard from disabled people who've read it?

RIVA: By and large, very positive. So far, I haven't heard much. I'm sure the critiques will come, and there are certainly things that can be critiqued. But the support has been great. The conversations have been great. I imagine that when it's out in paperback and it starts to hit schools, that I'll be able to have a lot of really interesting conversations with people who are reading it across the country. I mean, I'm getting a lot of really nice phone calls and emails and responses from people who read it and blurbed it. And I couldn't be happier about that. That's been incredibly sustaining. It [was] hard to write, because if I had written a book that was only for us, it would be a different book. I wouldn't have to do any Disability 101. And there are chunks of 101 in there that, yes, I [had] to write, but I knew that no one would understand what I was talking about if I didn't fill it in for a general audience. But also, I felt like the general audience is, by and large, the people who are so behind the curve. And so I was walking this very thin line between talking to us and talking to them and talking to us and talking to them. And, you know, I guess time will tell where it landed.

But I did find myself so happy that the book was such a celebration of who we are. All over the country, outside of the country, I have got to keep talking more and more and more about us as a community, as a movement, as a culture. There were people who wanted me to kind of skip over that stuff and just keep talking about my personal life. I'm like, "No, the point is you understand the culture because of my personal life." I don't really care much that it was my personal life, but my personal life explains how I ended up doing what I'm doing. And that was what was important to me—to get to the part of bringing us to people's attention and talking about [the] originality and beauty and flexibility that I see all the time in who we are.

ALICE: What do you love about painting other people, especially disabled people?

RIVA: Oh god, everything! People's faces and bodies are so poetic, especially as we go through time and really occupy our bodies, where the person that you are shows more and more on the outside. I like looking at pictures of people when they're young and then looking at who they are when I meet them, and just thinking about that proto-person and now the one that I see. But the thing about disabled bodies—I finally figured this out, and I've been telling people this in interviews—what I find beautiful is that, because we are so often looked at and [because] we have to be so conscious of what our bodyminds need, there's . . . a presence that I find in disabled people, a way of, like . . . Sometimes, to me, so-called "normal" people operate their bodies like they're driving in the dark or something. Like they just . . . they don't know where they are in space. They don't know, like . . . they're just kind of going *galumph galumph* through the world. And there's a kind of blankness there for me that, I mean . . . Not everybody, obviously.

And disability, it's got such a . . . hmm. [It's] hard-won. You know, it's like something that's been—that has a patina. Like something you've touched and touched and touched and rubbed and worked, and—There's just these things that are not really verbal. But it's just something I see of, like, this lustrous presence, and that's what I love.

ALICE: Thank you for that. For the sake of this interview, could you describe this portrait you did for me, what the piece is made out of and also what the portrait looks like?

RIVA: Well, it's on something called mylar vellum, which is like a plastic that you can draw on. And it's about—I think it's something like seventeen by twenty-two inches, something like that. And we did it by having multiple conversations over Google Meet. So I was drawing you while we were talking, and you're looking straight out at me [with a] very intense, very communicative expression. People have remarked multiple times on how just sort of riveting your eyes are and how they are stopped cold by your presence, which made me really happy 'cause I felt like that's what you're like. So people have gotten what I had hoped. So you are wearing a, kind of a black-and-white track jacket that has zippers, and you're wearing your BiPap ventilator, which has sort of these lovely milky whites and blue tones in it, and then there's sort of a purple ring around where one of the hose attachments goes. So it's got some very lovely, sort of almost atmospheric colors. And then that's set against the sort of gold and pink tones of your skin color, your deep sort of almost reddish-brown eyes. And then behind you, you can see a little bit of your headrest and then a doorway to more of the apartment and some of the art that you have hung on the wall. And I then took the framing of a

Google Meet that I could see on my laptop, and I drew the actual framing device that you would see on the screen with the time. And the dock to my laptop is off to the right. So I tried to capture what we were doing, so it wouldn't just be a sort of random picture, to make the point that we were communicating remotely and to explore what that was like.

ALICE: Yeah, I mean, I think what's really interesting is, on Facebook several months ago, you posted a photo of that portrait, and I remember distinctly one of your Facebook friends said, "Oh, she looks so tired!" And that was her first impression of me, and I was like, "Wow, that's all they got out of it?!" And I thought that was really instructive, too, because everyone's gonna have different attitudes toward bodies and the way bodies age, and [bodies] are a reflection of what we've been through. But I thought that was a really fascinating response. I think she made a comment about the dark circles under my eyes. And I was really tempted to say, "You know, lady, if only you knew half the story!" But I didn't say anything because life is too damn short to comment on Facebook.

A sketch of me by the artist Riva Lehrer, 2020.

RIVA: Well, it's part of what I call "pain reading," which I have experienced with my portraits over and over. Which [means] as soon as somebody, a viewer, sees a wheelchair or a crutch or an adaptive device or whatever, it's like the idea is, I think, that, in ableist society, disabled lives are by definition full of suffering and misery. And if you even try to show a disabled person being happy or sexual or joyous or just complex, that ableist thought and perception will think that that thing is covering over the authentic suffering of the disabled person! And I feel like because someone could see your adaptive devices, like for [my Facebook friend], it kidnapped her ability to see you. And instead of actually seeing your face and the attitude of peace, which I thought was very strong, she went to this place that I've just experienced so many times with people looking at my work, like, "Oh, there's a crutch!" [*huge gasp*] and that provides everything for them. And I'm still working to get people to see something else.

ALICE: I think that's what is so important [about having] these different kinds of portraits out there. Because they don't always have to be explained, but there are always gonna be people who pick up on what you're trying to express. And then there'll be other people who just see the dark circles under my eyes! Which I think is fine. To each their own. Could you talk a little bit more about the evolution of your process? Because this summer you did a portrait virtually with me, which I believe [was] your first time.

RIVA: Right.

ALICE: But how did that change your thinking about portraiture and also the relationship you have with the person who's usually the subject of your portraits? Like how has it expanded or enhanced the way you relate to your subject?

RIVA: Well, starting from the beginning of when I started working with disability, bodies that weren't just mine, it was really important to me to give people autonomy. Because I knew that being looked at, for a lot of us, is really at the very least complex and often pretty painful and demeaning in the way that we're treated when we're looked at. And it was super important to me not to replicate that. But it's not like I walked in knowing how to do that. That took a long time of trying

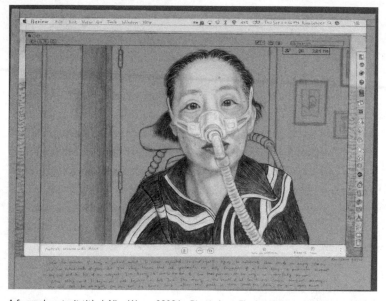

A framed portrait titled *Alice Wong, 2020* by Riva Lehrer. The handwritten text below the portrait reads: *After four decades of being a portrait artist I never expected to find myself trying to collaborate from inside an empty studio and from behind walls of glass. But I've always known that all portraits are only fragments of a human being, a particular moment in the self and the life of the subject. I'm having to work harder to see the person, so far away, so imperfectly known. Alice Wong and I began our work together in late June. This drawing is the result of at least six Google Hangouts meetings. She will still be emerging for me, hour by hour, long after this piece is done. Thank you, Alice, for your open heart.*

to be a better listener. You can always be a better listener. There are times I just blow it, but I really try. And to give people the choice of, you know—I'm not ever gonna force an image on anybody. It has to feel okay with them. And so I've tried various ethical structures to give people as much power as possible.

But the thing about working with you over Google Meet—and I wanna write a lot more about this—is that, first off, it made me think more about accessibility. I've been limiting my portraiture to people who could actually be here with me and who could . . . manage my home, which is not accessible enough for a lot of the people I know. Like my bathroom isn't accessible, and my elevator is tiny and won't accommodate a power chair. So it's really been limiting who I could work with, but I wasn't thinking my way around it. So this was one way, first off, I'm like, "Oh my god! Not every portrait has to be the same kind of thing. You can change your methods based on . . ." Even when [the COVID-19 pandemic] is over, I want this to continue.

But also longing and separation and loneliness. And everybody complains about Zoom and other videoconferencing platforms like Google Meet, and yeah, if I've been on it all day, I get pretty burned out. But I am sitting here looking at you, and I'm really happy to see you. I'm so happy to see you, and I'm happy to be seen. And I just feel like, "God, all these whiny people!" You know, I live alone, and video calls are the only times now when I get to look at someone and they get to look at me without any masks or any distance. I'm grateful for this.

Westward Ho

A 2020 interview by Grace Bonney with me and Sandy Ho, founder and co-organizer of the Disability and Intersectionality Summit, about Sandy's and my friendship for the book Collective Wisdom, *a series of intergenerational conversations. This conversation has been condensed and edited for clarity.*

GRACE BONNEY: How did you two meet each other and become friends?

SANDY HO: So, back in the day [*chuckles*], I think this was around, what, like 2011 or '12 maybe. I don't really remember. But I was, at the time, a program manager for a Thrive mentoring program, which was based out of Easterseals Massachusetts. And the program was the first of its kind in the state of Massachusetts that worked with young women with disabilities between the ages of fourteen and twenty-six who were mentored by older women with disabilities. So that was a different aspect to that program, because I think usually mentoring programs for youth with disabilities pair them with nondisabled adults. And so, out of this program, one of the activities I had the mentees and mentors do was to write letters to their younger selves just to try to get to know each other, get them talking about issues that, you know, maybe would've been a little bit more challenging to bring up right away. And through that process, I was googling for other women with disabilities.

And this was definitely during a time in my life where I was just kinda coming into that identity as well, figuring out what it means to be a disabled woman, a disabled young woman. And that was when I came across Alice Wong's work. Yeah! And I don't really know what sort of pushed me over the edge to just send a cold email. [*laughs*] 'Cause I was like literally, you know, this rando person just kind of getting started in the disability community. And I sent Alice an email, just like, "Hey, we're doing this Letters to Thrive project [on Tumblr]. I would love to meet you." And then, surprisingly, Alice responded.

ALICE WONG: And the rest is history! And I think for the most part nowadays, I'm much less likely to respond to all the rando emails. But I think Sandy caught me at a good time and a good year [when] I was more receptive! [*chuckles*]

And I do remember getting the email from Sandy and that her project, the Letters to Thrive, was such a lovely project because, you know, it is about uplifting youth, but it's also about what are our hopes and dreams, and really having this conversation with our past. And I thought, *Oh my goodness*. Like, what a gift it is to have this Letters to Thrive project on Tumblr. I know we're dating ourselves because it's Tumblr. But the fact that these are valentines to ourselves, I thought, well, what a lovely gift to give people a chance to share their stories.

So I think Sandy asked me if I would be interested in submitting something, and I told her—I'm like, "Oh, I just happen to have an essay that came out in an Asian American studies journal called *Amerasia*." I think this was 2017, and it really was one of the first times I wrote an essay about who I am as a disabled Asian American. And this was a special issue on disability and elders.

And that's where I think our friendship started. It's really just through exchanging information and kind of learning about Sandy's work. And I was just so impressed by the way that she really cares about disabled youth. She works with a lotta young disabled women and young girls and is just, like, such a cool person. And I'm just like, "Okay, this is somebody I know I'm gonna be friends with." And I think it was pretty instantaneous. What do you think, Sandy?

SANDY: Yeah, I think that the fact that there was such a response from the Tumblr. So after the young women and their mentors from the program gave me permission to post their letters, it was really just meant for the program, you know, for each other to easily read each other's letters and share things. What I did not expect was just an outpouring of other submissions from disabled women from across the country, from around the world. And the things that were being written about—including Alice's story as well, as she shared—sort of really clued us all into the fact that we have a community of support, of just a sense of pride and a sense of solidarity among each other.

I think Alice was one of the first disabled Asian American folks that I became friendly with in a genuine and meaningful way. And what I mean by that is like, this was not a friendship that was forced upon me by a social worker or a guidance counselor or a teacher or a parent. It was just very natural. I was ready to come into this space. Alice was, very luckily [for] me, receptive, and that helped a lot. And that's something that I always stress to young people, is that their community's always gonna be there when they're ready. That's our responsibility as mentors and as older folks.

GRACE: Can either of you remember a moment in time when you realized that your friendship was going to be something really meaningful in your life?

ALICE: Hmm. Well, I feel like we've been friends for quite a few years, but I feel like this year especially—just for me, I think, with the pandemic but also just, you know, all of the things that we've been involved in—that we've really kind of been there for each other. Like, there are text messages and these ways to just check in with one another and just give each other a space to kinda just vent and let our hair down and just, like—we don't have to talk about activism. We don't have to talk about disability. We can gossip. And I know I've relied on that. This pandemic has just accelerated with a lot of my relationships where I feel like you really do see who you can rely on. And I feel very grateful for that, you know.

And oh, I just wanna clarify. I just realized the essay I wrote in *Amerasia* was in 2013! Yikes! So I think when Sandy reached out, it was probably a few years after that.

SANDY: I think, in terms of me, the moment when I was like, "Okay, Alice is not just a resource for me, but more is somebody who I can maybe call a friend," is she definitely made it clear to me that she's there to give me the answers to the questions that nobody else in our community is talking about. And so what I mean by that is as somebody who's spent most of my quote-unquote "career" on restricted income, being an activist means that you don't have the traditional nine-to-five job. And figuring out, you know, when you get invited to do train[ings] or present, she constantly has been one of the folks who's reminded me that I have value beyond just being somebody who is there to be the diversity token or to give these inclusion trainings . . . that the work that I'm putting out is meaningful in both its content [and] also to just add to the content of what we're trying to build.

And just all of those kinds of really difficult things about, well, how much money do you request for an honorarium? Or, you know, how do you tell your parents that actually, you have no interest in grad school, and you just wanna do this activism thing for a while? Like, these are really difficult conversations that I think can have a big influence on somebody's early disability community activism career. And I think there's many folks in our community right now who may not have that person, and I hope that they find that person. Because having somebody in your corner who's gonna cheer you on constantly and give you the no-B.S. answers that you need, that's really key.

ALICE: Yeah, I think a lot of it is about strategy, you know, like figuring out the landscape and how to navigate it. And I think that's where I have been on this Earth a little bit longer than Sandy, and I have made my mistakes, right? I've definitely racked up some experiences, and I value these intergenerational exchanges, but with the people that I trust. Not everyone, right? Like, this is clearly mentoring. I don't even see our relationship as a mentor-mentee because it's really about two equals, even though sometimes Sandy refers to me as an older sister. And I guess in the bossy-pants way, yes! I can be an older sister. And I already am an older sister of two younger siblings. So this comes very naturally.

But I see Sandy as absolutely my equal, if not more, because I see her as the future, you know. And this is really something that's important to me, is how do we make sure that the next generation of disabled activists really just take on the world, you know? I do think, with my own kind of sense of mortality and stuff, like, what can I impart? What could I share that's gonna be useful? Especially insider stuff, you know, stuff you can't say publicly that would at least give Sandy and the people that I care about a leg up, you know, just whatever else I could do to be of service. And that's part of my own kind of sense of service, [but] it's not really out of obligation, right? It's out of, not to be corny, but it's really about love: the love of our people and just making sure that people feel seen and heard and supported.

'Cause I think for so many in our community, even now, a lot of young people are just still very isolated, right? They're still not politicized. They're not—they're not even interested maybe in getting involved or identifying. And that's okay, too, right? Like that's, you know, no one should ever feel obligated to do that. But I think for those who are interested that they are hungry for connection. And I don't think that it's . . . it's just because we're Asian American we have this automatic frame of reference because, you know, we're all not the same. I think very much we're lucky that our personalities matched up, you know, in terms of our love of food and just all sorts of things. So I think that's something else I wanna resist, this pigeonholing. Sandy and I have laughed about this—there is sometimes this weird presumption that all Asian American disabled people know each other or that we're all, like, buddies. And we're not. But with Sandy and I, yes, we are.

And one of the things I'm really most proud of in terms of just seeing her grow in her leadership is with the Disability and Intersectionality Summit that Sandy organized and created. This started in 2016, and it's a biennial event. There was one in 2016 and one in 2018. The one for 2020 was canceled and became virtual and prerecorded in 2021. And I just think it's the most amazing and powerful example of community organizing, and I respect Sandy so much for her style and leadership. She asked me to serve on their steering board for the last two events, and I was able to witness the way she was able to just develop consensus, working with all kinds of people, dealing with all kinds of conflicts and headaches that come with organizing an event. But she really has a commitment toward disability justice and amplifying multiply marginalized disabled people. So that, to me, is really heartening, and it makes me feel good just to be adjacent to that.

SANDY: Thanks, Alice! One of the most powerful moments for me was in 2018. The Disability and Intersectionality Summit was something that's always been centered in Massachusetts. But then that year, we also had the satellite San Francisco conference as well. And one of the things that we did was to celebrate and honor the first collection of essays that Alice had self-published, the *Resistance and Hope* anthology, an e-book. And to be able to a) have the privilege to be an organizer is one thing, but then to also be able to celebrate the work of your friends and include that in that niche . . . and then to uplift and to elevate, too—those are the moments where it's like, okay, this is why we are friends. This is why we work in community, and we see each other as co-schemers in each other's plans.

And I wish I could've been there in San Francisco at the time, but I was, of course, in Boston. But then shortly after that conference, I flew to Chicago and then took the California Zephyr train from Chicago to San Francisco. And I did it because a) I wanted to visit the disability community in Chicago, and they've got great folks at Access Living. But also because it was something that I always wanted to do in my life, to visit [San Francisco]. San Francisco is viewed as the birthplace, if you will, of the independent living movement, of disability rights. And so it was something that I wanted to do very much for myself. And of course, doing my work around the Intersectionality Summit and the community that came from that, I wanted to visit so many of my friends that I'd never met in person until that moment.

And so getting to meet Alice in person after that conference was incredible. Like, she was so welcoming with me to her home. This is what Alice does. You think she's gonna do one thing, and then she just levels it up times a hundred. And, you know, she really showed up with her friends and community there to just sort of be like, "Hey, this is who we are. This is what we're doing. This is what we're about." And it was great to just not talk about activist work but just sort of be together.

ALICE: Yeah, I love to entertain, and I think the gift of our friendship is that we're so privileged to be able to have this space. And I think about how I have not left my home since March, and I think about those times I was lucky to have parties or just have gatherings. And then yeah, I'm like, "Wow." At least Sandy and I got together once when she was over here and we got to meet up multiple times. At least we had that, and that, to me, is really—a really special moment.

I don't know, Sandy, if you wanna talk about it, but in 2016, as the summit was about to start in October, I got a chance to do a Q and A with you. And it was a way to promote the summit and to encourage people to attend. And that was actually maybe—correct me if I'm wrong—but that was the first time you identified as a queer disabled woman. So I think that might've been significant for you, but do you wanna talk about it in terms of just, like, what that meant for you, or if that meant something to you?

SANDY: Yeah, I think that having somebody who is not only going to cheer on your work but cheer on your just personal process as well is really important, and that's been so key to our friendship as well. That that moment of identifying as queer in a disability space and having that be seen as something that I felt comfortable to do, clearly, and so much of that is because I knew Alice. I knew her platform and what she was about as a person, and that trust is not stressed enough in friendships and community organizing work in particular. Because without that trust, we don't have activists who are gonna be able to take those risks, right? And I think that's part of what helps our community to continue pushing ourselves. But that moment, for me, was something that like, I think it was a long time coming, but it was just a matter of finding the space and the person and the platform to do that on. I didn't want it to just be some long, drawn-out Facebook post or a tweet thread. But it meant something to me to be able to do that in a way that I knew would not just be respected because it's Alice, but it's also something that I knew would get out to folks who are also looking for that representation as well.

ALICE: And I think that, to me, also showed me kinda like how our friendship has evolved, in the sense that you felt safe to do that. You know, it wasn't like something I asked or just, you know, 'cause I didn't know. I just wanted to interview you. But the fact that you felt comfortable and safe enough to do that, that was meaningful for me. I think that's ultimately . . . the world we wanna create: this sense where everybody can just be their full selves and not have to explain anything or just worry about anything. That's the future, that's what we're working toward. We're not really there yet, but I think, you know, constantly about this idea of building toward justice. And I think this is just one way that—one example of us showing the world all the different ways that we can just support each other in that collective effort. So, yeah, that's kinda just the beauty, too, right? That we can all kind of show up for each other in these big ways or obvious ways, but also a lotta ways that are not apparent as well. I think that's what happens in friendships, too. It's that ebb and flow.

GRACE: That's so lovely. I'm curious. I think that this can be a tough question to answer, but what do you hope that your friendship brings each other?

ALICE: Since I am older than Sandy, I think one thing I really do hope in terms of our continued friendship is just to help Sandy realize all her dreams and goals and to really encourage her ambitions. Because I wanna see her succeed in whatever she wants to do. That, to me, is one of my personal goals of making sure that Sandy realizes she has so many choices and talents, and she brings a lot to whatever she wants to do. And however I can facilitate that in a subtle way or not so subtle way, that, to me, is one of the things that I hope is part of our friendship, is the gentle nudging of, like, "Apply for this." "Try that." "Do this." And again, this is the bossy side of me, but, you know, I think we all need somebody who has that other perspective, right? Sometimes we talk ourselves out of doing things because we think, *Oh, I'm not—maybe I'm not the right fit* or just *Maybe it's out of* *my lane*, things like that. But I'm gonna be that secret person that whispers in Sandy's ear like [*loud whisper*], "Do it! Do it!" Yeah, I can be creepy. If that's what it takes, I'll be creepy, you know. And I love it. I'll text her, like, a creepy GIF, you know, whatever it takes. I'm just ready for Sandy to take over the world, and I'd like to help lay the groundwork for that.

SANDY: Yeah. That groundwork, by the way, also includes Alice promoting a hashtag every now and then that is #WestwardHo, because she is adamant about me moving to California, okay?

ALICE: Yeah. So, eventually, Sandy is going to relocate to the West Coast. And I'll just say, totally randomly sometimes, "Westward Ho." I'll just pop it in a text: "Westward Ho. Don't forget: Westward Ho." It's not happening yet, but it's in the works. And I think the universe will provide, but yeah, #WestwardHo is one of my guerrilla campaigns. It's Westward Ho 2024 or bust!

Year of the Tiger Crossword*

ACROSS

2 Watch it jiggle (6)
3 Hot yoga (6)
5 A form of love (6)
9 Northerners (12)
11 I *heart* _____ (2)
14 Resistance is futile (7)
16 A lifeline (8)
17 #____TheVote (4)
18 Cross-training routine (12)
19 It's alive! (8)

DOWN

1 Cassandra-esque (6)
3 Every day (8)
4 Care is _____ (14)
5 Suck on it (7)
6 Hoosier city (12)
7 "Greetings, Mork!" (8)
8 Not so easy (9)
10 A fave word (4)
12 Shady scam (8)
13 Peachy keen (8)
15 Show me the money (9)

---

* For accessibility, the number in parentheses after each clue indicates the number of letters. Answers can be found on page 371.

Lunar New Year Memories

I wonder what it was like for my parents to move to Indianapolis from Hong Kong without any friends, family, or familiarity with American culture in the 1970s. Two years after they arrived, they became first-time parents with me and later parents to my two sisters, Emily and Grace. One central part of missing home is longing for Chinese food traditions. When I was in grade school, our family took weeks off and went back to Hong Kong for Lunar New Year, and listening to Shandongnese spoken loudly by extended family, smelling incense and diesel fuel in the crowded streets, and filling my belly with the best food were my strongest Hong Kong sense memories.

One of our family trips to Hong Kong during the month of Lunar New Year. We are visiting Victoria Peak, the highest hill on the island and a popular tourist attraction. *From left:* Dad, Mom, me, my paternal grandmother 林國芬 Lín Guó Fēn, and my sister Emily.

...

During the weeklong celebrations, a revolving door of guests visited my grandparents' two-bedroom apartment in North Point, bringing gifts such as fruit or alcohol and 紅包 hóngbāo, lucky red envelopes with embossed decorative gold designs, for the kids. The amount a kid received was based on a complex social calculus of the giver's proximal relationship with their family, with stinginess or generosity as variables. My sisters and I never experienced this jackpot before, and we carefully stored all our envelopes in a shoebox for a major shopping spree. Reader, I never got that shopping spree—Mom took all our red envelopes and bought us a Texas Instruments Speak and Spell "toy" without our knowledge. Can you spell *j-u-s-t-i-c-e*? I can spell it, but I still don't have it. To quote from the film *Heathers*: "Oh, the humanity!" I can still taste the umami-less betrayal today.

With the guests who flowed in and out of the apartment came plates of fish and chive dumplings made by my 婆婆 pópo grandmother, who made everything à la minute. Chinese food has to be hot and fresh, and hospitality dictated a continual flow of dumplings until the last guest left. I remember seeing pópo cook in a small, crowded kitchen and being so tired afterward she didn't have any appetite to eat. Because of the Patriarchy, she usually ate dinner last because she was always cooking successive dishes in the heat (turning on the air conditioner was a rarity). I think about my pópo and whether she got to eat steam-filled dumplings bursting with savory juices only as a child, not as a wife or mother. Did she even get to dip her dumplings in soy sauce and vinegar, or nibble at a clove of raw garlic as accompaniment? Who served her and encouraged her to eat more in her later years?

Sometimes I see my mom tired after she makes dumplings, but with our family, everyone except me participates in making them (I used to peel shrimp, but I am retired). Mom is in charge of making the dough and filling (the most important parts). Dad rolls the dough into long, thick ropes and cuts them; then he creates individual wrappers by rotating the coin-shaped dough with a flick of a wrist while the other hand rolls them with a wooden baton. Each wrapper gets gently tossed onto the countertop with a dusting of flour, then Mom and my sisters take the wrappers before they get stuck together, add the filling, and fold the edges into a scalloped pattern. I am the self-appointed documentarian, taking photos and videos so that we no-longer-young-ones can save these memories.

When the Center for Asian American Media collected oral histories about Lunar New Year in 2015, I interviewed my mom, the second most extroverted person in our family, so that our Chinese American story could be preserved for the future. Preserving something doesn't mean it is trapped in the past. Preservation of a recipe or a food tradition is a guide for, rather than an arbiter of, "authenticity." Like any fermented sauce, time adds flavor, nuance, and depth to stories. They remain alive and available for our nourishment.

Mom (*left*) and me in a small recording booth at StoryCorps San Francisco, which closed in 2018.

Some families ski or camp together; Wongs make food and eat together. Talking about, planning, or dreaming about the next meal and remembering meals from the past—this is our love language, cultural wisdom, history, and family legacy.

ALICE WONG: My name is Alice Wong. I am forty years old. Today is February 12, 2015. We're at the San Francisco Public Library at StoryCorps, and I'm here to interview my mom today, Bobby Wong.

BOBBY WONG: My name's Bobby Wong. I'm sixty-five years old. And today is February the twelfth, 2015. I'm also at the San Francisco Library.

ALICE: And you're here to talk to me! [*laughs*]

BOBBY: Yes, my daughter. Yeah, my oldest daughter, Alice Wong.

ALICE: Oh, yay. So, today, you know, we're gonna have a chat about our memories and about the Lunar New Year and about the different ways we've celebrated it in the past and today.

BOBBY: Okay.

ALICE: So, tell me a little bit about where you were born. And when you grew up, what was 新年 xīnnián, Lunar New Year, what was that like for you?

BOBBY: Okay, I was born in Hong Kong a long time ago—

[*Alice chuckles*]

BOBBY: —in 1949. So, in Hong Kong, it's, you know, before I immigrated to the U.S., we celebrate Lunar New Year. It's a major holiday for the Chinese. So—

ALICE: It's like the biggest.

BOBBY: The biggest.

ALICE: Bigger than 中秋節, zhōng qiū jié, Mid-Autumn Festival.

BOBBY: Yes, yes. Yeah. Because this is the day for the family reunited together. So, it's—how to say it . . . I would say bigger than Christmas, has a similar meaning. But that involves the whole clan, you know, village.

ALICE: Yeah.

BOBBY: And then province, state, city, and the country to celebrate all together on the same day.

ALICE: So it's really kinda like the biggest important day of the year, at least, for Chinese people.

BOBBY: Yes.

ALICE: So tell me, how did you celebrate it as a kid, or what are some of your fondest memories regarding xīnnián?

BOBBY: Okay. Yeah, when I was a kid, I don't have to prepare anything for the New Year.

[*Alice laughs*]

BOBBY: Everything—my mother will prepare that. All I have is fun. And the things I like the most is eating the money dumpling that is only once in a year for the Lunar New Year.

ALICE: How would you say that in Mandarin, "money dumpling"?

BOBBY: 錢水餃 qián shuǐjiǎo. Yeah.

ALICE: And do many people, other people, do that? Or was that just something your family did?

BOBBY: This only pertains to the northern part of China.

ALICE: Ah!

BOBBY: And I don't know if, you know, other northern people does this.

ALICE: Uh-huh.

BOBBY: But I know the—

ALICE: Shandong.

BOBBY: —Shandongnese, Shandongnese, yeah, do that.

ALICE: And we're both—both you and Dad are 山東人 Shāndōng rén [Shandongnese people], and it's so funny that, you know, you guys met in Hong Kong.

BOBBY: Uh-huh.

ALICE: And there are so few northern Chinese people there. So it's pretty unique to have northern traditions in Hong Kong, right?

BOBBY: Yes.

ALICE: So what is a money dumpling and how does it work? And tell me about your fun memories with it.

BOBBY: Okay. The money dumpling is—how to say it—during Lunar New Year, the tradition is to prepare ten things. Ten means perfect. Like candy, this and that, or obviously, money is the important thing. And then you only put ten dimes in the dumplings.

ALICE: Mm-hmm.

BOBBY: And then you make a lot of dumplings for the whole family, about five to ten people, you know, and then you only have ten dumplings mixed in it. So it was really fun to poke to see which dumpling has something hardened, you know, with your chopstick—how to say—[*chuckles*] put it in. And, "Oh! This one must have the coin, you know, the metal inside," you just pick right away.

ALICE: So it's like an eating treasure hunt.

BOBBY: Yes. Yes. Eating treasure hunt.

ALICE: And how many hundreds of dumplings would you make, say, for your family? I mean, how many dumplings would you make in one meal?

BOBBY: Okay, we have six people in our family. My mom will make one hundred fifty to two hundred.

ALICE: Oh my gosh!

BOBBY: So, because you've got to have leftovers for next few days because we don't want to run out of things, so you've got to make more. Yeah.

ALICE: It seems like New Year's, definitely, the one time you share your prosperity, even if you're poor, right? It's all about new clothes—

BOBBY: Yes.

ALICE: —and eating a lot and having guests over and celebrating, right?

BOBBY: Yeah.

ALICE: So even people who have modest means, do they usually get a new outfit every New Year?

BOBBY: Oh, yeah. Yes, yes.

ALICE: What else did you do during the New Year? Did everybody in your family get new outfits?

BOBBY: Yes. Yeah. The—how to say—I grew up in a poor family, but during New Year, all the kids in the family have new clothes. And sometimes, I remember at one point, my parents went out and borrowed money to make a feast and buy new clothes for us.

ALICE: Wow. And that was pretty common among poor people, right?

BOBBY: Yes, mm-hmm.

ALICE: In terms of you do what you gotta do to keep up that tradition.

BOBBY: Yeah.

ALICE: Even if it puts you in debt a little bit.

BOBBY: Yeah, yeah. You try to pay off the debt before the New Year, and then you, after you pay off, then you can borrow some for the New Year!

ALICE: So pay off last year's New Year's debt to go into debt again for the New Year!

BOBBY: Yeah. [*laughs*] Coming year. But when we have more money left over, then we will always have a red color. Red color, red flower print, something like that, yeah.

ALICE: And what is symbolic about the color red in Chinese culture?

BOBBY: I think the red means happiness.

ALICE: Mm-hmm.

BOBBY: Yeah, like a wedding everything is red. And New Year and the posting, writing paper, all red. And so, we wear red clothes. Not totally red, but just one or two garments are red, like a red hat or red blouse, something like that.

ALICE: Mm-hmm. It's a meaningful color in Chinese culture.

BOBBY: Yes. Yeah.

ALICE: And it's also a lot of posters that go up, or signs that go up, that you post on New Year's Day. What are some of the characters on the signs?

BOBBY: Like double happiness, 囍, means 喜 xǐ, happiness, twice. And then 恭喜发财 gōng xǐ fā cái, wishing someone prosperity and good fortune.

ALICE: Mm-hmm.

BOBBY: Those are the few characters we wrote. And we wrote poems and posted them on both sides—both sides of the door.

ALICE: In Chinese calligraphy, right?

BOBBY: Yes.

ALICE: And that is another kind of tradition, too, right? This kinda artwork and things and then posting them. Because, basically, anybody can do that, right? They just—all they need is ink and paper. So anybody can do that, right?

BOBBY: No, no. How to say it . . . This also shows your family's education status. So if you lack education, then you don't write it by yourself. You purchase it.

ALICE: Ah.

BOBBY: Or you ask people who're famous who's good to write the poem, write good calligraphy. You ask for it.

ALICE: Wow. So it really is kind of like an outward showing to everyone that this is who we are. This is, you know, our status. Or no?

BOBBY: Not really. Because everyone does the same. Yeah, everyone does the same.

ALICE: But you can tell the difference, with some people, they actually have calligraphy skills.

BOBBY: Yes.

ALICE: And other people have store-bought products.

BOBBY: Right, store.

ALICE: So there is some difference, right?

BOBBY: Yeah, yeah, yeah. The writing, yeah, yeah. You can see that kinda like I see the status of the family, yeah.

ALICE: The education level.

BOBBY: Yeah, yeah.

ALICE: And I remember the paper is always so pretty because it is always red with flecks of gold, right?

BOBBY: Always.

ALICE: It's always, like—I remember seeing that as a kid, and it's, like, such pretty paper, right? And yet, it's very common and cheap, right? Or is it—

BOBBY: No, no. The red paper with gold is most expensive. Yeah. Lots of people don't use that.

ALICE: Really?

BOBBY: Yeah, expensive.

ALICE: I remember 爺爺 yéyé, Grandfather, used to do calligraphy, and I remember seeing that beautiful red paper that's handmade as the background against the large black calligraphy. It's always just so elegant.

BOBBY: He used the best paper to show off his writing, his artwork.

ALICE: Yeah. Yeah. He had a whole setup on the dining room table with his brushes, and you could smell the ink. You know, it's [a] very distinctive smell. And he didn't like to be bothered. I know one time, I annoyed him, and he got mad at me.

BOBBY: Mm-hmm.

ALICE: It's a sweeping, smooth motion. He never stopped. So it's very intense, right?

BOBBY: Yeah, yeah.

ALICE: I mean, it's like you can . . . I think I remember you and Dad saying, like, you can see the energy of the writing based on the calligraphy. And that was really cool, I thought.

BOBBY: Yeah, yeah. Because doing the calligraphy, you have to use 氣功 qìgōng, "life energy," to hold your breath and then hold the brush. So you have [to] prepare everything in—

ALICE: Your mind.

BOBBY: —your mind and how to—where to lay down words and where to go. And sometimes even the space, you had to be right. Otherwise it doesn't—

ALICE: Look right.

BOBBY: Yeah, it doesn't look right. So that's why you need a hundred percent concentration. So that's why he [didn't] like people to bother him while he was writing.

ALICE: Especially a pesky grandchild.

BOBBY: Yeah.

ALICE: But I remember, like—I mean, that sounds like a very spiritual, meditative thing, right? You have to be really in the zone to do calligraphy. That's not something many people have.

BOBBY: Yeah, yeah.

ALICE: And it's a tradition that most people—

BOBBY: That's kind of lost.

ALICE: Simplified Chinese is more commonly used now.

BOBBY: Yeah.

ALICE: Like, calligraphy is definitely not simplified characters. There's so much kinda symbolism and art and history that's embedded in calligraphy.

BOBBY: True. True. Especially this computer age. We use a computer to write now. We don't even bother to write characters by hand anymore. Because takes—

ALICE: Too long.

BOBBY: Time, yeah.

ALICE: Too many strokes.

BOBBY: Yeah. [*laughs*]

ALICE: But I think we kept up the tradition about the money dumplings. So, you know, one of my favorite memories that you and Dad brought from Hong Kong, but really from Shandong, is when we were young in Indiana, and you used dimes.

BOBBY: Yes.

ALICE: And I remember we would hunt for them, and you wouldn't let us. Every single one that we poked, we had to eat.

BOBBY: Yeah.

ALICE: So you can't just go poking around!

BOBBY: Yeah, yeah.

ALICE: And sometimes we'd stare at the dumplings, too, to see if there's an outline and look for the bigger ones. But that didn't always work, either.

BOBBY: Yeah.

ALICE: But it seems like it's another way to kind of encourage eating.

BOBBY: Yeah.

ALICE: And encouraging eating is a big part of Chinese culture, wouldn't you say?

BOBBY: Yeah, I agree to that. After immigrating to the U.S., then we [were just a small] nuclear family. So I purposely make less, less dumplings. So easier for the children to get into the prize, you know. So after you get one money dumpling, then you will get a prize. The prize usually is a red envelope with money inside.

Me holding three red envelopes during the Year of the Rooster, 2017. I will never be too old to receive a 紅包 hóngbāo, never.

ALICE: Mm-hmm.

BOBBY: Yeah. So just encourage you to eat. The more you eat, the better, so. [*laughs*]

ALICE: So my memories are—and we still do it today—you know, there's a really nice division of labor. Mom, you always make the filling, which is a filling made with 韭菜 jiǔ cài, which is Chinese chives. They look like long blades of grass. One year you grew some in our backyard, but our lawn mower thought it was grass and mowed them down! It's super pungent, very savory. And that's really a thing northern Chinese people eat, right?

BOBBY: Yeah.

ALICE: Yeah. So then the filling is a combination of minced pork, shrimp, the chives, and ginger. I don't wanna give away your recipe, but soy sauce, ginger, and a little sesame oil. So it's made into a filling.

BOBBY: Mm-hmm.

ALICE: And you and Dad would make dough by hand. And also, the dough would be cut in two, rolled into strips, and then cut into very small, like, you know—

BOBBY: Round pieces.

ALICE: Round pieces. And each round piece would be hand-rolled into a dumpling wrapper, the kind you see in the grocery store. But each one was hand-rolled by you or Dad. And as we got older, we helped out, too. Now, Emily and Grace are now—

BOBBY: Learning, learning.

ALICE: They are, they're learning. They haven't gotten down the filling part, but they know how to wrap.

BOBBY: Yeah.

ALICE: Which is a big deal, because it's a real skill to take a flat piece of dough, put in a nice amount of filling, and to be able to use your fingers and pinch it into a beautiful-looking dumpling. And we've seen—

BOBBY: And the dumpling has to be plump enough to—

ALICE: Sit up. It has to be three-dimensional.

BOBBY: If you don't have enough skills, your dumpling will lay flat.

ALICE: That's right.

BOBBY: Yeah.

ALICE: And that's the mark of a good dumpling, that there's enough body. Because when you eat it, you need a lot of dumpling filling. You don't want a bunch of dough. And we've had guests come over, other Chinese friends, and when they would wrap their dumplings,

A photo of our dining table and a bamboo tray that came from my grandmother. The tray is holding six rows of plump dumplings ready to be boiled. Lucky red envelopes with gold decorations are taped in a row for each person who discovers a dime in their dumpling. The envelopes have varying denominations, so you have a chance to be extra lucky if you pick one with a hundred-dollar bill!

we would see how everyone has their own method of wrapping them.

BOBBY: Uh-huh.

ALICE: I mean, sometimes we'd have a little contest [to see] who can wrap best and—

BOBBY: And fastest. [*chuckles*]

ALICE: But—your dumplings always look the most plump. They're always standing up. They're always very cute, and the seal is very good.

BOBBY: Yeah, yeah.

ALICE: But I think, you know, everyone has their own style, too, though.

BOBBY: Yeah.

ALICE: Maybe the worst thing about dumplings is when they break in the water. That's always unfortunate.

BOBBY: Yeah.

ALICE: But usually, you—

BOBBY: But not me! [*laughs*]

ALICE: Not you, no! Not you, Mom!

BOBBY: I'm the professional! [*laughs*]

ALICE: You are. And you're teaching Emily and Grace really well, too.

BOBBY: Yeah.

ALICE: They're pretty decent.

BOBBY: Yeah, they have improved, each time, yeah.

ALICE: Yeah. And now that they've mastered . . . well, they're mastering—

BOBBY: The rolling.

ALICE: —the rolling and dough and the pinching and the stuffing of the dumpling, one day, they're gonna have to do the filling.

BOBBY: Yeah, stepping up. [*laughs*]

ALICE: Now, do you think that's the toughest part of making dumplings, because it takes so much experience to balance the flavors?

BOBBY: Mm-hmm. I think the dough, making the right combination in the filling, is the most difficult.

ALICE: The seasoning.

BOBBY: The seasoning, yeah, is very important. And also the dough, you got to make the right consistency. Not too soft, not too hard. You know, that also.

ALICE: So Emily and Grace are just at the beginning stage, so hopefully they will have a chance to start really practicing.

BOBBY: Yeah, yeah.

ALICE: Because, you know, I do think about how we're so lucky to have parents who are immigrants who really do know the traditional ways.

BOBBY: Mm-hmm, mm-hmm.

ALICE: And this is the one thing that, you know, we can definitely pass forward, right?

BOBBY: Yeah.

ALICE: This culture of ours. And it's really through food, right?

BOBBY: Yeah, yeah. But I have been doing the dumplings for over forty years. So I see your two sisters are showing interest, interest in carrying on this tradition. So, with time, their skills definitely will improve, and hopefully this tradition will be carried on.

ALICE: Yeah, I think for us it's, you know, it is about family, and we do have dumplings other times of the year. But it's always like a treat, right?

BOBBY: Mm-hmm.

ALICE: Because it's, like, it involves so much labor.

BOBBY: And the whole family can participate.

ALICE: Yeah. There's always somebody who boils the water.

BOBBY: Yeah.

ALICE: And then there's always somebody to do, like get the dough ready. And, you know, this is like something for everybody to do.

BOBBY: Yeah, yeah.

ALICE: And it's always also the additional sauces and kinda—

BOBBY: Vinegar.

ALICE: —condiments.

BOBBY: Yeah, yeah, yeah.

ALICE: So there's usually, you know, I guess as northerners, we also eat, like, ground garlic, which I love. Dad would crush raw garlic and make kind of a paste with salt, and it's, like, super salty, super strong. Dad will eat whole raw garlic cloves with our dumplings. And cucumber smacked with the flat side of a cleaver marinated in some vinegar and minced raw garlic (again). So this is what's really unique about northern Chinese, that we love garlic.

BOBBY: Yeah.

ALICE: But you just eat a little bit of it with your dumplings. And then the other condiment that we use is like half soy sauce, half vinegar. And that gives it a little bit more of a kick, because the dumplings can be pretty savory and rich, but it's nice to have a little zing on the side with the vinegar.

BOBBY: Yeah.

ALICE: So who taught you how to make dumplings?

BOBBY: Obviously, it's my mother. First of all, she requires lotsa help, labor, you know—

ALICE: Uh-huh.

BOBBY: —child labor to help her do some carryout, some jobs for the dumplings, so.

ALICE: So what was your job when you were younger?

BOBBY: I started with rolling the dough, yeah, rolling into small round pieces. That's the first thing you learn.

ALICE: Uh-huh.

邱淑萍 Qiū Shū Píng, my maternal grandmother

BOBBY: Then the second thing is you learn to wrap. After you pass those two tests, then you start to learn how to knead the dough. And then the last thing is to mix the ingredients, put in the seasoning.

ALICE: Yeah.

BOBBY: That's the very last final test.

ALICE: That's the hardest part, don't you think?

BOBBY: Yes, yes, yes.

ALICE: So what did you learn from your mom in terms of how to make the best dumpling filling? Or did you just watch?

BOBBY: Yeah, mostly by watching. Once you watch enough, then you kinda like memorize, you know, what to put in and how much. Then, by the time for you to do it, then you were just kinda like mimic those steps. Then you can taste it before it's wrapped, so.

ALICE: So when you were young and your mom still made them, did you ever make the filling, or did your mom always make the filling? Did you ever have a chance to make the filling for your family?

BOBBY: No, no.

[*Alice chuckles*]

BOBBY: Only my mom handles that, because sometimes if I made it, I could ruin the filling, you know?

ALICE: Right. So she wouldn't risk it.

BOBBY: Yeah.

ALICE: But anyway, she always was in charge of the filling.

BOBBY: Yeah. And the dough, too. Yeah. Only when I move here, I have to do it myself. So, I kinda like, oh, okay. Doing this way, that way. Yeah. Kind of, oh, too salty this time. The next time, put less salt.

ALICE: You know, and when you and Dad moved to Indianapolis, in the early years, in the mid-1970s, there was a small Chinese community and a Bible study group you were a part of. And a lot of them were overseas students at college.

BOBBY: Yeah. Mm-hmm, mm-hmm.

ALICE: And you would usually, during New Year, have people over, right?

BOBBY: Yeah, yeah.

ALICE: And being so far away from home, what did it mean to have a taste of home for a lot of these people?

BOBBY: Yeah. So, because I'm part of the church group for outreach for the overseas students, and because they don't have family during holidays, especially Chinese New Year, so I invite them to come. And I just prepare the dumplings and other dishes, and so we can have a fun time together and they won't be that homesick.

ALICE: Yeah. And they're especially homesick because, you know, Lunar New Year is such a big deal, right?

BOBBY: Yeah, yeah.

ALICE: And do you feel like they appreciated the dumplings?

BOBBY: Mm-hmm.

ALICE: That they probably on campus don't have any real Chinese food.

BOBBY: Yeah.

ALICE: But to taste dumplings must've been quite a treat.

BOBBY: Yeah, yeah. Because in those days, Indiana still didn't have that huge population, you couldn't get good Chinese food, especially northern Chinese. And that the most students I have over were the northern people. Because the southern people will go to another family, and the northern people come to our home. So we have the same traditions and the same food.

ALICE: Yeah.

BOBBY: So they really enjoy that and treasure that.

ALICE: Yeah. I'm sure it must be really sad when—even for you and Dad—to be away from so many of your relatives, especially in the beginning. Because later on, many of our relatives moved to the U.S.

BOBBY: Yeah.

ALICE: And we're around more family members. But in the very beginning, it was just you, Dad, me, Emily, and Grace, and that's it.

BOBBY: Mm-hmm, that's it.

ALICE: And everybody was in Hong Kong.

BOBBY: Yeah.

ALICE: So what was it like for you in terms of . . . Did it feel weird to celebrate Lunar New Year with just a small group, or was it, like, just something you had to do?

BOBBY: It was—how to say—of course, you need to adjust when you are in a new place. So, I think I believe I adapted pretty quickly and made the best out of it.

ALICE: Mm-hmm.

BOBBY: And also, we have the church community. You see Chinese people there. So, I think it makes the transition easier so you don't miss home that much.

ALICE: Yeah. In a way, the Chinese church became our extended family.

BOBBY: Yes.

ALICE: And, you know, one thing I think was really great when I was young, and I remember in the second or first grade, you and Dad would actually take us out of school for four weeks.

BOBBY: Oh, you remember that? [*laughs*]

ALICE: Oh my gosh, you can't do that these days, now.

BOBBY: No.

ALICE: But you would, I think when we were seven or six, you took us out of school for the entire month of February.

BOBBY: Mm-hmm, yeah.

ALICE: We would go back home to Hong Kong and celebrate New Year.

BOBBY: Yeah.

ALICE: And what a treat that was, too, because not only did you guys get to go back to your families and meet with your relatives during this important holiday, there was a chance to expose us kids to the tradition.

BOBBY: Yes. Yeah, that's the purpose. Yeah. So, because when you were in kindergarten, first grade, and second grade, it was not a big deal to arrange for you to do your homework overseas.

ALICE: Ugh. Homework.

BOBBY: But later on, you have to stay in school, yeah.

ALICE: What happens is that on the day of New Year, so many visitors, their friends and family, come into our house. And you just greet them and host them. And I don't know how pópo did it, but she had round after round of steaming dumplings made.

BOBBY: Yeah, yeah.

ALICE: It was just a two-bedroom apartment. I don't know where she kept all of the dumplings!

BOBBY: Yeah, yeah, yeah.

ALICE: But I mean, every time a guest arrived—

BOBBY: You have to—

ALICE: —that you gave them freshly made dumplings!

BOBBY: Yeah.

ALICE: And she did this for the entire day.

BOBBY: Yeah, yeah. This would usually last a week, too.

ALICE: Yeah. I mean, it's like I remember just the day, but it's like a whole week.

BOBBY: Yeah.

ALICE: So you have a whole week of parties.

BOBBY: Mm-hmm.

ALICE: And you guys would go out at night, have really big, fun dinner parties with mah-jongg afterwards.

BOBBY: Mm-hmm.

ALICE: But the fun thing about being a kid is that—you never get this in Indiana—

BOBBY: True, true.

ALICE: —that every visitor would give the kids a hóngbāo, a red envelope with some money!

BOBBY: Yeah.

ALICE: And that, as a kid raised in the U.S., it's like, "What?! You get money on this holiday?!" It's like, all you have to do is be a kid and say, "恭喜恭喜發財 gōng xǐ, gōng xǐ fā cái!" "Happiness and prosperity!" And you'd get a red envelope. And I remember one of the fun memories . . . some of the visitors would give you a Hong Kong ten-dollar bill. Which is, as I remember, the exchange rate is about $1.50.

BOBBY: Mm-hmm.

ALICE: And then some people would just give you a coin. I'm like, "Aw! This coin!"

[*Bobby chuckles*]

ALICE: And then some people would give a fifty Hong Kong dollar bill. And I'm like—we're like, "Whoa!"

BOBBY: Yeah, it depends on the relationship.

ALICE: Yeah! And that, to me, was like . . . They didn't even know us, but because we were the grandchildren of pópo and yéyé, they just gave it. And they gave out a lot of envelopes because they were gonna visit other people, too.

BOBBY: They have different stashes.

ALICE: Oh!

BOBBY: So according to their relationship with the person they visit, they will pull out [*laughs*] the "correct" one, you know?

ALICE: You don't wanna mix them up.

BOBBY: Yeah, yeah!

ALICE: And tell me about why it's so important for the bills to be brand new. Because I remember even in Indiana when we were young, you made a point when you prepared to give out hóngbāo, and you went to the bank to actually get crisp brand-new bills.

BOBBY: Yeah.

ALICE: And why is that?

BOBBY: So everything's new: new clothing, a new beginning. So you get

Me holding up a dime with a piece of chive stuck to it. I found the dime in a dumpling during Lunar New Year many years ago. I am smiling because I know this means I will get some lucky money. The thrill never gets old. I am unable to eat chive dumplings with pork and shrimp, but that doesn't mean I'm not in it to win it. I still hunt for dimes, and after selecting a dumpling, one of my sisters will eat it on my behalf. This is what I call adaptive gaming.

new money. Yeah, especially for the money dumpling, you definitely want to use new coins. So, I also—how to say it—disinfect the coins even if they're new.

ALICE: Yes.

BOBBY: Yeah. Before I wrap.

ALICE: Don't worry, people. It's not dirty money.

BOBBY: [*laughs*] Yeah.

ALICE: I think as a kid, I could eat about fifteen, ten to fifteen, I think, to try to find the coin.

BOBBY: Yeah.

ALICE: That's a lot. But I remember Dad and our uncle Simon, they could, during those—

BOBBY: Eat thirty, forty, yeah.

ALICE: —in one sitting.

BOBBY: Yeah.

ALICE: But Dad can't do that anymore!

BOBBY: Yeah. So, let me give you a secret. When I boil those dumplings, because I know which one I put the money in, I save some portion of money dumplings for the kids' platter, so it's easier for you guys to pick it out.

ALICE: Ahhh!

BOBBY: Otherwise, you cannot compete with them, you know—

ALICE: Yeah, there's no way.

BOBBY: —ten compared with eating forty, you know. [*chuckles*] There's no comparison.

ALICE: So the plate you gave us, you knew you had—

BOBBY: Has more, more chances for you to get money. [*laughs*]

ALICE: Aw, you're too nice, Mom.

BOBBY: Oh, yeah. That's what Mom's for. [*laughs*]

ALICE: But I think that definitely was, I think, one of the most . . . When I think about being Chinese American, I think about food and I think about dumplings.

BOBBY: Mm-hmm.

ALICE: Because that is something that's so uniquely Shandongnese of us. And this tradition is one of the few things that we actually do regularly. I mean, we're not super-traditional people, and yet do the repetition of having a meal.

BOBBY: Mm-hmm.

ALICE: That's really what is . . . something we've been keeping alive.

BOBBY: Mm-hmm, mm-hmm.

ALICE: So, in a way, you know, what do you want in the future? What's your hope about continuing food traditions for our family?

BOBBY: Yeah, for us older folks, older Chinese folks, especially northern people, the Shandongnese, we don't say "I love you."

ALICE: Right.

BOBBY: And we cannot say that word, but we just show it through our action by feeding you. Giving you good food makes you healthy, those types of things. So my job is to continue feeding you guys, and hopefully you guys learn all my trades so you can continue the family—continue this tradition in your own families in the future.

ALICE: Yeah, I really hope so, too, 'cause I do think about the future and how we will lose this real important link, you and Dad. Because I think everything we learned about Chinese culture, about Shandongnese culture really, comes from you two. And it's a very particular view based on you two. And you know, we will lose that thirty, forty years from now, and it's on us to carry it forward.

BOBBY: And you can simplify. You don't need to follow 100 percent

Mom (*right*) and me. Photo taken by Yosmay del Mazo after our recording session for the Center for Asian American Media's Lunar New Year Memories storytelling initiative at StoryCorps San Francisco in 2015.

because I don't follow 100 percent what my mother did. And because life is so hectic, fast-paced for young people these days, you can keep a little bit, you know. Maybe not the hand-roll handmade dough. You can purchase the ready-made.

ALICE: Nah, not as good!

BOBBY: [*laughs*] Oh, you have to add to it!

ALICE: But the memories of, I think, the best meals are really special.

BOBBY: Just to eat together. Main thing is to gather together.

ALICE: Sharing. You're eating the love. You're not saying the love.

BOBBY: Yes. Yes. You are right!

ALICE: That's the Chinese way.

BOBBY: Okay!

ALICE: Thanks for talking with me, Ma.

BOBBY: You're welcome. Happy Lunar New Year.

ALICE: Yes, 新年快乐 xīnnián kuàilè!

BOBBY: Xīnnián kuàilè!

Proust-ish Questionnaire

AN EXCLUSIVE INTERVIEW WITH ALICE WONG BY ALICE WONG

1. What is your idea of perfect happiness?

Snacking and guffawing with my sisters, Emily and Grace, and our friend Rani. Having fancy afternoon tea with tiny sandwiches, warm scones, clotted cream, and jam. Meeting up with friends for coffee. Family meals at a dining table laden with food.

2. What are your greatest fears?

Spiders. Drowning. Not having assistance for my daily routines. Power outages. Emergency evacuations. Being unable to communicate during a medical crisis or an accident.

3. What are your current favorite lip colors?

Chanel's Le Rouge Duo Ultra Tenue in "Daring Red," The Lip Bar's lipstick in "Merlot," Yves Saint Laurent's Rouge Pur Couture lipstick in "Rouge Unapologetic," and NARS's Powermatte Lip Pigment in "Don't Stop."

4. Which cat resembles your personality the most?

The Pallas's cat (*Otocolobus manul*), a small wild cat with light gray fur, small ears, and a stocky body. This cat looks both aggressive and grumpy.

5. Favorite internet cat?

Jorts the Cat on Twitter.

6. Which quote from a fictional T.V. character do you love?

"This is my design." —Will Graham, *Hannibal* (2013)

7. What is your love language?

Long, slow blinks (like a cat's). Writing letters and postcards with pretty stickers and stamps. Sending gifts to friends for no particular reason. Making people laugh. Feeding people.

8. What sounds do you love?

Thunder, howling wind, and rain violently pelting against a windowpane.

9. What is your latest favorite podcast?

Las Culturistas with Matt Rogers and Bowen Yang. DING DONG!!

10. What musician are you obsessed with right now?

Bruno Mars. I don't know what took me so long. The man is talented.

11. What are your strongest qualities?

Curiosity. Snarkiness. Knowing what I like and don't like.

12. Who do you despise the most?

checks PERSONA NON GRATA folder Too many to name.

13. What do you consider to be overrated virtues?

Punctuality. Neatness. Exercise. Daily routines.

14. On what occasion do you lie?

Many.

15. What do you most dislike about your appearance?

Flaky scalp and skin. My bony bits.

16. What do you like most about your appearance?

Lips. My lips are my best physical asset.

17. Which words or phrases do you most overuse?

Abundance, joy, capacity, ableism, resonate, problematic.

18. What or who is the greatest love of your life?

Meeeeeeee!

19. What is your next professional ambition?

To find an angel donor or a funder who will give me money to open an office so I can create a space to work and celebrate disability culture. And to hire an executive assistant, because I really need one!

20. If you could change one thing about yourself, what would it be?

Learn another language, like Spanish or Mandarin.

21. What do you consider your greatest achievement?

Staying alive. Seriously.

22. If you were to die and come back as a person or a thing, what would it be?

A petty ghost to haunt all my nemeses and mess up their shit.

23. Where do you go for coffee, and what is your order?

Sightglass Coffee in San Francisco, and I usually get a latte to go.

24. Where would you most like to live?

Tokyo or New York City (without the winters).

25. What is your most treasured possession?

My memories or, as I call them, *murrrmories*.

26. What do you regard as the lowest depth of misery?

Participating in a means-tested public program such as Medicaid, because there's nothing that makes you feel more powerless and dependent on the state than when you're trying to live in the community with autonomy and get your needs met, prescriptions covered, and services and durable medical equipment approved. Yes, it's a lifeline, but as a sole lifeline it is also a bureaucratic ableist misery.

27. What is your motto?

Fuck the fuckers.

28. What are you grateful for?

To live in this time period. For my friendships and relationships. Creative freedom. Flexibility with how I want to spend my time.

29. How would you like to die?

Surrounded by friends and family in a room with a roaring fireplace. After eating a spoonful of coffee ice cream, I am wrapped in an electric blanket with a bunch of cats lying all around me. I can smell lemons in the air as I fall into a deep, painless final rest.

storytelling

You got to make your own worlds;
you got to write yourself in.

—OCTAVIA E. BUTLER

We never know how our small activities will affect
others through the invisible fabric of our connectedness . . .
In this exquisitely connected world, it's never a question of
"critical mass." It's always about critical connections.

—GRACE LEE BOGGS

Remembering is one way to resist erasure.

—MIHEE KIM-KORT

Storytelling as Activism

A discussion with Longmore Institute director Catherine Kudlick for the fifth annual Longmore Lecture in Disability Studies (April 3, 2018). This conversation has been condensed and edited for clarity.

The Paul K. Longmore Institute on Disability at San Francisco State University is named after the late Dr. Paul Longmore, a disabled historian and activist who famously burned his book, The Invention of George Washington, *because the royalties put his Social Security benefits at risk. Later the Social Security Administration changed this ableist and punitive rule with the Longmore Amendment. Today the Longmore Institute showcases disabled people's lived experiences, history, and culture through public education, scholarship, and events such as Superfest, the longest-running international disability film festival in the world.*

CATHERINE KUDLICK: It's super great that you're here. And I'm so honored to be in the position of interviewing the interviewer. It's daunting and exciting.

ALICE WONG: I'm not ready! [*laughs*]

CATHERINE: So we're going to talk for about forty-five minutes, Alice and I. We have some questions. Could you tell me about how you met Paul Longmore and how he got you out here?

ALICE: Yeah. I do want to really thank you all for being here in person, and everybody online, and everybody with the Longmore Institute. You know, I am so lucky that I knew Paul Longmore. A long time ago in the 1990s, I was an undergrad at Indiana University–Indianapolis. I lived in suburban Indianapolis. In the Midwest, feeling very isolated, disconnected, as I read about disability studies and learned about the independent living rights movement, I knew that I wanted to head west. I knew that the Bay Area would be like, you know, the place that I belonged. And, you know, as I looked at grad schools, one of my sociology professors, Dr. Carol B. Gardner, knew Paul. And she just gave me his phone number. His home phone number! [*laughs*] And I was like, here I am, just feeling like a little Midwest suburban mouse, calling up this guy, Paul Longmore. And we had a conversation. I was just like, just asking him, like, "I'm a disabled student who's applied to various programs in the University of California system (U.C. San Francisco, U.C. Berkeley, U.C. Santa Cruz), and I'm considering U.C. San Francisco." I was like, "What are your thoughts? Can I do it?" He was like, "You could do it. Just come on over. You're going to love it here."

At that time, I was just, like, you know, so unsure. It just felt like it was such a risk, and I really did not know whether I could do it or not. And Paul had this, like, the best amount of, like, confidence. And he welcomed me without even really knowing me. And that gave me a sign about the power of the disability community, because I didn't really have that community growing up as a disabled person in Indiana. And I knew that's what I was looking for. So I'm eternally thankful, because in a lot of ways, he was my first introduction to the Bay Area disability community.

CATHERINE: That's great. Thank you. So, Alice, everybody has that moment, that first moment, when you become an activist. Do you remember yours?

ALICE: Well, you know, I do think that just, before I answer that, I do think that, as a person born with a disability, I've always been an activist, whether I wanted to be or not, just for the fact of living and existing in a nondisabled world. I do think that—I've said [this] a few times in the past—I was an accidental activist. And I think about the first time I really got into activism was when I came out here for grad school at U.C. San Francisco. And I got involved with a campus organization founded by three disabled and Deaf students [Michele Gomez, Maria Lopez, and Dana Odom]. It was called the Disability Interests Group. It was a coalition of faculty, staff, and students at U.C.S.F. And it was really just the first time ever that they formed this in the late '90s. And we realized at that time there were a lot of issues that no one was addressing. People were going around creating solutions for themselves. And we weren't really looking at things from a systemic level. So what was really great that came out of that was that, after several years of having conversations with administration and a dialogue, we were able to have the chancellor establish [a] university-level advisory group on disability issues. And they are now tasked with looking at the policies and procedures at U.C.S.F. And that, to me, shows the power of coalition building, but also the need to be really strategic and to be really patient as well, because a lot of these changes don't happen immediately.

CATHERINE: That's great. So what about the activism with the Disability Visibility Project? Because that's another kind of activism. It's not the protests on the streets and whatever. But talk about that and your decision to do that work and come up with the idea.

ALICE: Yeah, I think the D.V.P. kind of started because I was really frustrated by the lack of disability representation, not only in history but also in media and pop culture. Where are our histories? Why aren't our stories in the mainstream?

So I kind of have always been a fan of StoryCorps, which is a national oral history nonprofit. At that time, they had a location in San Francisco. And I went to an event and they talked about community partnerships that they have with Bay Area organizations. So I went up to them afterwards, and I asked if they had any partnerships with the Bay Area disability community. They were like, "No, we don't." I'm like, "Did you know how rich and amazing and how powerful our community is?" So since they didn't have one yet, I thought, *This could be my thing.* This could be my way of utilizing StoryCorps, because they already have an infrastructure. Anybody can go in there to tell their story. It's free, and you have the option of having it archived at the Library of Congress. And that, to me, was the hook. It was giving all of us a way to tell our own stories, in our own words, without waiting around for a historian to find us significant. And the idea of capturing the zeitgeist and leaving this for future generations is just really exciting to me.

I had very modest goals; I thought this would just be a one-year project. I would just meet up with my friends. I would interview people that I thought were fabulous that not everyone knows about. And I really wanted to capture these stories because it's not really about the big names. It's about everyday people. But that to me is a form of activism, is to really amplify our lived experience.

This clip is from a D.V.P. oral history. It was produced by our local public radio station, K.A.L.W., and broadcast on their show *Crosscurrents.* You will hear the host of the show, Hana Baba, introduce a story about the 504 sit-in, featuring Jessie Lorenz and Herb Levine. And this was produced by Allison Lee for K.A.L.W.

HANA BABA: This is *Crosscurrents.* I'm Hana Baba. Protesting has long been a part of Bay Area culture. From the recent Black Lives Matter marches, to the AIDS activists of the '90s, to the antiwar demonstrations of the '60s and '70s. Then there's the fight for disability rights. The 1973 Rehabilitation Act made civil rights protections for disabled Americans part of federal law. But enforcement of that law lagged. So in 1977, activists staged a nationwide sit-in at federal buildings across the country. In San Francisco, that sit-in lasted for twenty-five days, resulting in regulations making it illegal for any federally funded program to discriminate against people with disabilities, basically the forerunner to the Americans with Disabilities Act of 1990. Herb Levine became an impromptu protester in that 1977 protest when he and a friend stumbled across the San Francisco sit-in and decided to stay. Levine and two other protesters managed to sneak out of and back into the building, despite the guards' close watch. Levine shared his story with friend and ex-coworker Jessie Lorenz. They talked in the StoryCorps booth at the San Francisco Public Library.

JESSIE LORENZ: Tell me about the clergy.

HERB LEVINE: [*laughs*] Well, you know, the guards kept whittling down the numbers. People would want to leave, take a trip, take a walk around the block, go home or something. And so every time they did that, they would say, "Okay, nobody gets back [in] but attendants and clergy." And we actually had some clergy there. There was a guy, Norm, who was a minister. And he came around Easter, and they had eliminated the attendants. They said, "No. Now the only people who can come and go are clergy." So I went out to do a run to get some razors and shave cream and [*bleep*] shit like that for people. And I slept in my own bed that night at home. And then the next morning I came back, and I knocked on the door. The guards came, and they started to say, "You can't come in here." And I said, "Oh, you know, I'm not really here to come in at this moment. Thank you. I'm Reverend Levine [*Jessie Lorenz laughs*], and I'm here to ask if my choir has come? We're here for Easter services for the group." And I hear him go over to the desk where all the other guards were and say, "I don't know, some reverend." You know, they called upstairs, and he said, "No, they're not here. Would you like to come in and wait?" And I said, "No, that's perfectly okay. I'll wait outside for a little while." And I waited outside, and who the hell should come tooling down the block in their wheelchairs but Jim and Gina Ann. And I thought, *How the hell did they think they were getting back in?* And I remember, I think I said something to them like, "Now just don't say anything, just follow me." I knocked on the door, and I said, "Two members of my choir are here. I think it's time for us to get going and get organized." And they let us in.

JESSIE: [*laughs*] Oh my god. That's awesome. That is such a great story.

[*music*]

CATHERINE: So, okay.

ALICE: I love that story.

CATHERINE: It's such a great story. How would you connect your activism with this activism that's described in that? Because obviously you felt something. Even, you know, loving that story, you have a connection with it.

ALICE: Well, I do think this kind of story is an example of all the people who are never fully known in history. It's like, these are the people, every group is made up of so many people that are never acknowledged. And I think stories like this really just show all of the humor and the joy and the labor and just the ingenuity of what happens when people come together and people are determined. And that to me is a really beautiful thing. That to me is, like, what I love about being part of the disability community, because people don't realize how savvy and how smart and how innovative we are. We really are truly the real disruptors, right? Disabled people are the real hackers of society. And that to me is, I think, a form of activism as well. It's a way of being, to carve out, negotiate, and navigate through this world.

CATHERINE: Yeah, and to navigate with things that are thrown at you, and you have no idea where they're coming from or what they are. And suddenly you have to do something new.

So you can tell, from all these things that Alice has been doing, that the other form of activism that's unacknowledged here is that it's—[it seems] Alice is at the center, but she's not. She creates scenarios where other people can shine and show their activism and their stories and their experiences. And it's an amazingly powerful thing, because it's not "Alice Wong wants you to think this." It's the world that needs to know this. And it's a very subtle and very wonderful, wonderful thing.

And I want to end by asking you to leave a question for our audience, something that you would want the audience to ponder.

ALICE: So I am actually enjoying this process more than I thought I would. [*laughs*] And you've been very gentle with [me,] Cathy, very gentle, very benevolent!

So the late Harriet McBryde Johnson once said—called storytelling a "survival tool." She writes in her book *Too Late to Die Young*, "Stories are the closest we can come to shared experience."

I think of storytelling as a chance to know ourselves better, to really question who we are, where we've been, and who we want to be. Each person has an entire universe of stories inside of us. So my question to you all is, what is your story, and how do you want to share it with the world? If you aren't ready to share, tell your stories to yourself and let it nourish and guide you. Most importantly, your stories should please you and you alone. And when you are ready to share it, it'll be out there with other disabled narratives, pushing back at the status quo.

BIG
PUSSY
POWER

Excerpt from:

Diversifying Radio with Disabled Voices

Transom blog (May 10, 2016)

Radio was something I always enjoyed. I never considered it as something within my reach as a creator of media and stories.

When I started my Community Storytelling Fellowship at Making Contact, I prepared by reading articles from Transom and the Association of Independents in Radio (A.I.R.) about interviewing, storytelling, and production. I felt more intimidated as I read advice on "how to do radio," especially since some parts were very physical (e.g., holding a microphone close to a person for a significant length of time). I wondered, *Where do disabled people like me fit in the radio community? Why don't articles about diversity in radio ever mention people with disabilities?* Al Letson's 2015 Transom manifesto explores the default straight white male voice. It resonated with me immediately, and I'd also add that the default human being on radio is able-bodied as well.

Good Voices/Bad Voices

Radio can be a familiar friend, a source of knowledge, a marker of time and place. But as a cultural institution, what constitutes a "good voice" in radio reflects and transmits cultural norms and structures. By accepting the default "good voice" as one that is able-bodied, one that is pleasant, clear, articulate, and devoid of any markers of disability, you erase disabled people, rendering them the Other (or, in fancy terms, the "subaltern"). The media and cultural studies scholar Dr. Bill Kirkpatrick wrote about the problematic nature of the invisibility of disabled voices and bodies in radio in a 2013 book chapter, "Voices Made for Print: Crip Voices on the Radio":

> There is no shortage of self-evident reasons why non-disabled voices thoroughly dominate radio, not least of which is the commercial imperative: broadcasters want listeners to stay tuned, therefore they find speakers and speaking styles that audiences are willing to listen to, with voices that listeners can easily understand and find pleasing to the ear. While undoubtedly sensible as a matter of capitalist logic, however, we need to question the aesthetic reasoning at the root of this supposedly listener-centered approach to speaker selection as well as the idea that "pleasing to the ear" is somehow a sufficient explanation for the absence of disabled voices on the radio . . . We cannot begin to expand the range of permitted voices on radio without simultaneously undermining the ideologies of ability and disability that disqualify those voices in the first place.

In the broader discussion of diversity in media, I see parts of myself included as a disabled woman of color. But more often than not, disability is not included because many do not regard it as a culture.

For radio, this is total bullshit. If you think about it, disabled voices are the missing instruments in this symphony that is public media. Letson stated in his Transom manifesto: "Stories are told that are incomplete, cultures are discredited because they don't conform. We are a symphony with one instrument playing all the parts. To make the symphony as dynamic as can be instruments must be given to other players."

The conversation on diversity needs to expand in several ways: first by including people with disabilities and other marginalized groups and acknowledging their cultural contributions, and secondly by conceptualizing diversity as disrupting institutions, practices, and structures rather than the symbolic inclusion and hiring of diverse people.

Diversity is an often-used word—everyone knows it's a social good—but it has to be meaningful and recentered on those who have been excluded and made invisible. I really like what Chanelle Adams wrote about her vision of diversity on college campuses in a 2016 article for the *Black Girl Dangerous* blog, and it applies to everywhere else as well: "This 'just add and stir' model for instant-diversity is flawed. . . . I want a diversity that does more than change the faces that surround us from white to Brown and Black, but also demands issues that affect our communities are brought to the forefront." This is the difficult business of diversity—the nuts-and-bolts, granular-level stuff. I don't have the answers, but I can share my story and experiences as a disabled person and a radio newbie.

Story of My Voice

In 2015, I became interested in radio as a result of a community partnership I formed with StoryCorps focused on recording the stories of people with disabilities. I had concerns about people who would be excluded from participation owing to the audist nature of oral histories. As I figured out ways to provide options and access for people who communicate visually or nonverbally, I thought more about the medium of radio and whether disabled lives, voices, and bodies are considered part of the public media landscape.

Even with a healthy set of lungs, my lung function has steadily declined because of weakening diaphragm muscles that are responsible for the act of breathing. In fact, I had a medical crisis when I went into respiratory failure due to sleep apnea. My diaphragm needed support, and that's when I started using noninvasive ventilation: the BiPap pushes breaths of air into a person's lungs at a set rate and volume; these breaths enter the body through a tube and mask. I became Darth Vader.

A big part of my identity, ego, and self-image is centered on my voice and writing. I had to confront my discomfort and accept my new sound and body, which has become increasingly cyborg-like as time goes on. To paraphrase "You Get Proud by Practicing," a beloved poem in the disability community by the writer and activist Laura Hershey, a woman who also used a BiPap, I continually work on regaining a sense of pride by practicing.

Even with my politicized disability identity, I have to remind myself that the problem isn't solely located in my body but in society and my internalized ableism. I also have to remember I am not alone, that I am part of a large community of disabled people with vocal differences. One particular community is Did I Stutter?, an online project that challenges the assumptions behind stuttering. Its website states:

> We understand disability and stuttering not as an *individual* defect, but first and foremost as a *social discrimination* against certain forms of human speaking . . . Stuttering is only a problem—in fact is only abnormal—because our culture places so much value on efficiency and self-mastery. Stuttering breaks communication only because ableist notions have already decided how fast and smooth a person must speak to be heard and taken seriously. An arbitrary line

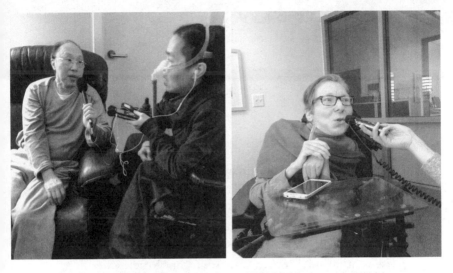

Two photos side by side. *Left:* I am pictured (*right*) holding a recorder, which I am pointing at my dad. I am testing equipment before I go out into the field to conduct interviews. *Right:* Alana Theriault, who I interviewed for my first audio story for Making Contact Radio, "Choreography of Care." Reaching into the frame from the right and holding a recorder close to Alana's mouth is the hand of my coproducer and mentor, Laura Flynn.

has been drawn around "normal" speech, and that line is forcefully defended.

Like all cultural institutions, radio enforces normalcy. This normalcy is centered on the ability to hear and speak "well." With the exception of a few radio shows by disabled people (e.g., *Pushing Limits* on K.P.F.A., *Disability Matters* on Voice-America) and a growing number of podcasts by disabled people, you don't hear a lot of people who sound different because of disability on public radio. It's time for people in radio to think critically about messages they are transmitting by excluding certain voices and lived experiences.

Symphonic Disabled Voices

On radio, I want to hear people who . . .

    lisp

    stutter

    gurgle

    stammer

    wheeze

    repeat themselves

    pause when needing to breathe

    make noises when they talk

    salivate and drool

    communicate, enunciate, and pronounce differently

    use different speech patterns and rhythms

    use ventilators or other assistive technology

    use sign language interpreters or other people who facilitate speech

    use computer-generated speech

    . . . I want to disrupt what's thought of as the default public radio voice. I want to challenge listeners as they ride the subway, jog on their treadmills, and drive on their commute. Even if the sounds and words we create might require greater concentration and attention, I believe our stories are worth the effort.

Cripping the Instruments of Radio

How do we create inclusive radio environments where disabled people are presenting, producing, or in charge of programming and administration? First, you need to start with organizations that practice what they preach. Making Contact is committed to social justice and the amplification of marginalized voices, and that is reflected in its support for first-time radio producers. Lateef McLeod, Making Contact's first Community Storytelling Fellow, is a disabled person who uses an augmentative and alternative communication (A.C.C.) device. Listening to his story and knowing that he produced it was a revelation. These are the kinds of stories I want to hear, and hearing his encouraged me to apply for Making Contact's 2015–2016 fellowship. I began a ten-week fellowship in October 2015.

How do disabled people take these instruments and make them ours by "cripping" them with our culture? When disabled people "crip" a space, they are transforming a space with their presence, culture, bodies, and thoughts. I wasn't sure how I would actually "do" radio, but I wanted to challenge myself and get uncomfortable. Creating a story that profiles the lives of disabled people from the San Francisco Bay Area offered me a chance to tell a story in a new format and learn new skills while covering a subject that is immensely important to me.

During my fellowship, I used some practical and real-world ways to crip the instruments of radio:

- **Usage of existing resources and infrastructure.** One of my main concerns was the physical activity of recording interviews and sound. If you are a radio producer, just imagine needing assistance every time you take your headphones on and off. I thought ahead and lined up interviews before my fellowship began and went to StoryCorps to record them. I used its free facilities, which included a facilitator who monitored sound levels and operated the equipment so I was free to focus on the interview. Plus, I left with a high-quality audio file that I could use and edit for my radio project.
- **Accessible and free tools.** Before my fellowship, I used Audacity to edit oral histories for presentations. Audio editing programs that are open source, free, and easy to use are critical in allowing all kinds of people to experiment and produce radio, not just professionals with the money and access to software/hardware.

- **Flexible logistics.** My mentor and coproducer, Laura Flynn, was willing to come to my home during our weekly meetings, so I didn't have to schlep from San Francisco to Oakland, saving me time and energy. This was a huge benefit and made my participation possible.
- **Asking for help.** Many aspects of recording are physically difficult. Holding a microphone, especially close to a sound or person, may be inaccessible for me as a wheelchair user with limited arm strength. The length of time holding a device during an interview is just too much for me. I asked Laura to come with me to two interviews to hold the microphone so that I could get "good tape" and room tone.

As I started recording ambient sound and interviews, I also had family members help me in various ways. They turned sounds on and off as I recorded them, inserted earbuds so I could check the sound levels, and took me to interviews, just to name a few activities. I usually have no problems plugging a cord into a U.S.B. port, but I struggled to connect and upload audio files to my laptop by myself.

I'm used to asking for assistance with my daily activities, but it's a balancing act since I have a lot of other competing needs and responsibilities.

What Can Radio Stations, Media Organizations, and Newsrooms Do?

The onus is on radio stations and organizations to adapt and be creative. Having people with disabilities behind the scenes and on-air will bring valuable perspectives and expertise.

Al Letson's manifesto outlined different ways organizations can become more diverse, starting with engagement: "Letting them know they are valued, letting them hear themselves in your local programming. It's going into these communities physically—being a presence. . . . What makes a station diverse is the work it puts into the community." Radio can become more diverse and accessible; both can benefit the workforce and the listenership. Here are some examples of next steps:

- Include people with disabilities as an underrepresented group when you recruit for applicants in radio academies, workshops, internships, or fellowships.
- Budget for accessibility so that shows can include transcripts for audio clips posted online. Without text transcripts, radio excludes people who do not hear and people who process information better in text or visuals. A budgeting model is the Broadcasting Accessibility Fund, an independent and impartial funding body that provides grants to advance accessibility to broadcasting content in Canada.
- In your job postings, include a statement about a commitment to accessibility and accommodations in addition to the language on diversity.
- Feature stories about people with disabilities in your local area; commit to at least one story a month or a week, or have a "beat" specifically on disability from a disabled person's perspective.
- Sponsor projects, form partnerships, and get involved with community-based disability organizations as part of your diversity initiatives.
- Engage and recruit people with disabilities who already host shows on local community radio or podcasts.

Advocating for diversity is one thing, but the implementation and intention behind it can be tricky and fraught with pitfalls. A diverse and "disability-friendly" workplace isn't achieved by hiring a single person with a disability, much less several people with disabilities. In a 2013 journal article in *Seattle Journal for Social Science*, Dr. Jennifer Lisa Vest described her experiences in academia and cautioned:

Diversity is a word that does not offend, does not highlight inequality, does not refer to historical injustices, or point the finger or lay blame. *Diversity* has a certain neutrality about it that makes it palatable. . . . Without explicit dialogue and action on ending oppression and privilege, diversity programs cannot change racist, sexist, homophobic, and ableist beliefs and practices.

Action, dialogue, and community involvement are key to successful social change. My experience at Making Contact encompassed all three elements, culminating in the creation of my first story ever: "Choreography of Care." Public radio is slowly becoming more diverse. The voices of disabled people and their stories should be an intrinsic part of that process.

Choreography of Care

A segment from "Caring Relationships: Negotiating Meaning and Maintaining Dignity," an episode of the Making Contact *podcast (April 13, 2016).*

ALICE WONG: [*yawn, sounds of oxygen machine*] Hey, Mom, I'm ready to get up.

BOBBY WONG: [*Alice's mom, speaking in Mandarin*] Did you sleep well?

ALICE: Not too bad.

BOBBY: Okay.

ALICE: Can you turn off the oxygen and the hospital bed?

[*sounds of beeping machines*]

. . .

ALICE: I don't want to get up. But here I am, in bed, needing to get up and get in my wheelchair. From the minute I wake up, I am connected to people. Can't get away from it, even if I wanted to. Kenzi Robi is an artist in San Francisco who has multiple people that work for him. Like me, he's in bed when his attendant arrives.

KENZI ROBI: I have no use of my legs, so I am very dependent on my care providers. So when someone comes in in the morning, the first thing they need to do: wash their hands, get gloves, and then check and be sure I'm clean ... and I can't urinate unless someone inserts a catheter inside my bladder, and I need to do that several times a day.

ALICE: When you need help with almost every aspect of your life, it changes the way you relate to others. I got a chance to talk with some of my disabled friends in the Bay Area, exploring their relationships with people who help them with their daily activities. Kenzi says it's different each time he trains a new attendant.

KENZI: And I've had people that are able to be directed and able to be taught the procedure within thirty minutes or two hours, and I've had other people who feel like, "Well, why are you picking on me? Why do I have to change my gloves? You are wasting material." And I have to tell them that the gloves are disposable, I'm not.

ALICE: Some people have spouses and family members as their attendants, whether they're paid or unpaid. Ingrid Tischer lives in Berkeley with her husband. Here's their typical morning.

INGRID TISCHER: When we get up, he's the person in the household who sort of gets the day started by making the coffee, starting the breakfast. Um, and I sleep at night using a BiPap machine.

ALICE: A BiPap machine helps a person breathe.

INGRID: So I get up and sort of take care of that. This is funny, but I would say in the time that I've been married, it's probably been the first time in my adult life when I could wear pretty much anything I want, or do something with my hair without it being a big deal, and he can help me button things, pull things on, zip things, and then tie my hair back if I want. He's really good-natured about it ... the way, you know, he makes it nice.

[*sounds of Alice meeting up with Alana*]

ALICE: Another Berkeley resident, Alana Theriault, has been living independently for thirty-four years. She employs six attendants and extra backup workers for shifts throughout the week. They go where she goes, including the home and out in the community.

ALANA THERIAULT: I hate driving on the freeway, but they're all very good sports and drive me where I need to go and then bring me home, set me up with a snack, help me open my mail, do whatever paperwork of the house, make dinner, and they leave at 6:00 p.m. And at that point, I have a little downtime, which is nice.

ALICE: Having privacy can be hard when you need assistance often.

ALANA: I don't have enough alone time now. I have the care hours that I need, and that's fabulous, but at the same time, I don't have the alone time that I miss. I miss that now.

ALICE: Anyone who uses personal assistance is part director, choreographer, and actor. Patty Berne is the executive and artistic director of Sins Invalid, a performing arts group in Berkeley. She compares her work to how she gets her needs met:

PATTY BERNE: Like, seriously, people are like, "Where do you get such skills?" I'm like, "Well, do you know what it takes for me to get dressed every day?" Like, that is a production, so of course I can manage, like, a show, you know? 'Cause, like, I produce an event every day when I'm dressed and fed and comfortable.

ALICE: It's choreography, right?

PATTY: Yeah! Oh my god, yes.

ALICE: Being disabled and using personal assistance isn't a solo act. It's an ensemble production where relationships are the key to a successful show.

[*sounds of Alice talking to her mom*]

One pivotal scene in my daily drama is how I gotta have my coffee every afternoon when working from home.

[*sounds of coffeemaker grinding*]

Since I can't make it myself and I'm picky about my coffee, I communicate clearly and supervise my mom, who is one of my attendants. My addiction to coffee is at stake and it must be satisfied. For Alana, it's all about teamwork.

ALANA: I try to foster relationships between the workers. It's nice because usually I have two to three days of training, and then maybe one or two attendants are involved in that training, so right off the bat, they meet each other. That'll encourage them to say, "Huh, I don't know, maybe we should call so-and-so, find out how we deal with this problem," or I encourage them to call each other when they need a sub, so it's not just all on email.

ALICE: There are lots of ways disabled people express thanks to their attendants. Showing gratitude can go a long way.

ALANA: Once a year I host an attendant appreciation dinner where we go out. I think . . . as I build relationships with them, they care about me and I care about them.

ALICE: Care *is* involved in the work of personal assistance, but it's impossible to ignore the power dynamics. Rachel Stewart, who lives and works in Alameda, describes the give-and-take nature of the relationship.

RACHEL STEWART: I'm still learning, and I think that, like you said, it's a very fine line. It's also letting people know when the line has been crossed. It's like, "Okay, I really need you to be on time because I'm going to pee in my pants unless you're here on time." Just being really frank and up front with people is really important and being honest but also showing your appreciation. Yeah . . . it's a hard one to navigate.

ALICE: Navigating these boundaries can be tricky, especially if your attendant is also a family member. Ingrid describes the understanding she has with her husband, Ken.

INGRID: I don't ever have to be concerned, for example, that one of us is going to use our argument to sort of get back at the other one in the course of assisting me with something. I think it's important for the health of the relationship, because at some point Ken is going to need help from me more than he does now. I think that we have a foundation of knowing what each other's limits are and what we will not transgress. That's what the health of the relationship is built on.

ALICE: Appreciation, trust, communication, and a shared sense of responsibility can keep relationships strong between attendants and disabled people. Keeping balance between your actions and your politics is another vital aspect. Patty recalls a time when she supported her attendant.

PATTY: You know, one of my attendants, unfortunately she recently broke her wrist, and rather than be like, "Okay, you're disposable, I'm just going to hire somebody else," I hired an assistant for her, to help with the pieces of the routine that she couldn't do anymore, because that makes sense, right? So it's just . . . how do we meet our needs collectively? It's really cool 'cause these nuances of the [disability justice] movement that she didn't realize I was contributing to, the routine now that she's doing it one-handed, she's like seeing now: "Oh, yeah, that's how Patty supports her own balance."

ALICE: For Patty, this is an example of disability justice in action. Communities can create collective access and no one is disposable. Jessica Lehman is the executive director of Senior and Disability Action in San Francisco. She tells me when she first connected disability justice with domestic workers' rights:

JESSICA LEHMAN: What happens in my home is, you know, just a little piece of that big picture that I'm talking about and committed my life to. And it just felt like the best example of the personal as political, and what an opportunity I have to learn and to live my values, to tie together what I care about, to bring the values that I put out into the world, to really feel that in my own body and in my own home, and to be able to work on that with other people.

. . .

ALICE: Hey, Mom? I'm ready to go to bed now.

BOBBY: [*speaking in Mandarin*] Okay. You ought to sleep now, it's so late.

ALICE: Can you turn on the hospital bed?

BOBBY: [*in Mandarin*] The bed? Okay.

[*sounds of the air mattress machine turning on*]

ALICE: Can you turn on the oxygen, please?

. . .

ALICE: Well, it's time for me to go to bed. As my mom turns on my oxygen machine and my air mattress, I'll leave you with these final thoughts: Disabled people and their attendants are both vulnerable *and* resilient. Our relationships and well-being are linked. How we treat each other is a reflection of the kind of world we want to live in. Our labor has value. We are stronger together.

Tiger Tips on Interviewing

Before

Take your time deciding on whom you want to interview. Follow their work, collect links about them, find their contact info and other details such as pronouns and bio.

Invite the person with enough specifics without writing a novel. Include the purpose of the interview, what you would like to discuss, an approximate amount of time the interview will take, and a date and time or a request for their availability. If there are different ways a person can participate (e.g., email, video, phone), make that clear so they don't have to ask. Ask the person if they have any access needs or accommodations. If this is for a research project or event, be up front about honoraria! End the message by thanking them for their consideration, welcoming any questions they might have, and linking to your website or previous work so they can check you out.

If the person declines, thank them for responding. If they don't respond, leave them the fuck alone! I might follow up after a few weeks, but I am careful not to pressure or harangue someone. No guilt trips or questions on why they declined. Move on and don't be an asshole about it.

If the person says yes, then huzzah! Now the work begins.

Confirm the date, time, mode of communication, and any accommodations they requested. Some people prefer to have questions or topics sent ahead of time. I think of this as a form of access, because people can feel nervous about being interviewed and may want to spend time writing notes to prepare. Not everyone is experienced in talking about themselves, and it's important for you as the interviewer to make them feel as comfortable as possible. If you are a journalist and have a policy of not sending questions ahead of time, you should make that clear. Also, let the person know if you plan to record the conversation and/or condense their responses in the final piece.

Send the person a calendar invite with any links or information on how to participate. Send a reminder one to two days before the interview.

In the lead-up to the interview, prepare in a way that works for you, depending on how well you know the person. Draft a few questions or topics you want to cover. Ask yourself:

- Based on what you know about the person, what interests you most?
- If the person has been interviewed before, are your questions going to feel repetitive or involve something they are tired of talking about?
- Are your questions open and broad enough to give the person the freedom to share what they care about?
- If you want to talk about something specific, what details or references should you refer to if needed?

During

At the beginning of the interview, thank them in advance for their time and labor. Ask if they have any concerns and for permission to record. Set the person at ease, and mention they can pause, take a break, revise a response, request anything they want left out, and stop at any time during the interview.

Curious cat, activate! I like to start with asking the person to introduce themself briefly. How they identify can help you describe that person in your piece. It's also a way to ease into the conversation.

You did the homework, but now it's time to listen and go with the flow. Think of a HANG IN THERE kitty poster. The interview is not a time for you to give your opinions or dominate. This is their time, and you are facilitating a vibe where they feel safe to share. Keep in mind:

- Let your curiosity be your guide. Don't cling to the questions if it seems like the person is not interested. They can feel it if you are genuinely into what they have to say.

- Listen carefully and prompt for more details or a related issue based on their response. There's no such thing as a perfect answer. Ask if there's something unexpected that you want to learn more about! Ask for clarification if there is something you are unfamiliar with, such as a term, acronym, name, or concept. Don't act like you know what they're talking about if you don't.

- If the person is going on a bit too long, find the right time to interject and say, "Thank you for sharing . . . I'd like to switch gears and ask you about . . ." or "I want to be mindful of the time, and I'd like to talk with you about a few more things . . ."

- If the person doesn't like a question or is annoyed by you, this is a good time to pause and ask how you can adjust or correct any assumptions or mistakes. Apologize and offer to discontinue if the person does not want to engage further.

- Listening and staying focused is at the heart of being a good interviewer. Being able to go to unintended places at the direction of the person is part of the exploration and exchange.

It's the unknown that can make a conversation thrilling and illuminating.

Near the end of the interview, be respectful of their time and check in with them. Here are a few examples: "We are almost at the end of our time, how are you doing? Would you like to continue a bit longer?" "Since we're wrapping up, I'd like to ask one last question." "Before we end, is there anything else you'd like to discuss?"

After

Thank the person for participating, and mention that you will be in touch once the interview is ready. Encourage them to contact you if they think of anything they want to add, change, or leave out. Give the person an approximate date when it will be ready.

Before publishing, follow up with the person if there are any details that need double-checking, such as the spelling and pronunciation of names and terms, the current version of their bio, and any links they'd like to share; if they are okay with being tagged on social media; and if they'd like to review the interview ahead of time.

Send the person a link to the interview once it is published. Ask if there are any corrections that need to be made. Thank them again!

Like editing, interviewing makes me a better writer. Interviews are part of my chosen cross-training storyteller regimen that does not require spandex or sweat. With interviews, I learn how to create space that offers both the subject and myself the chance to listen and grow from our exchange. The genuine enthusiasm and interest I have for other people are apparent for the listeners/readers of my interviews. The thrill of discovery from interviewing someone carries over as I try to make that same space for myself and channel that energy inward as I figure out who the fuck I am and what the fuck I really want to say. I wish I were as confident about my writing as I am with my interviewing skills. Much of my writing process is about asking myself good questions, and this is something anyone can develop through practice.

Podcasting as Storytelling

A discussion with guests Geraldine Ah-Sue, Cheryl Green, and Sarika Mehta on the Disability Visibility *podcast, episode 100 (April 3, 2021). This conversation has been condensed and edited for clarity.*

SARIKA MEHTA: You know, Alice, I think we've had this conversation a number of times and with all of your guests, about putting disabled voices on the air, which is not a luxury afforded to people. You have to have a radio voice to work in radio and podcasts and this, that, and the other. And people train their voices in such a way that we can't sound like ourselves anymore. And what does that mean when the whole point is storytelling, and we have to sound a certain way when we're telling our stories? What does that mean? It means we're not authentic, is what it means. So I love the idea of people just having the ability to be themselves and tell these stories that are really poignant or give so much history of culture and understanding family and understanding why we are the way we are, why things are the way they are.

And to that effect, because, obviously, there's populations that cannot access something that's just that you hear, especially if you're not a native speaker of English, or if you don't hear or for any—or maybe if your children [*laughs*] are being very loud in the background, you know! God bless the transcripts that are a part of this [and] the stories that envelop all of this. We have to make our medium of radio and podcasting, of audio, accessible to everyone. And that's really one of my passion projects.

ALICE WONG: Yes, thank you for that. And when I first started and [was] kinda doing the planning and just thinking about this podcast—2016, early 2017—I really did wanna start off with transcripts. You know, I know that there's a lotta different issues [for] independent podcasters who are like, "I don't have the money. I don't have the time. How do I do this?" But I did a lot of intentional planning and budgeting, and just, you know, I personally made a commitment to do that. Because it would be just incredibly silly and basically hypocritical if I did a podcast centering on the disability community without transcripts.

And I do think that, Cheryl, your podcast, you were one of my role models. And you were somebody that I reached out to early on, and you were just so helpful for me just starting, like understanding the mechanics and the process. So I just wanna give you a shout-out, because, you know, there have been disabled podcasters way before this podcast. And I just am kinda constantly trying to learn and refine my processes. But also, you were so generous with your experience and expertise. So thank you for that.

CHERYL GREEN: Oh my gosh. Well, since it's audio only, you can't see me with my eyes closed and my cheeks flushed. Thank you, Alice. And I . . . When you were developing this podcast, you were developing it, I think, in secret! Because I actually had you on my show, and this goes back to what Sarika was just saying—is that I did an episode on my show about disabled voices. So, when I'm on my show, I feel like there's a disabled person on the show 'cause I'm there. But I don't have a disabled voice. You don't hear disability in my voice most days. Some days you do, but I usually don't record on those days. And you were the featured person in my episode about the power and beauty and wonderfulness of having just what Sarika was saying, like having authentic disabled voices on the air. And this whole time when I was interviewing you, you were already planning your podcast, and I had no idea. And then [*laughs*], and then you . . . It was just amazing.

Mine came out, and then yours came out. And I was just blown away and so completely thrilled and happy to do anything for you any time, Alice.

GERALDINE AH-SUE: I am reflecting on what Sarika and Cheryl have shared and your question. And I'm just thinking . . . Yeah, I remember thinking about, having met you and thinking about radio and thinking about this medium, just thinking about the stories and the content of disability and how we consume that content and who we assume the audience is. And what a struggle it is to really get a voice that sounds disabled on the air or on podcasts to a really large audience. And I was really excited to sort of—to be on that journey with you and within myself.

I think hearing from you about your, I don't know, your feelings about being a newbie, I remember it brings back to me, like, I am still incredibly terrified and intimidated. And as somebody who is working on a podcast that centers around disability stories and disability culture as a producer who does not identify as a disabled person, I'm often really . . . it's just often, often, often, all the time, sort of these moments for reflection and change and reflection and change. And working alongside you and being invited to be part of that process and part of that learning for myself with you as my mentor in a lot of ways, again, sort of has just really changed my life. And it's really just, I mean, what a privilege it is to sort of get to live this life in this way, you know, and come and be awake in this way.

I also, working with you—I don't know if this is gonna come later—but I was also reflecting on how laid-back you are as a boss! [*laughs*] I feel like I have always really . . . I admire that and appreciate that about you. And also, there's something that I'm learning about from the disability community and disability culture: sort of this, you know, this, my training in go, go, go and productivity, and like even this term, like *hit the ground running*, like all of those things, you know? I have just learned so much, I can't even begin to describe the depths of what I am learning, continue to learn, have learned through this process.

ALICE: Thank you for that. You know, I was also kinda nervous, too,

Photos of Cheryl Green (*left*), Geraldine Ah-Sue (*center*), and Sarika D. Mehta (*right*)

about just being kind of the supervisor/boss in the fact that I pretty much knew my vision, what I wanted out of each episode, and the fact that I give each one of you notes and kind of a sense of what I would like in terms of the editing of an interview. But really, I wanted to give you, all of you, kind of that freedom to play as well, kind of just enough guidance but not, like, micromanaging.

And I think another thing that I was very intentional about was really building in as much flexibility as possible. And this is why, for some people who are listening, people who were former guests probably, [they] wonder, *Why did it take four months for my episode to come out?!* And that's because I work very much in advance, and I take my time. Because I'm working with audio producers. I'm making sure that I have my text transcript. I have all these little elements that I wanna put together, and I have the luxury of not being a fancy-shmancy kind of podcast on a network. I have control over my schedule and my workflow. And I think that's just something that I learned from my own lived experience. How about you, Cheryl?

CHERYL: Whew, hallelujah. I remember feeling, physically, this wave come over me of relief and, like, fresh air when I found out that you were going to be doing a podcast. I love the way you do politics. I love the way you do culture. But I just had a sense of what you were going to bring to podcasting based on what you'd been doing with the Disability Visibility Project and [I was] just so thrilled that you were going to just dip into this world. And then to be part of it, I mean, yeah, there aren't actually words to describe what it feels like to be part of it, because it just transcends language for me.

ALICE: Oh, Cheryl! How about you, Sarika?

SARIKA: How am I supposed to follow the both of you? My goodness. I mean, like Geraldine was saying, I'm not a person who identifies as being disabled, and so to be asked to be a part of the community in this way is a huge honor. And the irony is you're saying that you felt like a newbie. I mean, I was walking into this like any other job where I'm terrified; I don't wanna screw up. More specifically, because I just wanna do my best work [*laughs*] for you, you know? And for this vision that you had.

So I think I started out nervous just because I wanted to do this job really well. I mean, to be honest, working for your podcast is the first paid gig in audio journalism that I've ever had. I've been in the field for over ten years, but this was the first paid job I ever had. When you work in community radio, you pretty much do whatever you want, which is great [*chuckles*], you know. It's a labor of love.

Despite that, I've worked adjacent to this community for almost ten years being a sign language interpreter. I learned so much! And I felt embarrassed that I didn't know these things already. I was learning and also like, well, *Why didn't I know this?* Because none of us know these things until you listen to the podcast!

And I remember other episodes where you and your guests were talking about the fatigue of either from a disability or from the fatigue of having to explain yourselves, whether you're going into a new job or requesting accommodations, whatever the case is. There is a fatigue and . . . or just I need an extension on a deadline because there's a fatigue. And it was something I might have [a] 1 percent modicum of understanding, because after having children, I had such a struggle in the recovery of my first delivery, such a struggle. I think I just never recovered. Then I had a miscarriage, and then I had a second pregnancy, or rather a third pregnancy, that was so difficult and terrible. And that was the entire time I was working for you! And you were so gracious and understanding.

So when Geraldine and Cheryl are talking about you as a boss and how laid-back and wonderful, I realized that you're another leader in this community who is saying we are human bodies, and we are not machines. And when things are not going well, we have to listen to our bodies and take things forward. And I remember feeling really bad that I couldn't meet a deadline, but you all, you guys, all three of you, you had my back.

ALICE: What questions do you have for me, and is there any kinda tea you wanna spill about me? Go for it, this is your time.

GERALDINE: [*chuckles delightedly*] I love this part. I don't know if I have any questions, but I do want to spill the tea that Alice is one of the best bosses or supervisors that I've ever worked with. If you, out there listening, are looking for somebody to feel really human with, Alice is your person. [*chuckles*]

SARIKA: Second to that. [*laughs*]

CHERYL: But also, Alice is your cat. Spilling tea is not usually like, "Let me tell you more excellent things about this person." But I have no tea to spill in the traditional sense of spilling tea. I mean, the thing that [*laughs*]—that I remember is I get very, very scared and nervous when I meet people for the first time. But you're so down-to-earth, and I quickly got over being terrified about meeting you. But I don't know how long it was into the working relationship that you started signing your emails to me with meows and mewls and other cat noises. Or maybe I started. I don't know who started it, but it's been going on for several years, and I just love it. You're [*chuckles*] so not intimidating, but having this work relationship that's got very healthy, very good boundaries, but then signing the emails with "meow for now," it's just—it's the best.

SARIKA: This is not about the podcast, but Alice was a guest on *United Shades of America* with W. Kamau Bell, when they did an episode on disability history. And I think somebody made it into a GIF or a meme or something, but Alice was talking about able-bodied actors portraying disabled characters, like, all the time. And then they win Oscars for it! It's a formula. And so Alice said something like, "Suck it, Hollywood!" [*laughs*] It just is like, if you ever wanna know Alice in one sentence, that. And I think at another presentation, somebody asked you . . . maybe it was about picking battles or something. But you're like, "I have no fucks to give!" [*laughs*]

CHERYL: "Eat more pie! Eat more cookies!"

SARIKA: [*laughs*] I do not have fucks, either!

ALICE: Well, you know, I think everything that's worth doing, we should try to have as much humor and pleasure and enjoy, you know. This podcast would not exist and would not be what it is without the three of you. So, I just [want to] make this very clear: this has been a partnership. And I think this is really something that I want everyone to know, that this has been a real creative collaboration. And I think it's where the best things come out, right? Just this magic. Thank you all for being with me on this journey.

CHERYL: Thank you, Alice.

SARIKA: Thank you, Alice.

GERALDINE: [*sighs contentedly*] Thank you, Alice.

ALICE: Mew, Cheryl!

CHERYL: [*gasps*] Meow, meow, meow! Meow meow, meow meow!

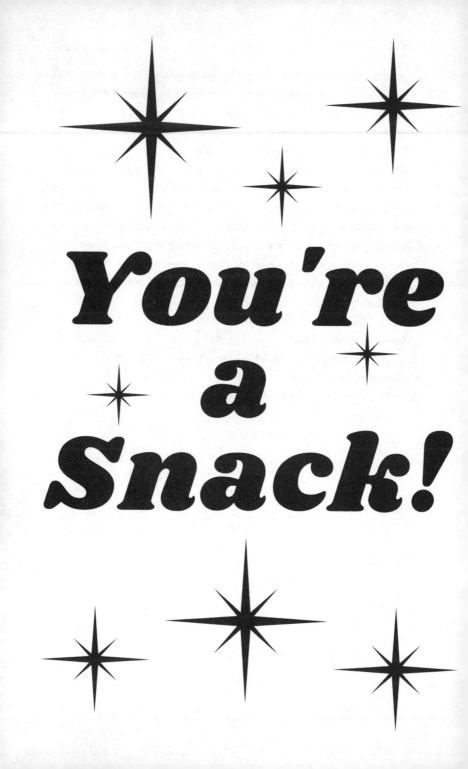

Letter to Asian American Disabled Women and Girls

Hello!

Hey there, I got your email, letter, tweet, or direct message. Or maybe I met you at an online event or at a party pre-pandemic. Or maybe I met your mom one time I was shopping, and she stopped me and cried, telling me how amazing it was to see someone like you out in public but older. Or maybe it was a friend of a friend who connected us because we both happen to be Asian American and disabled (we are not a monolith, and yet people presume we automatically have a lot in common). Either way, here I am, replying to you.

Thank you for sharing your story with me, your questions, and your request for mentorship. First of all, I see and hear you. I hoped things would be better in the twenty-first century, but it's clear that disabled people of color, including Asian American women and girls, still feel disconnected and alone. I did not set out to become a storyteller or activist, but it emerged organically as I struggled to find myself and my people. I hope my story and work help you imagine other paths, but please remember I am just one example. There is a lot of work ahead, and collectively we can succeed in our own ways.

Shit is hard, right? Growing up and becoming more comfortable in our own skin is a tough, nonlinear process. I am still working on myself as I imagine you are, too. In the midst of your challenges and searches, I hope you are taking time to find joy in the world. Building and nurturing relationships gives me joy. It might take a while, but you will eventually find people who have your back whether they have the same disability or come from the same culture or not. And maybe there aren't any solutions or immediate answers to the questions you're asking. All we can do is discover what or who makes us happy *now*.

We don't need a nonprofit to establish a community just for us . . . we don't need to identify, use the "right" words, or carry a membership card to be connected. We exist and that is *everything*! It's easy to say and harder to accept, but *you are enough*. In fact, if you're *too much*, rejoice in being *all that* and more. This may seem like a cliché, but *you do you*.

Do not feel obligated to represent or speak on diversity, intersectionality, or identity. There will be people out there who see you only in those narrow terms. Those are not your people no matter how nice and "helpful" they seem. You can talk and think about disability however you want, especially the uncomfortable, difficult, shameful, messy stuff. Fuck the rules. Fuck the model minority myth and respectability politics.

There will also be times you're made to feel like you can't be your full self, that you have to choose. Or that you have to be grateful to be in America because things are "better" here (on stolen land, by the way). Resist the notion that disability rights and disability justice in the United States are more progressive or a beacon to the world, because that's some capitalist colonizer bullshit. We can take the best parts of our cultures and let them inform our understanding of what it means to be human. There is wisdom and beauty from disabled people everywhere. We just have to look and have the humility to learn.

I appreciate the time and vulnerability it took for you to reach out to me. To keep it 100 percent honest with you, I am not your role model, mentor, or friend. I prefer to be your peer, colleague, or fellow troublemaker in the future. Role models create unrealistic expectations and an asymmetrical power dynamic; role models or icons can do more harm than good because they obscure the flaws and contradictions we all have. I've become increasingly uncomfortable over the years with the way people perceive me, because *it is a lot*. I don't want the fear of disappointing others to influence my decisions, because I am accountable to myself first and foremost. Setting boundaries and being clear about my time and capacity are ways to protect myself, and I encourage you to do the same when you are ready.

Living at multiple axes of oppression can be heavy. The many identities you hold and your lived experiences are not in conflict with each other; they make you sharp, whole, and extraordinary. You may not see yourself that way yet, but I believe in you and who you will become. No matter what happens, even if we never cross paths or speak again, I am grateful that we are in this universe together.

Your comrade,

Alice

Respect
My
Time

About Time

After I get up from bed, it takes me a while to come alive, and this is similar to my writing process. I don't like to be rushed into doing anything, especially writing. I *love* to procrastinate. I procrastinate *hard*. Call it Dr. Rabbit/Mr. Turtle Syndrome. Deadlines exist, but I try as much as I can to build in as much time to prepare and adjust if things take longer. This is the ideal situation, although everything isn't within my control and some circumstances prompt immediate action and response. Before I start typing a single word, I go through thoughts, feelings, and ideas in my head and spend a large chunk of time focused on completely unrelated things. Tidying up my desk? Check. Scrolling through Twitter? Check. Deleting emails from my inbox and closing tabs in my web browser? Check. Volunteering to help other people with their projects? Check. Taking care of stuff for my health care, finances, and basic needs? Check. Wiping down my laptop and phone? Check. Sanitizing my hands? Check. Restocking supplies or looking at online sales? Check. Going down rabbit holes such as Korean cooking videos, tips for raising pet snails on YouTube, and Instagram accounts of cats? Check. Check. Check.

In the middle of these distractions, a vibe will emerge, a point I want to make, a phrase, a hook, a title for a story, an image. A connection or epiphany can happen while watching or reading something brilliant. By doing "nothing" and day-dreaming, I am actually composing, even if words don't immediately materialize. When I try to fall asleep at night, the best bits and bobbles tend to rise up. My hips and elbows have contractures, which means I cannot lie flat. I have a hospital bed where I can recline the upper and lower half of the bed, and I use a lot of pillows to position my body properly. With my muscles stretched out after sitting for more than sixteen hours a day, it is difficult to relax and fall asleep, and this is when my imagination goes wild. These elusive bits are glowing fireflies hovering above my bed within grasp. If it's a strong spark, I'll be able to recall it and scribble it down on paper,

A piece of paper with my difficult-to-read scribbles in black ink from June 17, 2021. I was working on the essay "As I Lay Breathing" and the introduction of this book. Words such as *oracles* and *conjuring* are legible.

add it to my Notes app or a Google Doc the next day. And if I forget it, that's okay, too. I have faith that my wanderings will lead me in the right direction eventually.

Procrastination is a creative practice; it sets me on autopilot, allowing other parts of my brain to refine my random, undefined ideas. Procrastination is also how I get my sicko kicks. I'll never be an M.M.A. fighter or someone who drives a car at one hundred miles per hour, but I can live recklessly by feeling the pressure of an impending deadline of doom. Homework was never my strong suit, and many a night I stayed up frantically finishing something. The internal Dr. Rabbit/Mr. Turtle tension pushes and pulls, operating with an unknowable logic and rhythm that I embrace rather than fight against.

Whether it's a blog post, an op-ed, or a book chapter, I interrogate myself during this embryonic stage of writing. *What do I have to say that is unique? Is this what I want to do right now? What are the risks in revealing another piece of myself to the world? What messages do I want to share with the reader? What do I want to learn and gain from this experience? When is my next snack break?*

These questions are set on repeat as I decide what to include and write in this very memoir. Intention and timing matter. There are personal stories that will remain dormant and private forever. There are stories that need to simmer and evolve. There are stories that should be told by other people instead of me.

After a healthy amount of procrastination, it's euphoric when words pour out of me, dribbling, splattering in messy directions like a melted hot fudge sundae. *Tap, tap, tappity tap.* Swirls of Very Important Thoughts and whipped Useless Blather soak up the page. More tapping. More deleting. Cutting and pasting. The rush fades, and this is when the *more* work begins: editing. In putting together this book, I realized that life is one never-ending edit. Sounds like a cheesy metaphor, but it's true! In writing about my life, editing is time travel, collapsing, folding, expanding time. Gathering disparate wispy threads into neat chapters and sections. Memories rearranged, pulled apart, de-emphasized. Secrets and fears erased in between drafts only to emerge again as tangents to be deleted or set aside. Invisible track changes that reframe a narrative only to be solidified, trashed, and reborn. Filtering truths until the most essential elements remain. Em dashes that link; ellipses that prolong. A constant telling and retelling until the act itself threatens to weaken the blood and guts of a piece. Editing is a dialogue with demons, ancestors, and the future; a witchy dark art that summons the forces of the universe into legibility.

Imposter syndrome and internalized ableism are subjects that I've talked about ad nauseam to the point when it bores me, yet as I wonder, *Who wants to read another piece about writing? Thousands of books have been written on the subject by actual literary, scholarly, M.F.A.-degreed, award-winning people. What's so original about my hot take on it?* I have no practical advice, nor do I speak from a body of literature on this topic. I am not well-read, nor do I extol a particular daily writing routine. Marinated in procrastination ooze, I reject the assumption that you need to exercise a particular writing discipline, which is entrenched in middle-class whiteness and nondisabledness. If a goal of reaching a certain number of written words per day works for you, great! If certain practices and tools help you, great! If not, there are so many other ways to write that should be celebrated and demystified so that people won't feel inadequate, "lazy," or unproductive, or the most pernicious of insinuations: unlike a *real* writer. Writing less, in compressed time periods, or in an atypical manner does not make the work any less. It is still work. Writing will always require practice, whether it manifests on the page, in scribbles and doodles, or in your mind.

Death and deep uncertainty are realities that disabled and chronically ill people know intimately. Living in a disabled body, where getting through the day and taking a shower are Olympic gold-medal-worthy achievements, adds a layer to the push/pull of writing. All this is tempered by the fact that disabled life, with its unpredictable crises, can upend and throw the best-laid writing plans into a dumpster fire. Privilege is being able to keep to a prescribed timetable without fear of paying the rent, being in pain or becoming sick, losing health care, and taking care of your family and yourself.

The sense of urgency, of being in a world that values speed and quantity, and inhabiting this watery sack of bones, informs how, when, and why I write. "Ever since I bought my first journal so I could become my own historian, writing was an act to preserve myself against forces that tried to diminish and distort me," Emily Jungmin Yoon wrote in a 2021 essay about Asian American identity for *The Cut*. I do not write for representation's sake or to satisfy an audience's hunger for "authentic intersectional stories." I write when the spirit moves me. I write because it's fun, pleasurable, and dangerous. I write because it is my chosen form of resistance, self-preservation, and defiance. I write plainly and openly from the heart.

Every organism starts decaying from the moment of birth. Reaching my fourth Year of the Tiger lunar cycle, I wonder if my attitude toward time is wrong. I shouldn't treat time as a fleeting commodity or a scarce luxury I must capture and hoard as it slips through my clawed, bony fingers. The feat of getting to this age and being able to tell my story should be liberating rather than a *2 Fast 2 Furious: A Tiger's Tale* race against mortality. Because only death wins in the end. Slow or fast, people can find me in these words and the spaces in between long after I'm gone.

pandemic

This shit is bananas
B-A-N-A-N-A-S

—GWEN STEFANI, "HOLLABACK GIRL"

You better check yo self before you wreck yo self.

—ICE CUBE, "CHECK YO SELF"

Excerpt from:

I'm Disabled and Need a Ventilator to Live. Am I Expendable During This Pandemic?

Vox (April 4, 2020)

I t is a strange time to be alive as an Asian American disabled person who uses a ventilator. The coronavirus pandemic in the United States has disrupted and destabilized individual lives and institutions. For many disabled, sick, and immunocompromised people like myself, we have always lived with uncertainty and are skilled in adapting to hostile circumstances in a world that was never designed for us in the first place. Want to avoid touching door handles by hitting the automatic door opener with your elbow? You can thank the Americans with Disabilities Act and the disabled people who made it happen.

Technology, accessibility, and a hard-core will to live shaped me into a cyborg oracle ready to spill some hot truths. I am tethered to and embedded with a number of things that keep me alive: a power wheelchair, a noninvasive ventilator that is connected to my chair's battery, a mask that goes over my nose attached to a tube, metal rods fused to my spine. How I sound, move, and look elicits pity and discomfort by many in public. This is the norm.

My family and I have been sheltering in place for over three weeks in San Francisco. As the news warns of overcrowding in hospitals and scarce resources push hospitals to consider rationing care, I'm deeply concerned. Already, disability rights groups have filed complaints that some states, such as Alabama and Washington, are making triage recommendations that discriminate against people with disabilities. While the federal health department's Office for Civil Rights released a bulletin on nondiscrimination during the pandemic, I'm still worried. The ethical frameworks for rationing often put people like me at the bottom of the list.

Bioethicists and philosophers like Peter Singer, a utilitarian philosopher infamous in the disability community as someone who advocates for our erasure, have applied cool, rational, elegant arguments and thought exercises on who should live and die during crises like this. But where are the disabled doctors, bioethicists, and philosophers in this global conversation? They actually exist and need to be heard and involved, like Dr. Joseph A. Stramondo from San Diego State University, who wrote a blog post for *The American Journal of Bioethics* about triage and the coronavirus:

> There is a significant body of empirical evidence showing that there is a substantial gap between a disabled person's self-assessment and how their quality of life is judged by folks that have never experienced their disability. Some prominent bioethicists even refer to this as the "disability paradox." To me, there is little paradoxical about disabled people valuing their own life more than it is valued by non-disabled people making judgments based on stereotype and stigma. To conceptualize it as paradoxical is to wrongly assume that disability inevitably diminishes well-being.

Eugenics isn't a relic from World War Two; it's alive today, embedded in our culture, policies, and practices. It is imperative that experts and decision makers include and collaborate with communities disproportionately impacted by systemic medical racism, ageism, and ableism, among other biases.

The debates on health care rationing unveil how our society devalues vulnerable populations. Draft guidelines from various states and health systems identified people with dementia, cancer, intellectual disabilities, and many other preexisting conditions as those who will not benefit from treatment, compared with younger, healthier, nondisabled people. Dr. James Keany, an E.R. physician at Providence Mission Hospital in Mission Viejo, California, was quoted recently in the *Los Angeles Times*: "As it stands in the U.S., if your family member is adamant that you would want everything done and you're ninety years old, wearing a diaper, severely demented, you would get put on a ventilator . . . Most countries consider that malpractice because what are you saving that person for?"

Everything is personal and political for me. I know people with cognitive and developmental disabilities. I use disposable briefs when needed and require total assistance with my personal care, such as eating, dressing, and bathing. Were I to contract coronavirus, I imagine a doctor might read my chart, look at me, and think I'm a waste of their efforts and precious resources that never should have been in [short supply] to begin with. They might even take my ventilator for other patients who have a better shot at survival than me. All these hard choices that doctors have to make primarily hurt those hit hardest, not the people who present as worthy investments of scarce resources. Who gets to make these hard choices and who bears the brunt of them is a matter of inequality and discrimination toward protected classes.

Even the notion of "quality of life" as a measurable standard is based on assumptions that a "good" healthy life is one without disability, pain, and suffering. I live with all three intimately, and I feel more vital than ever at this point in time because of my experiences and relationships. Vulnerable "high-risk" people are some of the strongest, most interdependent, and most resilient people around. We may still face significant disparities in political power, which result in being left out of policy making, but we know how to show up for each other. Disabled communities, queer communities, and communities of color have been hustling and providing mutual aid since time began. Many of us know the safety net has gaping holes and the state will not save us, so we're going to save ourselves with abundance, wisdom, joy, and love.

Disabled people are not acceptable collateral damage in this pandemic. I want to believe that the future is not just mine but ours. When one of us falls through the cracks, we all suffer and lose something. Time and ventilators are scarce, but we have the creativity, moral courage, and collective power to shape a world that has space for us all.

Excerpt from:

Freedom for Some Is Not Freedom for All

Disability Visibility Project blog (June 7, 2020)

Freedom for some is not freedom for all. As a high-risk disabled Californian staying at home in San Francisco, I am not jealous that people are enjoying bars, beaches, and parks. I am angry seeing so many people outdoors not wearing masks or social distancing. As various cities and states begin to ease their shelter-in-place restrictions, I fear for the millions who will be left behind.

The public is incredibly eager to get back to "normal," even as thousands of people continue to die in congregate settings and institutions such as nursing homes, detention centers, prisons, shelters, and psychiatric, residential, and other long-term care facilities, out of sight, out of mind. I am perplexed by the lack of urgency in response to people trapped in institutions and congregate settings who face maximum risks with minimal protections. Many are my disabled kin— they are part of the disability community, segregated and isolated in the name of "safety" and "care."

One of the first widely publicized COVID-19 outbreaks happened at a nursing home in Kirkland, Washington, with 142 cases and thirty-five deaths from February to March. As of June 4, more than 43,725 people in long-term care facilities have died from COVID-19 in forty states, with New York reporting the highest number: 6,237 according to the Kaiser Family Foundation. All these numbers come with names, faces, and families, not just body bags. What number will be high enough for people to care? This is a complete political and moral failure.

The federal government is considering rolling back infection control requirements in nursing homes, which prevent or stop the spread of infections with procedures such as having standard practices for hygiene and handling equipment. A 2017 analysis of nursing home data by the Kaiser Family Foundation reported at least 40 percent of the nursing homes had at least one infection control deficiency that year. At least eighteen states have laws or governor's orders that protect nursing homes from lawsuits and/or criminal prosecution related to the pandemic. New York and New Jersey so far are the only two states to provide immunity to corporate officials in the nursing home industry from civil lawsuits and some forms of criminal prosecution. Governor Gavin Newsom received a request in April from a group of hospital and assisted living lobbyists for a sweeping executive order granting broad immunity from civil and criminal liability, which was objected to by advocates from the disability community.

Governors need to launch investigations into outbreaks at all congregate settings, mandate reporting of infections and deaths, enact universal testing for all workers and residents, provide adequate personal protective equipment, increase wages and protections for workers, and deny the nursing home industry the legal immunity it is demanding. In a video from May 6, 2020, featuring the late Stacey Park Milbern, a disabled activist and a founder of the Disability Justice Culture Club, she warned, "There has to be checks and balances on hospitals and nursing homes. Otherwise, disabled people, especially people of color, are left alone in a system that already doesn't care about us."

Congregate settings do not ensure safety or care. By design, institutions do not allow us to know about the conditions of the people incarcerated inside. These institutions are allowed to operate without transparency and accountability. They render people as less than human, subject to exploitation, abuse, and neglect.

The systems that exist now don't have to remain the same. We must dismantle the nursing home industry that places profits over lives while endangering workers and operating with inadequate oversight and regulation. And we must work toward decarceration and deinstitutionalization because these systems are dangerous, inhumane, and unjust.

Safety is an illusion and privilege for the very few. Knowing that asymptomatic carriers are out in public, the time it takes to develop a vaccine or treatment, and the possible changes in the virus, I will remain at home long after any orders are lifted because I simply do not feel safe. I am deeply concerned about the resurgence of institutions as the "best and only" option for people with significant medical and care needs, including those who have survived COVID-19 and continue to experience long-term symptoms.

As a disabled woman of color, my life is unavoidably high risk. I fight to be seen while knowing I'm one infection, medical crisis, or policy change away from institutionalization or death. This pandemic lifted the veil on what kinds of people are considered "acceptable losses" in the name of saving the economy: Black, brown, indigenous, poor, disabled, older, fat, chronically ill, unhoused, incarcerated, and immunocompromised people, just to name a few.

Right now, Black people are risking their lives protesting against systemic racism in the face of both the virus and state violence. Fighting for justice and liberation requires the abolition of all systems that oppress and punish us for merely existing.

No one is disposable or invisible. We can't look away from these deaths while enjoying the sun and sand. By the sixtieth anniversary of the A.D.A., I want to see older and disabled people fully integrated into the community with robust supports and services. This is my American dream; it's a vision that requires creativity, political will, and a radically inclusive culture in how we design our infrastructure, policies, services, and programs. Freedom to live in the community is a human right. One day, everyone will truly belong.

Excerpt from:

Cooking in Quarantine

SHELTER-IN-PLACE JOOK

Al-Jazeera (March 26, 2020)

Jook, also known as congee, was the ultimate comfort food for me as a Chinese American kid growing up in Indiana. We would eat it for breakfast with an array of small dishes, like ground fried fish or pork floss, thousand-year preserved duck eggs, pickles, shaobing (sesame-covered Hot Pocket–like pastries), or youtiao (fried sticks of dough).

Another popular variation is to make jook with a whole chicken until the meat falls off the bone and a bunch of green onions and ginger. Jook was also something served plain when I was sick; it filled my belly when it could not handle anything seasoned or oily. It could be thick like oatmeal or soupy, depending on your taste. I always enjoyed the thicker consistency and would scoop large bites with a traditional blue-and-white ceramic Chinese spoon patterned with little translucent grains of rice.

As my parents and I started sheltering in place in March 2020, our rice cooker remained our constant friend throughout these rough times. It never lets us down and allows us to cook a meal in one pot set at the perfect time and temperature. The variations are endless with jook: savory, sweet, vegan, gluten-free, vegetarian. Using stock instead of water will give more flavor and not require any additional salt. It is a dish made for frugal times and can be supplemented with fried dumplings, boiled eggs, peanuts, kimchi, or anything crunchy on the side for a heartier meal. In my childhood memories, steaming bowls of jook mean comfort, healing, and sustenance—all the things we need right now during the coronavirus pandemic, with such uncertainty and no end in sight.

For a simple meal that can use a wide range of pantry items and leftovers, jook can get you through another day. You can make jook on the stove, in a rice cooker, or in a slow cooker like an Instant Pot, following the manufacturer's instructions.

Shelter-in-Place Jook

INGREDIENTS

1 cup short-grain white rice (you can use short-grain brown rice if you soak it for two hours before cooking)

6 cups chicken or vegetable stock, or water

1–2 cups greens: fresh or frozen spinach, sautéed kale, bok choy, chard, or any other green you have handy

1 cup chopped protein: cooked tofu, beef, ham, chicken, duck, sausage, ground beef, bacon, canned fish, rehydrated dried scallops, or pork

Garnishes: chopped green onions, thinly sliced ginger, sesame seeds, kimchi, peanuts, or boiled eggs

Optional: sautéed peppers, onions, or mushrooms; edamame; diced butternut squash or sweet potatoes; or shitake mushrooms

DIRECTIONS

Rice cooker instructions

1. Rinse the rice in the rice cooker bowl. Drain and rinse again. Do this 3 or 4 times, or until the water runs clear.

2. Add the cooking liquid and let the rice soak for an hour before turning on the rice cooker.

3. Select the congee or porridge setting on your rice cooker. Press START. If you do not have a congee setting, just hit the COOK or START button, then come back and check on the rice in 45 minutes.

4. Once the timer beeps, add the greens, protein, and any optional ingredients.
5. Close the lid and leave it on STAY WARM mode for another 30–45 minutes.
6. Serve with garnish either topping the jook or on the side.

Stovetop instructions

1. Rinse the rice in a bowl. Drain and rinse again. Do this 3 or 4 times, or until the water runs clear.
2. Transfer the rice to a saucepan with a lid. Add the cooking liquid and bring to a boil.
3. Lower the heat, cover, and allow to simmer gently for at least 45 minutes and up to 2 hours. Check on it every half hour or so.
4. Once the jook has reached the consistency you want, add the greens, protein, and any optional ingredients.
5. Serve with garnish either topping the jook or on the side.

slow
the
fuck
down

It's My Body and I'll Live If I Want To

A discussion with Ana Marie Cox on the With Friends Like These *podcast (March 27, 2020). This conversation has been condensed and edited for clarity.*

ANA MARIE COX: Alice, welcome back to the show.

ALICE WONG: Thank you for having me back on!

ANA MARIE: And in case people are wondering why I am interviewing Darth Vader, I guess people should know you are a full-time vent user, correct?

ALICE: That's right!

ANA MARIE: I wanna bring up something that's a much more personal aspect of the situation we're dealing with now, which is this idea that we don't have enough medical supplies to go around. We've already seen in Italy doctors admitting that they have to make choices about who lives and dies. As someone who's on a ventilator, I'm sure every time people talk about the shortage, maybe, I don't know, what happens for you? When you hear people talk about this massive shortage of ventilators, how does that feel for you?

ALICE: Yeah. I mean, I've never heard *ventilators*, like that word, uttered so many times—

[*Ana Marie laughs*]

ALICE: —on the national news. I'm like, "Seriously? Now we're talking about this? Okay." I think, first of all, people don't really even know what they do and there's different types. I'm using one that's called a

BiPap, and it's what's called a "noninvasive ventilator." I wear a mask over my nose, and it helps me breathe. And I have— It's part of my body. It's, you know, I cannot sleep, breathe, and do much of anything without it. So, already, even with, let's say, a regular cold or bronchitis, you know, it wipes me out. I have very little reserve in terms of just being able to fight off infection and just recover.

And hearing these stories all over, it's just, you know, it really hurts, actually. I think it's very traumatic in the respect of just my own sense of just mortality. And, you know, I've always felt vulnerable, and I've always been aware that I'm a marginalized person, but when people, so casually, are so ageist and ableist with this Darwinian [mindset], kinda like people laughing about the coronavirus or people just making a joke that "You know, don't worry. Most of us will recover."

ANA MARIE: Mm-hmm.

ALICE: Yeah. When they say "most of us," they're talking about, like, the average nondisabled person. So that's— Again, they're not talking about the people who are really gonna be impacted, and they kinda forget that there's a lot of us of all different ages; it's not just older people. So it shows time and time again when we have these major crises, who does our society really value?

ANA MARIE: Mm-hmm.

ALICE: And clearly within this capitalist framework, certain people are much more valuable than others, and we see that with the guidelines that various health care systems and states are creating right now, where they have to decide who gets services, who gets treatments, who gets ventilators. And a lot of these measures are based on our ideas of what is valuable. And again, people like me who rely on others for help, who rely on technology like this, are not given the same benefits and the same chances, even though we want to live just as much as anybody else.

ANA MARIE: I mean . . . it just must be something else, if it's— I can imagine how traumatic it is just to see people be casual about the disease itself. But the other thing that I imagine—I hope this isn't too triggering right now—is that people are talking very casually and in the open about who lives and who dies. They're talking about having to make that decision, people just kind of bring it up. And unfortunately, this is a decision people—again, able-bodied, nondisabled people—probably do not realize that kind of decision gets made a lot, right? Like, doctors deciding this person's quality—quote "quality of life" will not be good. And so, therefore, I am not going to give the kind of care and attention to this person as I would to someone whose quote-unquote "quality of life" is going to be better. I mean, this must be . . . I mean, I would be terrified, I guess. This is . . . I would be—I would be very . . . scared. And maybe you are 'cause you live with this. So I don't wanna assume anything, but . . .

ALICE: No, and I think it's just this is something that I've lived with since birth. I think this is something that a lot of people—especially people with disabilities, but also, let's say, people of color, women—I mean, we have not been served by the health care system well at all. I mean, there's such a history of bias and discrimination that's really resulted in deaths.

ANA MARIE: Mm-hmm.

ALICE: And this is just another huge amplification of it. And again, I wanna bring up this paper written recently by Samuel Bagenstos, who teaches at the University of Michigan Law School. And he wrote about the ethics of and the laws about disability-based medical rationing. And he says that this whole idea of scarcity is basically a result of societal decisions, right?

ANA MARIE: Mm-hmm.

ALICE: That there was a decision to not have a stockpile of ventilators, right, in times of emergencies. You know, these are all political decisions. There are decisions made by institutions and individuals to use preexisting conditions as criteria for denying people the use of ventilators. So none of this is like some sort of neutral, abstract thing. It's all very much political and very much a reflection on who gets to make these decisions and who has been left out of the political process.

ANA MARIE: How would you like people to be thinking about this scarcity issue? I mean, unfortunately, it's too late, too late for a lot of things. It's too late for us to create a stockpile of ventilators. It's almost— I hope it's not too late for the creation of more ventilators, although capitalism seems to be having some . . . throwing a wrench into that as well. So it looks like we will be facing scarcity, a scarcity— Actually, let me rephrase that. We will be facing a scarcity that affects able-bodied white people. [*laughs*]

ALICE: [*sarcastically*] Yeah. And I'm so worried about the able-bodied white people out there.

ANA MARIE: Yeah.

ALICE: [*more sarcastically*] Yeah. I'm really scared for you all. I'm just, you know, hopes and prayers.

[*Ana Marie laughs*]

ALICE: [*even more sarcastically*] Hopes and prayers! For all you white nondisabled people out there, all you cisgender white middle-class folks, I'm just, I'm pulling for you! I am pulling for you!

ANA MARIE: [*laughs*] 'Cause part of your point is that people who are marginalized have had to deal with scarcity all the time: those ideas of triage and who gets what and how you distribute a limited supply of things. So what's happening now in our world is people who normally never have to think about scarcity are having to think about scarcity. But what can you offer? What perspective can you offer? Like what are the kinds of things you want people to be thinking about beyond what we should've been thinking about earlier? Which we should have.

ALICE: I think there . . . Okay. I don't really have any solutions, but I do know that when decision makers have the chance to really develop policies and guidelines to really be really thoughtful about how this reflects our collective values, what does it say about us as a people? And I know that sounds very touchy-feely, but I really do believe that there must be ways to practice the values that we claim to have. And I know that it's gonna be difficult. I know that there will be people that do not, will not, get the care they need. And there will be people who will face huge outright exclusion and discrimination. But also, I feel like there's a chance for all of us to step up and say there must be another way, that we must use our imagination, our creativity, and our political will. We gotta use—utilize everything we have.

And I feel like, you know, at this point, especially from the [Trump] administration, we haven't seen them really use everything they have at their disposal. I mean, for example, the Defense Production Act.

ANA MARIE: Yep.

ALICE: I mean, let's use that. Let's . . . You know, I don't understand this whole emphasis of the economy over humanity. I just don't fully understand why we care about the Dow Jones. It's just, you know, all this stuff that's not really gonna be much use if people are dead.

ANA MARIE: And also, I think that, unfortunately, you have some testimony you could give about relying on the kindness of institutions and companies to provide what is needed. Which seems to be what the administration is saying: "Oh, people will volunteer." And while I know people do volunteer and people make sacrifices for others all the time, I think you probably realize that to rely on such a thing is to abdicate responsibility.

ALICE: Absolutely. And also, again, asking for volunteers, asking for the private sector or philanthropy to help, it's unsustainable, right? We can't rely on them solely. But the federal government does have certain powers that should be extended and should be shared with, you know, at the state and local level. I mean, to see what states or local towns and cities are doing, they're like, "We're not waiting for you all. We're not waiting for the administration." They're just getting shit done. And I see a lot of people within the disability community providing mutual aid. There's so much voluntary collective care that's happening right now, which is heartening to see. I mean, it's just—it's beautiful, but it's also a really sad commentary that we cannot trust or rely on the state.

ANA MARIE: Alice, this is already personal for you, I know. We've already discussed some of the ways it's had an impact on you individually. But I wanna dive in a little bit more, 'cause, you know, it's funny. I've seen interviews with astronauts about dealing with solitary living. I've seen interviews with submariners about how to deal with living in close quarters. It's weird to me, Alice, how come no one's thought, *Oh, you know, there's a whole community of people who have to deal with* *the kinds of things that we're all dealing with right now. Why don't we ask them to lead us?* I mean, shouldn't you guys? [*laughs*]

ALICE: Yeah! I mean, again, why aren't we on the news every night? Why aren't we the pundits to give our opinions on this? You know what I mean? Really, it's amazing to see so many people finally learn, like, "Oh, I didn't know I could do a videoconference."

[*Ana Marie laughs*]

ALICE: Or "I didn't know I could have online classes," you know? You see all these amazing performers performing free livestreamed, and, you know, disabled people have been fighting for decades advocating, begging, just working so hard, saying, "We need these kinds of things." And, again, it's just really weird. I think this speaks to the ableism in our society where we don't really want to see what disabled and chronically ill and immunocompromised people are doing. We don't wanna think about the fact that people have different ways of doing things and that accessibility is not seen as a burden. You know, it really adds to everyone's experiences. And if this one small silver lining as something that comes out of this pandemic is the fact that people realize that there's different ways to have social gatherings, there's different ways for people to organize, there's a whole range of people doing amazing things from their home or their couches, on their beds. I hope that it awakens people that there have been people doing this for years now, just completely unrecognized and undervalued, who have so much expertise.

ANA MARIE: Alice, it is always a pleasure to talk to you. I think you bring so much to the table, and you always enlighten me and make me laugh. And I just, I hope the same things that you hope. I hope that this gives people a chance to rethink the way that other people relate to the world. And I hope you take care of yourself, Alice.

ALICE: Thank you, Ana Marie! And may the Force be with all of us.

ANA MARIE: [*laughs*] Thank you.

A High-Risk Timeline of Alice Wong, Proto-Oracle

Location: Earth, North America, California
Era: Pre-Outage

Welcome to the Oracle Archive, younglings. My name is Master Meow, and I have been a curator and librarian at this institution for two millennia—or, for some of our out-of-galaxy guests, 5.6 boops. You are all in the fifth form of your cyber-organic development, and this is the appropriate stage to share this exhibit about a dark chapter in Earth history before the Outage, which precipitated the Great Liberation. Ancient history can teach us much about our flaws as well as our strengths. It may be inconceivable, but there was a time when phages—or, as they were then called, pandemics—were rampant across various species. Some of you might have heard about the horrors of the Scarcity Games, and this is one example. The Oracle Archive was able to piece together a record from a Proto-Oracle named Alice Wong during her forty-seventh year of existence in the Earth year 2021. Using our latest methods, we found bits and pieces of her story through artifacts such as tweets, articles, emails, texts, images, and audio about what it was like to live through these times. If these terms are unfamiliar to you, refer to the codex on twenty-first-century communications. Please explore this exhibit with care, and let's gather afterward for a discussion on the connections between our ancestors and the way we live today. And don't forget to visit the gift shop on your way out.

January 20, 2021

"Vaccinating Californians 65 and Older May Last till June, Pushing Back Timetable for Others"

—LOS ANGELES TIMES

January 23, 2021

From San Francisco's vaccine notification system

Text Message
Yesterday 5:13 AM

Alice Wong we will notify you when Phase 1C is eligible for the COVID-19 vaccine.
Supplies are limited, so it may take months.
Reply STOP to opt out.

January 25, 2021

"California Will Prioritize COVID-19 Vaccine by Age, Not Occupation in Next Rounds"

—LOS ANGELES TIMES

January 29, 2021

Remarks prepared for an online press conference organized by Disability Rights California and other disability rights organizations

Hi, my name is Alice Wong. I am a disabled activist from San Francisco residing in District 9. I have not left my home since March of last year except once for a flu shot. If I am infected with COVID-19 I will die. I am not alone in this situation. Like other disabled, chronically ill, and immunocompromised people under sixty-five, being in phase 1C meant we were prioritized in the next round of vaccinations. Everything changed with the governor's announcement this week that would eliminate this phase and "scale up" with age-based eligibility. Age is not the only factor in determining risk. This decision by the Newsom administration is an act of violence and erasure toward groups disproportionately impacted by the pandemic. It is racist, classist, and ableist. And by the way, there are high-risk disabled people who are essential workers, immigrants, unhoused people, undocumented people, and in communities of color. I am filled with fear for myself and others. I also refuse to defend my humanity and prove my deservingness for the vaccine in comparison to other high-risk groups. High risk is high risk. For more stories by people in phase 1C, check out the hashtag #HighRiskCA on Twitter. You can also find me there at @SFdirewolf. Thanks.

February 4, 2021

Text notification from a vaccine standby app

Text Message
Today 9:53 PM

Thank you for subscribing to updates about extra vaccines near ▊▊▊ We will send updates here via text. Reply STOP to unsubscribe.

February 7, 2021
Text notification from a vaccine standby app

> Hi, this is Dr.B! You are the 8,285th person to sign up. We prioritize based on local government criteria and then order in line. We will notify you via text if a dose becomes available. For additional questions please refer to hidrb.com/faq

February 11, 2021
From the Disability Visibility Project

On January 25, 2021, Governor Newsom announced the elimination of the phase 1C priority group for COVID-19 vaccination in favor of an age-based approach in California. I created the hashtag #HighRiskCA to create visibility and space for high-risk people under sixty-five who will be devastated by this change. This is not a singular case; states across the United States have differing vaccination plans and prioritization of high-risk groups.

Here are some valentines you can share with your friends, family, and the special elected representatives in your life. Please encourage people to take action and demand prioritization of all high-risk groups including disabled, chronically ill, higher-weight, and immuno-compromised people, plus essential workers and un-documented, unhoused, and incarcerated people. High risk is high risk. We are not disposable.

VACCINE EQUITY,

**WILL YOU BE MY
VALENTINE?**

#HighRiskCA #HighRiskCOVID19 #NoBodyIsDisposable

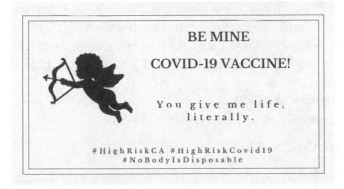

BE MINE

COVID-19 VACCINE!

You give me life,
literally.

#HighRiskCA #HighRiskCovid19
#NoBodyIsDisposable

I LOVE YOU, VACCINE EQUITY

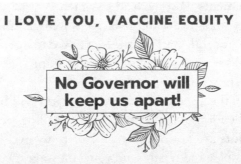

No Governor will
keep us apart!

#HighRiskCA #HighRiskCOVID19 #NoBodyIsDisposable

February 12, 2021

"California to Open COVID-19 Vaccine to People with Cancer, Obesity, Other Conditions"

—LOS ANGELES TIMES

February 15, 2021

Message sent to my primary care physician

Hi, [redacted],

The Department of Public Health issued a provider bulletin on 2/12 that reprioritizes high-risk disabled people under sixty-five for the vaccine. Could you inquire with the [redacted] vaccine clinic what the process is for someone like me to make an appointment starting 3/15 (per the bulletin)? I'm sure it'll take a while to get a response, but I wanted to see if you can help me get a head start. Thx!

February 16, 2021

Response from my primary care physician

Hi Alice,

I'm pretty deeply embedded in this process, and I think about you all the time as we, finally, get close to immunizing patients with medical risk factors who are under sixty-five. It's been difficult to watch as the whole system—federal, state, local—defaulted to age, so I (and many physicians and patients) am happy about this coming shift.

When the appointments are open, you will be able to access them on [patient portal] or by calling [redacted]. These slots are not open yet. I'll keep my eye out when they do open and try to send you a message. We also, as a system, will need to find a way to invite people who qualify. Thank you, Alice. Hope you're well.

—Dr. [redacted]

February 22, 2021
Email forwarded to me by multiple people

Hello East Bay community partner,

Some updates for you regarding the mass vaccination site at the Oakland Coliseum, 7000 Coliseum Way, Oakland, C.A., 94621:

As a reminder, this site will be able to administer up to 6,000 vaccines a day. The mass vaccination site should be open daily from 9:00 a.m. to 7:00 p.m. Staff will be at the site to direct traffic and assist with questions and translation. The focus of this vaccination site is to provide equitable access to safe, life-saving vaccines to California communities that have been heavily impacted by COVID-19.

The State is putting aside a block of appointments each day to ensure access and equity for BIPOC and people with developmental and other disabilities within 50 miles of the site. These appointments will be accessible by a specific access code. This code will change periodically based on demand. This code will be shared with [redacted], other disability leaders, and other equity advocates.

To ensure community members who are eligible to receive vaccines are best served at this site, the State wants [redacted] to be a key partner in reaching community-based organizations that can promote the availability of vaccines and help individuals sign up/register for vaccination appointments.

Eligible community members will be able to access vaccination appointment openings at the Oakland Coliseum by visiting the state's MyTurn website or calling the state's toll-free hotline at 1-833-422-4255. When confirming eligibility, it asks for an "Accessibility Code (optional)." **This is where you enter the code: For appointments on 02/22/2021–02/25/2021 the Oakland Coliseum code is: [redacted]**

(Eligible groups include phase 1A and 1B: Health care workers, paid caregivers, family caregivers, long-term care and skilled nursing home residents, individuals 65 and older, as well as education and childcare workers, emergency services workers, as well as food and agriculture workers. Any person in this category you identify can use the access code. People with developmental and other severe high-risk disabilities or underlying conditions will be eligible on March 15.)

Thank you for helping those in our community access the vaccine using this code where applicable. Thank you for your critical advocacy and commitment on setting the policies, and for carrying your hard work through to getting people vaccines.

February 23, 2021

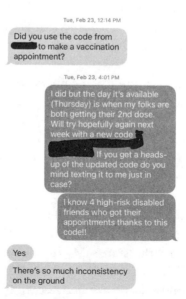

Tue, Feb 23, 12:14 PM

Did you use the code from ███████ to make a vaccination appointment?

Tue, Feb 23, 4:01 PM

I did but the day it's available (Thursday) is when my folks are both getting their 2nd dose. Will try hopefully again next week with a new code

If you get a heads-up of the updated code do you mind texting it to me just in case?

I know 4 high-risk disabled friends who got their appointments thanks to this code!!

Yes

There's so much inconsistency on the ground

February 24, 2021
Two messages from different people on the same day

Wed 1:04 AM

Are you up? New appointments available this weekend using the same code !

 Missed Audio Call
1:06 AM

Just saw yer message

👍 1

I am swooping in now like the apex predator that I am

OWLLLLLLLLS

2/24/21, 1:14 AM

Did you sign up to get vaccinated?? The codes actually work!

can't believe it

Your appointment is confirmed!

Hello Alice, your COVID-19 vaccination appointment has been successfully scheduled.

Appointment [number]
3qsgbaw1x

Patient
Alice Wong

Vaccination Location
Alameda County - CalOES (Drive Thru C)
7000 Coliseum Way, Oakland California. 94621

Your appointment date and time
Sunday February 28 2021 at 05:00PM

Your appointment date and time
Sunday March 21 2021 at 05:00PM

February 26, 2021

Text Message
Today 8:15 AM

Your vaccination appointment scheduled at the Oakland Coliseum has been CANCELLED. It has been identified that you are under the age of 65, and that you are in an eligibility tier other than Healthcare Worker, Emergency Services, Education/Child Care, or Food & Agriculture. At this time, vaccines are only available to individuals inside of these tiers.

February 27, 2021

Two separate conversations

The health equity code is for people w IDD and other disabilities and for BIPOC communities, but the intention was that people still need to be in current eligible phases

I'm worried about supply for 3/15. Next week we should expect some updates there

People encouraged me to use it so I am a bit confused

About how we can ensure that phase is smoother.

Sorry to hear about the cancellation. I'm hearing that all over— started this AM

And there were others I know earlier this week in my situation that got vaccinated

So they've tightened their verification per the phases to

iMessage

Hey, are you willing to lie and put 65+ on the form? There is a new code and appts available today, and they're not checking details when you show up.

Today 8:12 PM

I guess? I mean, are they going to cancel a bunch again?

It doesn't feel right but I am very conflicted

If you have a chance to share the latest code with me I'll think about it

A friend suggested I identify as an educator but that also feels very wrong

▇▇▇▇ this is wrong. I already entered my info once in MyTurn. It's not difficult for them to figure out the discrepancy.

Honestly it could work.

It's all just so wrong

AND what's right is that you have access.

Mmmm, nope

My Turn already has my data

Oh fuck.

People suggesting all these things they would never do for themselves

Like, just stop it with your guilt

Mmm yes I hear you.

This is not disability justice

No it is not. It is not.

Not the help or support I need

February 28, 2021
"Vaccine Equity Memes" posted on the Disability Visibility Project *blog*

I faced some ups and downs lately with my search for a vaccine appointment as a high-risk person under sixty-five years old. There are many others in California and everywhere in the same situation. Time is not on our side. When I feel defeated and frustrated, it helps to create something that makes me giggle. Feel free to share these memes along with some resources.

March 5, 2021

*A friend who is a leader in the California disability commu-
nity sent me a new code from the state vaccine-appointment
system. This time the codes were individual, one-use only, and
meant for people with disabilities. I grabbed a slot for my shot
like a bat out of hell.*

March 13, 2021

Moscone Center, San Francisco, 4:45 p.m. Pacific

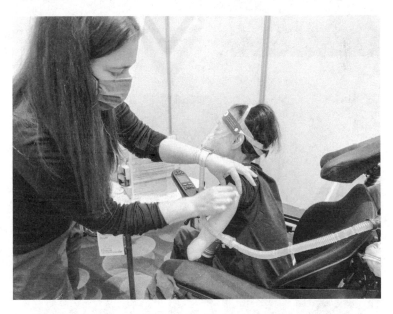

A nurse (*left*) administers a COVID-19 shot into the muscle near the top part of my left
shoulder. What a glorious day. What a fucking odyssey. I am indebted to the many disabled
leaders and activists who tried to make the vaccine rollout to our community in California
as equitable and accessible as possible. Afterward, to celebrate, my parents and I picked
up sushi for dinner.

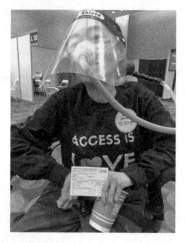

Smiling with great relief and waiting during the observation period after receiving my first dose of the COVID-19 vaccine with my ACCESS IS LOVE T-shirt on.

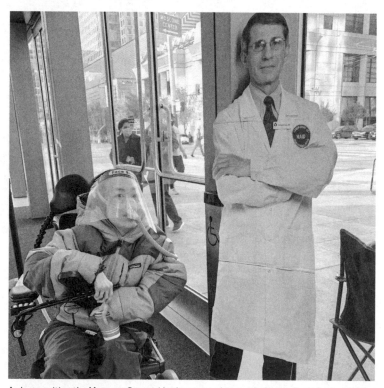

As I was exiting the Moscone Center, I had to get a photo with this cardboard cutout of Dr. Anthony Fauci.

. . .

Thanks for visiting the timeline of Alice Wong, Proto-Oracle. You can also explore the following exhibits about the twenty-first century from the Oracle Archive:

The Barbarity of Crowdfunding for Health Care

Who Gets to Breathe? Oxygen

Global Migration, Displacement, and Starvation: The Failure of Neoliberal Nation-States

In Praise of Peaches

When San Francisco's shelter-in-place order started on March 17, 2020, I did not feel as cut off from the world as many did since I already worked at home and maintained social connections primarily online. There were things I missed: going to Sightglass Coffee, my neighborhood café down the block, and running errands at Safeway and the bank, both conveniently within walking distance from my home in the Mission District.

Being outdoors, in the sun and open air, was unsafe for multiple reasons, with my only outing after lockdown being in October for a drive-through flu vaccine. The need for pleasure and deliciousness, coupled with predatory scarcity and fear, prompted me to savor the simple things that were within my grasp and to dream about what I missed.

I don't eat a lot of fruits and vegetables, preferring to focus on four main food groups: fat, sugar, caffeine, and carbs. But I make special exceptions for peak-of-the-season produce that is one of the dazzling gifts of living in California. That spring my friend Emily Nusbaum checked in with me after the death of my friend Stacey Park Milbern and asked if I would like a homemade peach cobbler or pie. A week later in June, Emily dropped off a golden-brown pie made with frozen peaches she saved from the season before. I stayed inside while Mom met Emily by the entrance of our building. The peach filling had the consistency of marmalade: gooey, warm, scented with cinnamon. It was such a sweet gesture of care, made with love in a time of sadness. I treasured this act of kindness, and it comforted me as many people collectively mourned for Stacey, a beloved friend, community organizer, and activist from the Bay Area.

Emily is a member of Peachful Easy Feeling, a team that adopted a tree at Masumoto Family Farm in Del Rey, three hours from San Francisco on land originally inhabited by the Yokut peoples. The team goes every summer and harvests a single tree that can produce up to four hundred pounds of organic heirloom Elberta peaches. "Elberta is one of those old fashioned, creamy, buttery smooth peaches with a bright yellow flesh and a golden skin when ripe," says the farm's website, adding that they evoke "memories of a family tree in the back yard or eating one a long time ago." Emily invited me to become a member of this team, and she offered to pick and deliver some of the peaches to my home in August.

Eating a fresh Elberta peach is indeed a magical, spiritual experience. Its flesh is firm and brimming with juice, sweet yet neither overly ripe nor tart, and its skin delicate so that I can gobble or blend the whole fruit easily. Cool. Succulent. Luscious. When I bite into one, I am connected with the infinite cycles of life and death that produced this fruit, the hands that picked and packed it, and the family and farmworkers who nurtured it. I travel through space aboard U.S.S. *Masumoto*, destination: deliciousness. The pandemic contracted and expanded my unstable world, but tasting that peach took me through a wormhole of joy. It eased my heart and gave me peace.

Emily brought the best of the summer to my indoor, socially distanced world. Our friendship is one of many examples of interdependence and mutual aid in the disability community. Pandemic notwithstanding, I wouldn't have the energy or ability to spend an entire day traveling to the farm and harvesting with Team Peachful Easy Feeling. This knowledge and the months of staying inside weighed on me as I devoured these peaches with my parents, who also have high standards for fruit. Ever since, we reminisce about these peaches as if they were long-lost friends whom we can't wait to see again next summer.

Am I overhyping these Elberta peaches? Did my salivating, Gollum-like desire for these precious golden orbs in a time of isolation intensify and distort my memories of them? Does it even matter as long as I felt pleasure and nourishment?

Team Peachful Easy Feeling first started with Emily, her friend Kathy Wage, and the Takeuchi family. The Takeuchis know the Masumotos from the Japanese American community in the Central Valley. Emily met Kayla Takeuchi during her time as faculty at Fresno State University through Kathy, a speech-language pathologist. Kayla is a young autistic nonspeaking person who did not have the means to communicate until she was fifteen, when she worked with Janna Woods, who introduced her to supported typing, a form of alternative and augmentative communication (A.A.C.). The group was formed to honor the memory of Janna and Emily's brother Jonathan, who both died from cancer several years ago, as a way to come together and do something beautiful each year.

Emily described eating a peach from the Masumoto Family Farm as "tasting the sun, the blossom that it started from, the bees that pollinated, the air, sky, and water." The cycle of living and dying is a reminder that we do not exist as humans divorced from one another and nature. Little did I know the cycle would continue in unexpected ways.

David "Mas" Masumoto emailed me out of the blue in January 2021 without knowing my ardent passion for Elbertas: "Thanks for all the work you do and your spirit. I'm an organic peach and nectarine farmer (and a writer) and the stories you capture reflect the true 'natural world' we live in (and eat in an organic peach!)."

As we corresponded, I learned that David was working on a book, *Secret Harvests*, about the life of his aunt, Shizuko Sugimoto, who, because of her disability, was separated from her family during the forced relocation and incarceration of Japanese Americans in World War Two. In 2012, David "found" her and, in doing so, discovered a family story steeped in secrecy and intergenerational trauma. I got to read an early draft of his manuscript and shared some feedback on disability history, language, and culture. What an exchange of abundance and generosity between Emily, David, and me, between our intertwined communities and histories, between living organisms on this planet!

Nurturing life requires care and connection. Like an orchard in full bloom, nurturing stories requires care and connection, too. The people we love who are no longer alive—Stacey, Janna, Jonathan, Shizuko—are still with us, and our stories about them are seeds planted with gentleness and hope for the future.

Sometimes a peach is just a peach. Sometimes a peach is a cosmic portal to relationships that sustain and tie us to one another.

Photos taken by my friend Emily Nusbaum at the Masumoto Family Farm during summer 2020

No to Normal

I was one of several keynote speakers for a 2021 online event, Night of Ideas, a celebration of culture, conversation, and community in the San Francisco Bay Area. The theme was "Closing the Distance," and these were my recorded remarks.

How do we close the distance? Access. Building and supporting access will bring us together as individuals, communities, and nations.

I am a disabled person living in the Mission District of San Francisco who uses a wheelchair and ventilator full time. Every day I experience the very real distance between myself and the nondisabled world, which, by the way, is the default we all exist in. The distance I am talking about is the ableism and exclusion embedded in our political, physical, and social environments.

A disabled person in a nondisabled world is forced to advocate for access, constantly having to provide proof and perform deservingness. When you're not in the center, you are subject to being doubted and under suspicion of getting unfair special treatment, when access is actually a human and civil right.

And lo and behold: in March 2020, when San Francisco announced the stay-at-home order, almost everyone had to adjust to new ways of working and connecting. For decades, disabled people who advocated for remote work and learning, for online conferences and festivals, for content in multiple formats, were told "It's too difficult" or "It takes away from the face-to-face experience." In this new reality where being close can be deadly, access suddenly became available because nondisabled people were inconvenienced and had choices taken away from them.

As a high-risk person, I have been out exactly one time in the last eleven months for a flu shot. Even with the arrival and distribution of vaccines to the Bay Area, I will continue to feel unsafe for the rest of this year because vaccines are not a panacea. Like so many other disabled, sick, and immunocompromised people, I fear that people will stop taking precautions, such as hand washing, social distancing, and wearing masks, because they are under the belief that vaccination will protect them 100 percent or that herd immunity will take care of us all.

Privilege is the distance. Access and the quest for justice are the ways to close that distance. Both access and justice require political will and the belief that everyone is interdependent and has value. That my well-being is tied up with your well-being. That access belongs to everyone.

However, this pandemic revealed how far we have to go, because hypercapitalism and white supremacy made the conditions in which marginalized communities suffer the most, are considered expendable, and face the greatest inequities in health care, education, employment, and housing.

But what if . . . we decide to not go back to normal . . . we learn from these difficult times and design a better world centered on access, care, and justice?

This would require San Francisco to acknowledge its complicity in fueling gentrification and structural inequality in our so-called progressive city. And this would mean acknowledging how certain populations have been harmed, criminalized, and disenfranchised by public institutions, such as houseless people, older and disabled people, undocumented people, poor people, and communities of color.

We all have the capacity to create access for one another. And while things still feel bleak, I have hope for the future, because we all have the potential to learn and grow if we close the distance together. I'll leave you with two questions to think about:

1. Who is missing in the spaces you inhabit, and why?

2. What can you do beyond being a "good ally" to advocate for access through actions and practices?

Thank you for listening.

FUTURE

When something can't be fixed then the question
is what can we build instead?

—MARIAME KABA

Let's fly.

—CAPTAIN MICHAEL BURNHAM, U.S.S. *DISCOVERY*

We are each other's
harvest:
we are each other's business:
we are each other's
magnitude and bond.

—GWENDOLYN BROOKS, "PAUL ROBESON"

MY DISABLED ANCESTORS

stacey park
milbern

ing wong-ward

erin gilmer

ki'tay
davidson

stella
young

greg smith

laura
hershey

barbara
waxman
fiduccia

carrie ann lucas

paul
longmore

harriet
mcbryde
johnson

Surrounding this tree are the names of people whom I consider my ancestors, people I knew of and people who were close to me. May they rest in power. *Clockwise from top right:* Ing Wong-Ward, Ki'tay Davidson, Greg Smith, Barbara Waxman Fiduccia, Carrie Ann Lucas, Paul Longmore, Harriet McBryde Johnson, Laura Hershey, Stella Young, Erin Gilmer, Stacey Park Milbern

Ancestors and Legacies

What do we leave behind when we are gone? Since I'm not dead yet, I have no idea. Disabled and other marginalized people know what it's like to live with loss and to grieve for people who died well before their time. This was true before the pandemic and will continue to be so. My dear friend Stacey Park Milbern died on May 19, 2020. I found out from our mutual friend, Leah Lakshmi Piepzna-Samarasinha, who texted my phone and messaged me on Facebook. A late riser, I missed a bunch of messages and found out long after many in the disability community. To catch up, I scrolled through Facebook, a place where Stacey and I were connected with other Bay Area disabled folks. One of my immediate responses was how performative some posts were about Stacey from people who barely knew her. Some disabled people wanted to organize memorials. Others wanted to push organizations to recognize her during that year's anniversary of the Americans with Disabilities Act. Very few were taking a moment to pause and center those who knew Stacey best. The rush to organize also placed an unfair pressure on people to respond rather than hold space to feel the shock and sadness.

My disdain for the white disabled people who so badly wanted to be "allies" with disabled people of color, who never understood Stacey's politics or disability justice and never supported her work while she was alive, ignited a flame in me.

As someone close to her but not within her trusted innermost circle, I wrote a remembrance, "Loving Stacey Park Milbern," that very day, because I wanted the public to recenter its attention on Stacey's actual words and work. This was my small way of honoring her while telling these so-called good allies to back the fuck off.

Stacey and I knew of each other in online communities for years and met for the first time in 2015 at the Ed Roberts Campus in Berkeley. We both had the same disability (or so I thought), and when Stacey looked at me and inspected my hand, she said, "I think you have a different type of muscular dystrophy because of your hand." I was taken aback and thought, *Who is this audacious bitch to say this to me?* And it turns out she was right! A recent genetic test indicated I have something even rarer, even though I have many similar symptoms. Thank you, Stacey, for not holding back and seeing things I couldn't.

This was classic Stacey, a funny and bold person who dreamed big. She was unafraid of saying exactly what was on her mind. Stacey was a person who loved ice cream, boba tea, and Mariah Carey as much as organizing mutual aid and building coalitions. Stacey also lived her values and politics, believing that no person should be left behind and that interdependence is the way forward, the solution right before our eyes.

Stacey is perhaps best known for being an activist, but she was also a beautiful writer. Over the years, she would post the most thoughtful and tender insights on Facebook. One post about ancestors moved me so much that I asked if she would be willing to expand on it in a guest essay for my website. Published on March 10, 2019, "On the Ancestral Plane: Crip Hand Me Downs and the Legacy of Our Movements" traced the lineage of Stacey's disabled ancestors through a pair of boot socks passed down from Harriet McBryde Johnson to Laura Hershey to her. Stacey wrote:

I do not know a lot about spirituality or what happens when we die, but my crip queer Korean life makes me believe that our earthly bodyminds is but a fraction, and not considering our ancestors is electing only to see a glimpse of who we are. People sometimes assume ancestorship is reserved for those of biological relation, but a queered or cripped understanding of ancestorship holds that, such as in flesh, our deepest relationships are with people we choose to be connected to and honor day after day.

I included Stacey's prescient piece in my anthology, *Disability Visibility: First-Person Stories from the Twenty-First Century*, with no idea that she would become an ancestor a few weeks before the book came out in June 2020. It continues to feel bittersweet, but it makes me happy imagining that people might learn about Stacey for the first time from that book. During various online events and interviews promoting the anthology, I could hear Stacey's *tee-hee, tee-hee* giggles cheering me on. I wish she were here to celebrate with me and the other contributors, but I know she already was part of it on the page and in spirit.

In 2021, Dr. Jess Whatcott from San Diego State University organized a feminist disability justice speaker series as part of the Bread and Roses Feminist Research Colloquia, inviting Leah and me to speak about Stacey and the practice of disability justice on a panel moderated by Dr. Joe Stramondo. I couldn't wait to do this with Leah, another anthology contributor, who knew Stacey much longer than I did. What a generous opportunity to gather and share wisdom together. After many emails, notes, and preparations for this event, on April 28, 2021, I was excited and ready. I woke up that day to a text from Leah: "Hey, are you there?" I had a sinking feeling that one of my biggest nightmares had come true.

I'd overslept and completely missed the event.

This was a first, a horrible first. I swore that I looked at my calendar the night before, noting the time I would need to get up, eat, and digest before the start of the event. Everything was in place, but my body had other plans: "Bitch, I am the captain now. Do you realize your nerve pain has been flaring up again, making it difficult for you to sleep and focus on stuff? Plus, you have been doing way too much. I know you want to be there, but I'm gonna pull the brakes and we're gonna stay in Sleepy Town. You'll thank me later. Byeeeeee!"

Leah, Joe, and Jess were understanding in a way that only fellow disabled, neurodivergent, and chronically ill people truly "get." I apologized profusely and was terribly embarrassed that I disrupted their plans and forced them to improvise with zero notice. While sleeping through an event is not an access need per se, the grace the three of them showed me could be characterized as *access intimacy*, a term described by Mia Mingus:

> Access intimacy is also the intimacy I feel with many other disabled and sick people who have an automatic understanding of access needs out of our shared similar lived experience of the many different ways ableism manifests in our lives. Together, we share a kind of access intimacy that is ground-level, with no need for explanations. Instantly, we can hold the weight, emotion, logistics, isolation, trauma, fear, anxiety and pain of access. I don't have to justify and we are able to start from a place of steel vulnerability.

I am still working through the guilt and disappointment in myself for missing this event. I didn't want to let Stacey or Leah, Joe, and Jess down. But I did, and in a strange, poetic way, that's okay. Stacey would have encouraged me to take care of myself and honor my needs. These are the values she lived by, and this experience reminded me of what I learned from her. Thank you, Stacey.

Being vulnerable, as well as honest, is the key to collective liberation. This is one thing I understand from the principles of disability justice. It is not something that happens overnight after buying a candle, listening to a podcast, or reading a memoir. It requires daily intentions, self-reflections, and support from the people who care about you. The thing about being vulnerable is that it also opens you up to pain, which requires additional emotional labor to process and respond to it.

I was horrified to see media outlets and other nonprofit organizations get the details about Stacey's life wrong in 2020 and again in 2021 on the first anniversary of her death, which also happened to be her birthday. Friends and family of Stacey had to demand corrections, reply in comments to posts, and spend time educating people for free on a day they should have spent remembering her with love.

And then a person had the caucacity to send me a direct message on Twitter, asking, "Possibly weird question—Do you know who got Harriet McBryde Johnson's socks after Stacey Milbern?" This person, a disabled journalist, wanted to pitch a radio story for the twentieth anniversary of "Unspeakable Conversations," Harriet's essay published in the *New York Times* on February 16, 2003. This essay, like Stacey's, means the world to me and is also in my anthology. I like to imagine Harriet and Stacey in dialogue with each other, ancestor to ancestor, in *Disability Visibility*.

I replied that this request was inappropriate and, like many of Stacey's friends, I was still in mourning. Again, in a time when emotions remained raw, anger boiled forth when I should have been able to rest and quietly celebrate her. The impulse to be gentle and treat others with grace comingled with the need to make clear in no uncertain terms that some people need to back the fuck off.

This was the reply I wanted to send but didn't, because that person is unworthy of my fire:

You . . . asked me . . . for information about the whereabouts of my beloved friend's socks for a fucking pitch because it would make an "interesting" narrative thread? These socks are sacred objects, and there's no way in hell I would share any contacts from her estate with you. Nor would I ask folks close to her on your behalf. How you do something is just as important as what you do. I have seen the way you treat others in the disability community . . . not just me. I fucking see you.

What do we leave behind when we are gone? Perhaps one part of my legacy is how I cherish the legacies of my loved ones. Stacey left a body of work in the form of writing, interviews, videos, poetry, images, a Bay Area disability justice collective, and more. She also built relationships that are as enduring and tangible as a single story or book. The real gift any person can give is a web of connective tissue. If we love fiercely, our ancestors live among and speak to us through these incandescent filaments glowing from the warmth of memories. Loving fiercely is real-time legacy building. Maybe that's the best way to honor people. One day I will have ice cream with Stacey and talk shit about people again. I can't wait.

THE PARASITE

TIGER TAROT

ARTWORK BY HATIYE GARIP

With the new moon arriving, expect emotional vampires to swoop in and attempt to sap your power. Cast a protective bubble while you can and safeguard your time, energy, and capacity.

As I Lay Breathing

June 3, 2021

Dear Diary,

I am very proud of myself. I recorded my first-ever audio essay on breathing for *Radiolab* today! I did it online earlier, but there was a technical glitch and the producer asked if I would be okay if they sent someone to my home. My chest tightened at the thought of it because *no one* has been in my bedroom/home office aside from my family since March 2020. Recording someone requires close proximity, and the person who came wore a mask and was as nice as could be. Could this be the start of my slow poking-out-of-my-snail-shell Hot High-Risk Girl Summer? Hmm. We shall see. Baby steps.

I can't wait for this piece to come out. Who gets to breathe? This is the question I want people to think about after listening to it.

Kisses!

. . .

June 11, 2021

Transcript of my audio essay "Breath," Radiolab, W.N.Y.C. *Studios*

I sense a disturbance in the air. My chest feels tighter, something is not quite right. And then I see it. Flames are licking the bottoms of trees . . . hundreds of miles away. From my home in San Francisco, I can sense a wildfire coming before most people because of how my respiratory system is built. My diaphragm, which is slowly weakening over time, gives me a heightened sensitivity to secrets in the air.

Because my diaphragm is weak, I use a ventilator to help push the air out of my lungs. Without this machine, my own [carbon dioxide] would gather in my body, and I would die slowly from a buildup of acidic blood. This nearly happened when I was eighteen years old and first experienced respiratory failure. My brain went fuzzy, and in the E.R., I remember seeing my arterial blood drawn from my body, starved of oxygen, thick and black as ink. But I clawed my way back and lived to tell the tale; that is, if you are willing to listen.

When the coronavirus broke out, many states ranked people like me, who need a machine to breathe, lower down on the list of those deserving medical treatment. New York went even further. According to the ventilator allocation guidelines on the New York State Department of Health's website, it says that hospitals are allowed to take people's personal ventilators and give them to other patients in times of triage if they seek acute care. In essence, they can steal breaths from people like me and give them to others.

But my body, which the state calls "broken," I call an "oracle." It's not just the distant flames that I can see before you. But it's the cold math that calculates the value of my life, an algorithm of expendability that—whether you realize it or not—can come for you as well.

. . .

June 14, 2021

Medical Device Recall Notification (U.S. Only) / Field Safety Notice (International Markets)

Philips Respironics

What is the safety hazard associated with this issue?

Possible health risks include exposure to degraded sound abatement foam, for example caused by unapproved cleaning methods such as ozone, and exposure to chemical emissions from the foam material. High heat and high humidity environments may also contribute to foam degradation in certain regions.

The potential risks of degraded foam exposure include: Irritation (skin, eye, and respiratory tract), inflammatory response, headache, asthma, adverse effects to other organs (e.g. kidneys and liver) and toxic carcinogenic affects [*sic*].

To date, Philips Respironics has received several complaints regarding the presence of black debris/particles within the airpath circuit (extending from the device outlet, humidifier, tubing, and mask). Philips also has received reports of headache, upper airway irritation, cough, chest pressure and sinus infection.

For patients using life-sustaining mechanical ventilator devices:
Do not stop or alter your prescribed therapy until you have talked to your physician. Philips recognizes that alternate ventilator options for therapy may not exist or may be severely limited for patients who require a ventilator for life-sustaining therapy, or in cases where therapy disruption is unacceptable. In these situations, and at the discretion of the treating clinical team, the benefit of continued usage of these ventilator devices may outweigh the risks.

If your physician determines that you must continue using this device, use an inline bacterial filter. Consult your Instructions for Use for guidance on installation.

. . .

June 15, 2021

Dear Diary,

Fucking hell. Like, fuck a duck. Huh. I cannot believe I found out about this recall yesterday on Facebook of all places. It's high-key disgusting that corporations like Philips recommend that people with BiPaps and CPaps just "discontinue use of your device and work with your physician," and people like me who need it for life-sustaining purposes are supposed to suck (ha) it up and weigh the risks if there are no other options. Basically, they're telling a bunch of us to be okay with inhaling toxic carcinogenic particles because our bodies and lives are fucked up already and no one cares.

Bloody, violent revenge fantasies are running through my brain right now. Meanwhile, I tweeted about it with the hashtag #SuckYouPhilips, and many people replied, saying they were never notified and they only discovered it on Twitter. Welp. I guess social media isn't all trash.

I always knew this pre-pandemic and for most of my life, but *no one will save us but us*. The state and the medical-industrial complex *was never designed to serve us*. How many examples and deaths will it take to get nondisabled people to give a fuck? The pandemic taught us that access opened up a little only because they, the nondisableds, were inconvenienced. As states are now opening up and removing mask mandates, there is an erosion of the small gains in remote learning/work, on-line events, curbside pickups, and delivery options.

I motherfucking survived 2020 and fought hard with other high-risk people in California for watered-down vaccine equity after being deprioritized this past February (fuck you forever and ever, Gavin Newsom). The very things I talked about in the *Radiolab* audio essay and pieces about disabled oracles are real! But oracles need to breathe in order to be heard (figuratively, of course). Maybe that's the point. They want to suffocate our truths in the midst of a mass disabling event. Are oracles nothing more than zombie dodo birds that refuse to go extinct despite everything?

Yeah, I know I should be grateful. And I am. Parents are good. Sisters are good. I'm still alive, but that's not really enough, is it? That's low-bar shit. Living is more than surviving and scraping by as if one should be grateful to have a pulse. The apocalypse has already arrived for marginalized folks who do not get to breathe and exist in the same space as others, whether it's because of white supremacy, the climate crisis, medical racism, settler colonialism, or systemic ableism. Water, air, breath . . . all essential and all for the privileged few. I want to Hulk out and burn shit down but, oops, fire will create smoke. More smoke, more particles, more problems.

Maybe I'll start some fires with my words and tweets.

Ta-ta for now, bitch.

. . .

June 15, 2021

Email sent 5:34 a.m. Pacific

Hi, [my respiratory care agency that provides equipment from various manufacturers],

I hope you two are well and that you don't mind me bothering you with a question. Did you see this letter from Respironics? They are recalling a lot of machines, including the Trilogy 100 that I use.

It's pretty freaky what's happening and the fact that I may be inhaling these particles. I do use the round white filters, and maybe that'll help keep those particles out.

Looking forward to an update from you with your recommendations and next steps.

Thank you!

Alice

. . .

June 15, 2021

Email received 3:16 p.m. Pacific

Hi Alice,

We are in the process of sending out notifications to all our patients.

But yes, you are correct, this recall is specific to the sound abatement foam used in the Trilogy ventilators and PAP devices.

The notice further elaborates that the foam degradation may be exacerbated by the use of Ozone cleaners. We never suggest Ozone cleaners, nor have we observed our ventilator patients using this as a cleaning method. If you do or you have used an Ozone cleaner, please stop, and let us know.

We can send you an extra bacteria filter with your resupplies as this gets all worked out!

Also, if at any time you notice any changes to the white filter, please let us know.

We have very limited information, other than Philips does not have replacement ventilators or PAP devices at this time.

This recall does not affect the Trilogy Evo, but Philips does not have that product available as well.

[Respiratory care agency] is doing everything possible to work with Philips as they guide us towards a resolution.

Kind Regards,

[name redacted]

. . .

June 17, 2021

Email sent 6:02 a.m. Pacific

Hi, [name redacted],

Thanks for the update, and yes, I would love more bacterial filters at this time. I have a DreamStation that I use at night (not serviced by your company), but I was wondering if it's safe to attach a bacterial filter if I use a heated humidifier, or would that cause the filter to mold?

And while it's great that the company doesn't use any ozone cleaners, the foam can still degrade and has me a bit worried, because I've had watery eyes for several years and just assumed it was because of the pressure of the air coming into my nose.

Thanks for responding, and I hope there will be more updates later.

Alice

. . .

June 17, 2021

Email received 12:08 p.m. Pacific

Hi Alice,

Yes, you are correct that the bacteria filter cannot be used with heated humidification as it will BLOCK the airflow if wet!

Not ideal, but you could remove the heater from the PAP device; that would expose the PAP outlet, that then the bacteria filter could be placed on. It would be "dry" PAP therapy.

The watery eyes are not all that uncommon with PAP devices or non-invasive ventilator use with certain masks, at certain pressures, since the eyes and nose have common pathways.

I had one patient where her left eye would bulge a bit under her eyelid each time she inhaled on the device!

I also recognize it does not make it less worrisome with this recall.

[Name redacted] can best assist with your resupply and bacteria filter.

We will keep you posted as we learn more!

Best,

[name redacted]

. . .

June 30, 2021

CERTAIN PHILIPS RESPIRONICS VENTILATORS, BiPAP, AND CPAP MACHINES RECALLED DUE TO POTENTIAL HEALTH RISKS: F.D.A. SAFETY COMMUNICATION

Talk to your health care provider about using an inline bacterial filter, which may help to filter out particles of foam, as indicated in the Philips recall notification. At this time, the F.D.A. does not have evidence of the safety and effectiveness of a filter for mitigating the foam risks, and the F.D.A.'s evaluation is ongoing. It is important to note the following considerations:

- Filters will not help to reduce exposure to certain chemicals that may be released from the PE-PUR foam.
- Filters may affect ventilator performance because they may increase resistance of airflow through the device.
- You should closely monitor for possible accumulation of foam debris on the filter or resistance-related problems in the breathing circuit after filter placement.

. . .

July 1, 2021

Dear Diary,

These recent exchanges from my respiratory care agency have got me thinking. My filters turn gray after use for a few weeks, sometimes sooner during the smoky wildfire season when they turn dark gray. How many black particles are embedded in there with dust and allergens? I'll never know. At night my throat frequently gets dry and irritated, causing me to cough, tear up, and awaken. Is it because I slept with my mouth open, or is it due to some particles of degraded foam as outlined in the "voluntary" recall notice?

The linings of my nose are all fucked up, along with my sense of smell after continuous years of wearing a nasal mask that pushes cold, dry air with force into my lungs during the day (heated and humidified at night only). Is this related to the toxic particles? Or is this just "normal" bodily wear and tear that I have to live with in order to breathe? It's not an option to stop using this machine, which has become part of my cyborg apparatus. So I guess there's nothing I can do now except change filters more often. Note to self: order more filters online and pay for them out of pocket in case of shortages.

The safety alert from the F.D.A. ramped up my anxiety even more, because I'd clung on to the naive hope that the filters could do *something*. It makes total sense that particles and other exposure from the foam could not be trapped by filters. Should I still order a bunch? I mean, it's better than nothing, even though it feels like hygiene theater, right? Shit. Shit. Shit. Fuck. Fuck. Fuck.

Around the time I turned forty, I started using my BiPap more often during the day, transitioning from nighttime only to almost twenty-two hours per day. As of the recall, I calculate that I have spent the last seven years, at twenty-one hours/day—that is, 53,655 hours—potentially breathing in toxic particles. The number is conservative, since I have been using different brands of BiPap machines including Philips Respironics at night since the age of eighteen. *Shiiiiiiiit.*

What does the future hold? Beats me, but the harm from a machine (and its manufacturer) that has extended my life and the lives of millions of people around the world is a depressing betrayal. I treasure each intake of air because I know the struggle whenever I aspirate or am sick with bronchitis. As I fight for access to inhale and exhale, I am forced to welcome untold numbers of particles into my body that can endanger my peripheral existence even more. I am an unwitting character in a eugenic horror movie based on real events.

Rage is treated as a gateway drug, something you have to be careful of before you get in too deep. I. Am. In. It. So far, rage has been a generative force balanced with rest and pleasure. But I gotta be honest, I am tired. *Tired!* One day I will be crushed by the weight of the world. That day hasn't arrived. *Yet.*

Maybe I should be a cephalopod in the next life, a colorful, soft, pattern-changing, bioluminescent creature with tentacles that extend beyond the outer limits. A creature that squirms away from danger and refuses to break easily.

Kisses!

Alice, your friendly neighborhood
future disabled octopus cyborg

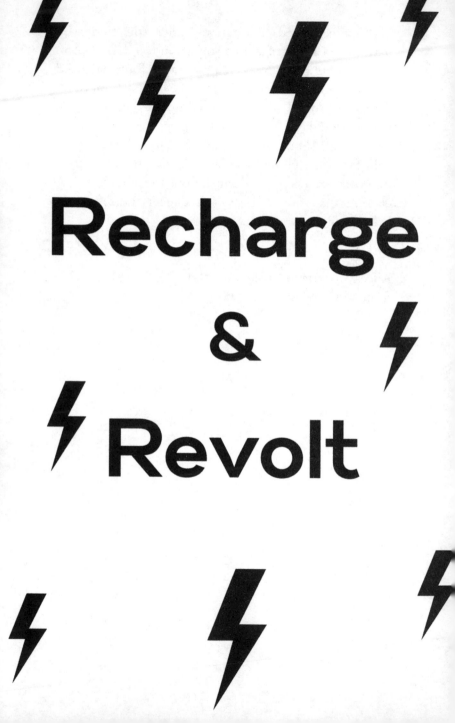

Recharge
&
Revolt

The Future of Care?

"'Care Bots' Are on the Rise and Replacing
Human Caregivers"

—ALEXANDRA MATEESCU AND VIRGINIA EUBANKS, *THE GUARDIAN* (LONDON), JUNE 3, 2021

"Where Do Infrastructure Talks Go from Here Now That
Biden's Negotiations with Republicans Collapsed?"

—JOEY GARRISON AND LEDYARD KING, *U.S.A. TODAY*, JUNE 9, 2021

"Bipartisan Group of Senators Say They Reached
Agreement on Infrastructure Plan"

—EMILY COCHRANE, *THE NEW YORK TIMES*, JUNE 10, 2021

"Biden's Pledge to Boost Home Caregiver Funding
Excluded from Infrastructure Deal"

—SUZY KHIMM, N.B.C. NEWS, JUNE 26, 2021

"What Happened When a 'Wildly Irrational' Algorithm
Made Crucial Healthcare Decisions"

ADVOCATES SAY HAVING COMPUTER PROGRAMS DECIDE HOW MUCH
HELP VULNERABLE PEOPLE CAN GET IS OFTEN ARBITRARY—AND IN
SOME CASES DOWNRIGHT CRUEL.

—ERIN MCCORMICK, *THE GUARDIAN* (LONDON), JULY 2, 2021

"Predicting Death Could Change the Value of a Life"

NEW TECHNOLOGY PROMISES TO FORECAST THE LENGTH OF YOUR LIFE.
BUT FOR DISABLED PEOPLE, MEASURING MORTALITY CAN PROVE FATAL.

—BRANDY SCHILLACE, *WIRED*, DECEMBER 28, 2021

Dream Dispatch

SOCIETY OF DISABLED ORACLES

Year: 2021
Location: Turtle Island, the returned land of the
Ramaytush Ohlone people (formerly known as
San Francisco, California)

Notes written by Alice Wong in preparation for a conversation with Ai-jen Poo and Alicia Garza on the Sunstorm *podcast (June 9, 2021) that were recently recovered from a sound packet on Mars. These notes have been deciphered, reclaimed, and processed by resident Oracles.*

Chorus

> Why do these institutions still exist? Why don't people see them as forms of incarceration that need to be abolished? Which systems and ideologies are perpetuated in rendering older and disabled people as invisible and disposable? How does capitalism pit groups that receive care against groups that provide care while it profits and exploits both? And what are the tensions between ageism, classism, and ableism that keep groups from organizing and supporting one another?

Response

> Care is infrastructure. Infrastructure is care.

> In the future, care infrastructure will be . . .

> One led and designed by disabled people and others who need care and/or provide care and based on their lived experiences.

One that is free, fully and publicly funded, and not means tested or linked to employment.

One that is rooted in a sustainably built environment with affordable and accessible housing and public transit.

One that doesn't require a person to verify and document their disability status every year to remain eligible.

One that is portable and not tied to residency in a given county or state.

One that includes home modifications, assistive technology, and durable medical equipment in home, educational, work, and public settings to facilitate full participation in society.

One where each neighborhood has a community hub of backup workers available for emergencies, cancellations, and natural disasters that does not require authorization or advance notice.

One that plans for geographic and demographic variation so that there won't be any underserved or underrepresented communities.

One that treats care as a normal part of the human life span and not a failure or weakness to need help.

One that fosters a culture that values the labor and expertise of care workers, treats them with respect, and gives them the pay and benefits that they deserve.

One that puts a primacy on self-direction of the individual, bodily autonomy, and dignity of risk rather than a formulaic, medicalized training that pathologizes disabled, older, and chronically ill people.

One that equates care with freedom, justice, love, and a social reinvestment in the potential of all kinds of people, however they show up in the world.

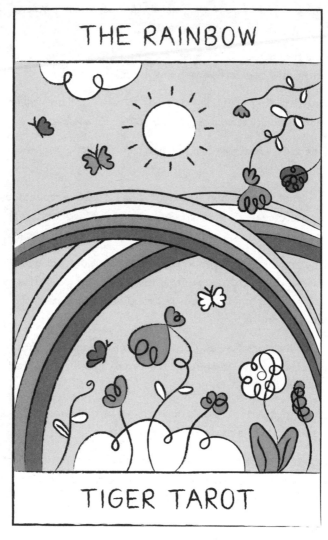

THE RAINBOW

TIGER TAROT

ARTWORK BY HATIYE GARIP

Double the abundance, opportunities, and joy awaits if you are open to it. Luxuriate in their warmth and good fortune.

How to Create a More Inclusive Future Post-COVID

An interview of me by Nikolay Nikolov for Mashable (March 3, 2021). This conversation has been condensed and edited for clarity.

In our society, some people matter much more than others. Conventional wisdom, especially by bioethicists, is the idea that the most resources should go to those who deserve it.

And I think there are so many layers of white supremacy, sexism, and, clearly, ableism and ageism. And this is really personal for me; this is just one reason I wrote and published a lot in 2020, to really push back at these narratives that are incredibly harmful to disabled, chronically ill, fat, older, and immunocompromised people.

I'm high risk, but I want to live, too, just like everybody else. But I think a lot of people who are not disabled just see me and think, *Oh my god. I cannot imagine living in your body, you must just have it so hard.* It is difficult, but what's really difficult is the way this world is constructed, the way inequality is institutionalized. The way certain people are penalized just for existing. Criminalized.

There are so many of us who live in nondisabled worlds, who are incredibly innovative, creative, and adaptive. And there's so much wisdom now by disabled and sick people about how to slow down and make things more flexible that I wish people paid attention to. If there's anything to come out of this pandemic, I hope that people realize that, for many of us, we have always been here, we have always survived. And in many cases, we have the solutions.

And I think a lot about these multiple waves of people whom I consider part of the disability community—people who are called "long-haulers" because, clearly, recovery from COVID can be a lifelong process.

One of the biggest things that's so toxic about ableism and capitalism is this idea that our worth is based on our productivity. We are interdependent. We know there's more to our worth than just whether we're taxpayers or whether we can work forty or more hours a week, and there are so many lessons to learn. We need to think about being more fluid and taking more risks, in terms of how we structure our daily lives, building in more accessibility and really listening to those who are most impacted.

And let all those people who are most impacted, from every marginalized community, be at the center of finding the solutions and making decisions. Because, frankly, when you've been harmed by systems and institutions for your entire life or maybe just recently, you know how to figure things out.

And I think, for people who've never had to deal with that, they're often the ones in positions to create policies, and this is a huge loss of opportunity. Some of the core requirements that many people with disabilities have requested over the years in terms of employment and education were, for so many years, sidelined on technicalities. Whether it's copyright issues, whether it's that the company I.T. system cannot handle too many requests, or whatever it may be. Now we've learned that we're actually able to meet those requirements very quickly, and when it comes to money and retaining students or a workforce, things can happen very, very quickly. They may not be perfect, but when they have to happen, they can happen overnight.

The future is one in which we need to really think about power: how power is shared, how power is obtained, how we create power. And I think about *Star Trek*, because I love the phrase "infinite diversity in infinite combinations." Because this Vulcan idea is really about how our differences make us better.

The whole pressure to return to what we think of as normal is something we need to let go. I want everyone to think about looking ahead as a real chance to rethink the world. To really reenvision the world, a world that is centered on justice, liberation, interdependence, mutual care, and mutual respect. There may not be a "post-pandemic" world at all, at least not anytime soon; we may be in this forever, and that can be deeply unsettling to many. Perhaps people should take this time to learn from the mistakes made in the past: how we were slow to act, how we were slow to believe people, how we distorted what freedom means. Freedom from a mask mandate doesn't mean shit if you're dead. I see the future as a time when we critically need solidarity with one another. We need to show it. We need to really understand that asking for help, needing help, is not a weakness. I think the only way we can survive is if we truly *believe and practice* that we're in this together.

A lot of disabled people have to fight for their futures today.

There are a lot of forces around us—technology, in particular—that don't want to fix us, that actually want to erase us at a molecular level; for example, human gene editing with a tool called CRISPR-Cas9.

This is something that is deeply concerning to me, because it really is about the future trying to disappear us, people like me—people who have what some think of as "bad genes." So these kinds of technologies and other really explicit ways to "fix" disabled people send messages that we don't belong in the future. And I categorically reject that.

Disabled people belong in the future. We're gonna resist as much and as hard as we can.

The Last Disabled Oracle

On August 6, 2020, I gave a talk titled "The Last Disabled Oracle" as part of Assembly for the Future, a project of the collaboration The Things We Did Next, based in Melbourne, Australia. The Things We Did Next was cocreated by Alex Kelly and David Pledger and produced by Not Yet It's Difficult and Something Somewhere Inc. One purpose of the event was to collectively imagine multiple futures. Attendees gathered in small groups and created dispatches from 2029 in response to my talk. Below is the script of my talk from the year 2029.

Welcome, everyone! It's 4:15 p.m. Pacific time in California, and I'd like to call to order the December meeting of the Disabled Oracle Society, North American chapter.

To describe myself, I am an Asian American woman wearing a black jacket with white stripes. I have a mask over my nose attached to a tube for my ventilator. While people are joining both online and in person, please help yourselves to some drinks and snacks in the back. Louise brought some Tim Tams back from her visit to Melbourne attending the Australian chapter's annual meeting last month. Please remember we have people participating online, on the phone, and through an all-new platform, Beep Boop. Be sure to follow the various streams from your device throughout our meeting today.

Since it's December and we're about to embark upon another decade in the twenty-first century, let's take some time to review the major issues and challenges we faced as disabled oracles. [Since our society's establishment] in December 2020, these nine years have been difficult with the coronavirus, the phage in 2024, and the increasing changes in weather patterns and global migration in the last five years. All of these crises have disproportionately impacted marginalized people, especially communities of color and indigenous, poor, older, and disabled people.

The planet is literally more hostile to people like us, and yet one of the greatest existential threats we face is from other humans who believe congenital disabilities are something to be fixed and eliminated through human gene editing, also known as H.G.E.

Eugenics has always been with us, but in the next ten to fifteen years, we know H.G.E. will be widely available to the public since the press conference this past August by McEdit, a multinational corporation planning to provide high-end boutique services for people who want to give their future generations the "best" chance at life. They didn't announce the date of their launch, but reports say it's likely to take place in 2030 or 2031 at the very latest. The fact that there was such fanfare and little opposition to McEdit means we have a lot of work ahead of us as disabled oracles.

What does the advent of McEdit mean for us? How do we, imperfectly perfect creatures, argue against these seductive narratives about being better, stronger, healthier? How do we address the very real ethical implications behind this technology?

Before we have a discussion on what to do next, let's go back and review some basics. This may be useful for some of our newer members.

Many years ago, the Center for Genetics and Society described human genetic modification as "the direct manipulation of the genome using molecular engineering techniques." This is often referred to as human gene editing.

There are two types of modification: somatic and germline. We are focused on germline modification, because it would change the genes in eggs, sperm, or early embryos. This means subsequent generations would also carry those changes.

CRISPR-Cas9 is one gene editing tool that became popular because it's fast, cheap, and accurate. CRISPR was used in 2018 by He Jiankui, a researcher who announced at an international conference that he had produced genetically edited babies in an attempt to make them resistant to H.I.V. He was sentenced to three years in prison for illegal medical practices in 2019.

At that time, germline modification was a red flag for ethical reasons, but it wasn't banned or regulated in every country. Over the years, tools such as CRISPR became more

sophisticated, and slowly opposition to the unknown consequences died down. Excitement around the science and possibilities of eliminating disease outweighed any questions
about the underlying assumptions about health, disability,
and difference. The idea of giving babies an advantage—
whether it's less likelihood of developing a disease or enhanc-
ing other traits—was irresistible to people with the means to
give their kids quote-unquote "the best." The *best* meaning a
life without a disability. And this is why McEdit and its subsequent competitors are on the horizon for commercial and undoubtedly militaristic purposes.

The Disabled Oracle Society began in 2020 in the midst of
the coronavirus pandemic, when sick and disabled people
sounded the alarm about the importance of wearing masks,
the value of accessibility, and the interdependence of all communities. It became very clear who was considered disposable
and who was not as institutions and governments were forced
to implement medical triage guidelines. The casual ableism,
racism, and ageism went unchecked in debates around restart-
ing the economy, with the terms such as *acceptable losses* and

DISABLED ORACLE
SOCIETY

EST. 2020

high risk thrown around as if those lives weren't worth living or saving.

The catalyst for the formation of the Disabled Oracle Society came from an article in July of that year from the *New York Times* as part of a series of stories marking the thirtieth anniversary of the Americans with Disabilities Act, a civil rights law for disabled people. An article by Katie Hafner titled "Once Science Fiction, Gene Editing Is Now a Looming Reality" featured several parents of disabled children, scientists, and bioethicists. And only *one* person with a disability.

My friend and fellow oracle Rebecca Cokley tweeted, "Hey @nytimes how DARE you have a writer who doesn't identify as DISABLED write about what CRISPR means for OUR community as part of your #ADA30 spread?!?! Your ableism really knows NO bounds."

When I saw that, something in me snapped. Here we are, disabled oracles since the beginning of time, warning society and telling our truths, being completely sidelined once again. This is nothing new or unique. Throughout history, marginalized, troublesome, or undesirable people were not believed or taken seriously. We elicit discomfort and disrupt people's binary ideas of normalcy. Our warnings have been silenced in order to uphold the status quo. Even when we make persuasive arguments, we are not at the center, despite our extensive scholarship and wisdom. For instance, I interviewed Dr. Jaipreet Virdi in August 2020 about her book, *Hearing Happiness: Deafness Cures in History*, and she said this about the future of cures such as human gene editing:

> There is no guarantee that genetic engineering will eradicate hereditary deafness nor any certainty that it will not cause any further complications. Moreover, this is essentially, at the core, a form of cultural genocide. To argue that this needs to be "avoided" at the level of genetics is an af-

front to generations of Deaf people who do not perceive
themselves to be genetic defects.

That was a brief overview of our origins, and I share this
because the mission remains constant:

We tell our stories and truths in our own words.
    We define who we are and our place in the world.
    We fight to be seen and heard.
    We live in defiance with joy and radical acceptance.

You elected me as the president of the Disabled Oracle Society this year, and I take this responsibility seriously. Friends,
I too am tired of defending my worth every day to people obsessed with having everything faster, shinier, newer. We try to
reach people where they are, engaging in a number of creative
ways. We assert the danger and uncertainty to future generations with altered genomes and how it will impact the entire
human race. We repeat our main talking points all the time:
all people have worth, no person should be left behind, and
technology is never neutral. We also try to point out how technology reinforces white supremacy, ableism, and all forms of
structural inequality. This is not new, with too many tragic
examples to list.

What else can we do? How do we love and hold each other
up so we keep on going as a community? How can we harness
our imagination to create the world we want to live in right
now and in the future?

At this time, I'd like to open it up for discussion and questions. Let me see . . . "Hi, I'm Emily from New York City.
What is the role of a disabled oracle?"

Thanks, Emily. It's totally up to you. What are you comfortable talking about? Just living your best life is a form of
resistance. As I mentioned earlier, I don't have the answers or

even a strategy yet on how to engage with McEdit and the millions who will become their customers. But I'm good at asking questions. I'm good at telling my personal story within a larger political context. In asking questions, I want people to consider other perspectives and why germline human gene editing is incredibly troubling and problematic for so many communities, not just disabled people.

Since we're almost out of time, here's one final question: "Hi, I'm Grace from Tempe, Arizona, longtime disabled oracle. I'm scared. What is the point of doing all this if we're going to become extinct?"

Thanks, Grace. I'm really scared, too. Things feel overwhelming and impossible every day. Just know that you have a choice on how much you want to do. I believe everyone has the capacity to change the world while we are still alive in big and small ways.

I'm reminded of this tweet from 2017 by Dr. Ruha Benjamin, a sociologist and author of *Race After Technology: Abolitionist Tools for the New Jim Code*: "Remember to imagine and craft the worlds you cannot live without, just as you dismantle the ones you cannot live within."

As disabled oracles, we continue to build and create on the knowledge and dreams of our ancestors. They left their mark on the planet, as will we. After we're long gone, we will show up in other ways. Someone will see and discover us, and we'll be speaking with them from the past.

I don't know if this helps, but think about the ancestors that mean something to you. Connect with the people close to you right now and the stories passed down by your elders. Know that we are in this together collectively and that our brilliance as oracles will not be denied. I call upon the power and wisdom of my disabled ancestors, such as Stella Young, Carrie Ann Lucas, Ki'tay Davidson, Ing Wong-Ward, Harriet McBryde Johnson, and Stacey Park Milbern. I have my memories and their words to guide me. And I hope this bit of advice brings you comfort, because we should embrace every single moment while we can. In closing, let's recite the motto of the Disabled Oracle Society:

> We are the past. We are the present. We are the future. We are forever.

See you all in 2030. Meeting adjourned!

Gather your intentions and share your wisdom everywhere.
The future is behind you, in the seeds you planted.

My Grown-Ass Disabled Person Make-A-Wish List

Become editor in chief of an imprint at a major publisher centered on disabled writers and editors.

Host, direct, write, and produce a weird, funny show about disability culture that is part *Reading Rainbow*, *Masterpiece Theatre*, and *The Muppet Show*.

Cofound a venture capital fund that invests in disabled founders, creatives, and entrepreneurs.

Co–executive produce T.V. shows, documentaries, and feature films.

Cocurate an exhibit on disability activist culture at the Smithsonian.

Work with a major cosmetic company to develop a new lip color, "Tiger Power," and be featured in its ad campaign.

Develop a Netflix series with Samin Nosrat about making and eating snacks.

Write a book about cooking, eating, and craving and have it published by 4 Color Books.

Partner with a local creamery for a new ice-cream flavor.

Take a private jet that will store my power chair safely to Tokyo with friends and family; stay in a luxury hotel; visit my friends Adam, Seiko, and Mizuki; eat *all* the things; and take a train to Nagoya to visit the Studio Ghibli theme park. And eat bento while on the train.

Portray a disabled character in a *Star Wars* or *Star Trek* series, such as *Star Trek: Lower Decks*, *Star Trek: Discovery*, *The Mandalorian*, or *Ahsoka*.

Begin a new career as a voice actor in animated shows like *Tuca & Bertie* or *Bob's Burgers* and in video games.

Throw a blowout fiftieth birthday party in 2024.

Feed a koala eucalyptus leaves and take a photo with one at the S.F. Zoo.

Be swept off my feet in a grand Jane Austenesque romance consisting of watching T.V., baking, going to the grocery store, and hot letter-writing.

Two words: *ghost sex*.

Thank You,
Mrs. Shrock

There is a difference between thinking about death and becoming obsessed with it. I was never supposed to reach forty-eight years old, my fourth Year of the Tiger. I knew this reality at an early age, and it haunted and shaped me into the person I am now.

As a baby I went from sitting to walking. I did not crawl because my neck could not hold my head up while on all fours. When the doctors diagnosed me with an undetermined type of muscular dystrophy, my parents told me they cried. It was a big deal to hear this and imagine my parents crying about something, anything. How frightening it must have been for them, new to the United States and new to parenting without any family support. How did information about muscular dystrophy translate in Chinese? How did they figure their way through the medical system and services I would need for the rest of my life? This is not my story to tell, nor is it my place to speculate about their response to an unknown prognosis for their child.

Thanks to P.B.S. shows like *Sesame Street*, *The Electric Company*, and *Mister Rogers' Neighborhood*, I skipped pre-school and went to kindergarten. Television taught me that *agua* means "water" and that when counting from one to twelve you have to sing and scat to a funkadelic beat accompanied by a cartoon showing a pinball bouncing around inside a machine.

At the time, I lived at 1033 West Seventy-Eighth Street on the north side of Indianapolis and attended Delaware Trails Elementary, which was nearby on Hoover Road. I had three wonderful teachers in a row: Mrs. Fisher in kindergarten, Mrs. Dixie Shrock in first grade, and Mrs. Sorrell in second grade. While I knew I was physically different from other kids the moment I started attending school, and the Individuals with Disabilities Education Act had passed only a few years before, I was mainstreamed and welcomed by these teachers.

Unfortunately I couldn't find any photos of Mrs. Shrock in my family albums. This is a photo of two other students and me in my second-grade classroom, which was taught by Mrs. Sorrell. It is my seventh birthday. Back in the 1980s, kids were allowed to bring treats to school to share with the class on their birthday. This year, Mom made egg rolls and brought Coca-Cola to class for everyone!! Reader, we ate this entire meal during class time, in addition to lunch. This was ah-mazing and far more special than a birthday cake! Mom also did this for my first-grade birthday, but it didn't continue after second grade with Mrs. Sorrell.

To my right is my best friend from school, Heather Lynch, who's posing adorably. You may not have noticed, but she is wearing supercool rainbow suspenders. I'm in the middle wearing a turtleneck and hand-sewn overalls Mom made me (which are featured in more than one photo in this book, strangely enough). Another classmate, Kirsten B., is to my left.

Mrs. Shrock was a particular favorite; she was kind, gentle, and good-humored. She genuinely cared for her students. There was a moment during story time when she took down her long brown hair, which was always up in an elegant chignon, and it was a Rapunzel-like, oh-my-god-she-really-did-that moment in my mind.

I would lag behind as my classmates lined up and walked to gym or art—they would assemble in two lines, and Mrs. Shrock would lead them to their destination, and sometimes it would be just me left behind in the hallway, slowly making my way alone. One memory that will always stand out from all my many enraging, traumatic, discriminatory, bullying, and embarrassing experiences during twelve years of primary and secondary education was a day when Mrs. Shrock asked me to be at the front of the girls' line, and when she guided both lines of students to another part of the school, she held my hand and supported me as I slowly walked alongside her. Walking together, in tandem—adult-child, nondisabled-disabled, teacher-student—we set the pace for the entire class. I have not felt that seen, safe, or cared for by a teacher since.

I reconnected with Mrs. Shrock in my twenties, when she reached out to me after discovering I was a student at Earlham College, a small, private Quaker liberal arts school in Richmond, Indiana, before I had to take a leave of absence a few months into my freshman year. I believe she had relatives who were alumni and might have seen something about me. We began exchanging holiday cards every winter.

Mrs. Shrock continued to teach first grade at Greenbriar Elementary School, only a few blocks from Delaware Trails, for over thirty years. Here is an edited excerpt of a letter I sent to Jamie Alexander, the interim principal of Greenbriar, and Dr. Nikki Woodson, superintendent of the Metropolitan School District of Washington Township, on January 1, 2013:

Dear Mrs. Alexander,

I am writing to commend one of your teachers, Mrs. Dixie Shrock. I do not know if your school or if the M.S.D. Washington Township has an award for teachers recognizing excellence, but please consider this letter as a formal nomination.

I recently listened to a story on N.P.R. about a student who tracked down his teacher after decades to say thank you to her. I want to formally share my thoughts with her colleagues and document my thank-you to this great teacher.

I was a student of Mrs. Shrock in her first grade class in 1980 at Delaware Trails Elementary. The school was torn down in 1981 or '82. One day as a second grader, I could not keep up with my classmates and was left by myself in the hallway. As I tried to walk back to my classroom, I tumbled to the floor due to exhaustion. I started crying, and Mrs. Shrock was one of the first teachers to come out of her classroom and comfort me.

Mrs. Shrock showed great care and affection for every student—I wasn't the only one who felt like she could do anything and was full of potential. For a student with a disability, this was an invaluable feeling to have at an early age before adults started imposing limitations. I was never made to feel different in Mrs. Shrock's classroom—I was simply part of a group of kids who were eager to learn.

Over the years I updated Mrs. Shrock with my life. Sometimes I wonder if it sounds like I'm bragging, but the real reason I send her articles or news items about me is so she knows she contributed to my success, just like my family and friends. What I meant to say in those cards was *Thank you, Mrs. Shrock. Part of who I am today is because of you. Some of my fondest childhood memories were in your classroom.*

The main messages I received from Mrs. Shrock as a student were the following: *I felt safe. I felt loved. I felt included.* Those feelings built a foundation for learning and self-confidence that I still possess today.

Dixie Shrock is an asset to the M.S.D. Washington Township and should be recognized as such. School administrators should reward teachers who remain dedicated to their craft and continue to imbue students with a sense of wonder and optimism.

Please accept this letter as an expression of gratitude from a former Washington Township student and congratulations to Mrs. Shrock for a lifetime of excellence in teaching.

During the beginning of the pandemic, I wondered how Mrs. Shrock was faring and if she retired. I sent her a copy of my anthology with a thank-you note (I love sending and receiving cards and keeping them as mementos). Unprompted, Mrs. Shrock shared this amazing story in a note dated July 16, 2020:

Dear Alice,

What joy, pure joy, when I received *Disability Visibility*. The goals in your introduction are thoughtful and powerful and formed through your experiences in order to shine a light. The power of perseverance was always present as we walked hand in hand wherever we went. One day, as we entered the cafeteria (the other students would trail behind us), you said, "Mrs. Shrock, [pause] am I going to die?" We kept walking for a few seconds. "No, you aren't going to die." I knew in that moment that you were always "figuring things out" at a much deeper level than those around you. I am so very proud of <u>all</u> the things you have done for others.

I have just resigned my position because of COVID after 42 years, so your book is the first on my list! Thank you!

You are always in my heart,
Dixie Shrock

I remember as a kid watching the Muscular Dystrophy Association telethons and not being able to imagine myself as a thirty-, forty-, fifty-year-old adult. How can I know what I will be when I grow up if I'm not expected to grow up? How do little humans process these concepts and emotions? The doctors and science at the time closed the door on my future, while key people like Mrs. Shrock ripped it wide open. Along with my family and friends (and technology, the internet, Medicaid, and other services), I have no doubt she saved my

A class picture from either kindergarten or first grade, so I am about five or six years old.

life. And I didn't even know it. This essay is a Venn diagram of our memories from 1980 in that little elementary school.

I am my wildest dream. The dream is not about "overcoming" a disability. The dream is about looking straight into the abyss and creating something out of nothing. Dreaming is infinite universe building. Thank you for everything, Mrs. Shrock. Thank you, six-year-old me, who was figuring out life and death in that weird brain of ours.

ALICE AT 6: Who are you?

ALICE AT 48: I am you.

ALICE AT 6: Um, you're old. *So old.*

ALICE AT 48: I know. Weird, right?

ALICE AT 6: When am I going to die?

ALICE AT 48: I have no idea, but I'm still alive and surprised by it.

ALICE AT 6: Can you eat anything you want and stay up all night?

ALICE AT 48: Pretty much. That's one of the good things about being a grown up, although I still feel like I'm your age. What else do you want to know?

ALICE AT 6: Is it scary being alive at your age?

ALICE AT 48: I'm not going to lie to you because we never had it easy. I have a lot of friends now and am doing all kinds of cool things. This makes life fun, but there will always be risk and danger. And, girl, the planet is in danger!

ALICE AT 6: What's so great about the future? Can you go to space and say "Nanu nanu" to Mork?

ALICE AT 48: Not yet, but it would be nice to float around and explore the planets. Maybe we could become friends with an alien.

ALICE AT 6: I knew it. Aliens are real. Mork is real. *Mork & Mindy* the T.V. show was just to get us ready for them. Do you get tired? I'm tired.

ALICE AT 48: I am still tired, probably more than you. I wish I wasn't, but things are worse with our body, but that comes from aging and our disability.

ALICE AT 6: That's not fun.

ALICE AT 48: Nope, it's not. Hey, you know Mrs. Shrock? I'm still in touch with her!

ALICE AT 6: Nice! What about my best friend from kindergarten, Heather Lynch?

ALICE AT 48: We're still in touch on Facebook.

ALICE AT 6: What's a face book?

ALICE AT 48: Nothing useful. Never mind! What else do you want to know?

ALICE AT 6: When am I going to die?

ALICE AT 48: Oh brother. As I said earlier, I don't know, but the not-knowing part isn't all bad. We can't know or control everything no matter how hard we try.

ALICE AT 6: Can we still get an Orange Julius and a hot dog? Mom and Dad get them for me whenever we go to Lafayette Square Mall. I like the salty and sweet.

ALICE AT 48: I wish we could, kid.

ALICE AT 96: Um, hello? Is anyone there?

ALICE AT 48: Whaaaa? Is that us? We look great!

ALICE AT 6: Are you a witch?

To be continued in the forthcoming *Year of the Tiger: The Fur Will Fly* (Vintage Books, 2070).

Future Notice

At the tender age of ninety-six, in the Year of the Tiger 2070, Alice Wong died. Oracle, storyteller, cyborg, trouble-maker, activist, night owl: Alice was the firstborn daughter of Henry and Bobby Wong, who emigrated from Hong Kong to Indiana in the 1970s. Alice moved to San Francisco in 1997 for graduate school and the Bay Area disability community. San Francisco became her home for many decades. In 2014, Alice founded the Disability Visibility Project, which led to a blog, a podcast, and a series of books, television shows, feature films, and documentaries.

In 2026, Alice became the editor in chief of the first disability-centered imprint for a major U.S. publisher. Along with many other disabled editors, writers, and colleagues, the imprint helped usher in what is considered the first of several golden ages of disability publishing.

As with many people who came of age during the 1999 *Olmstead* decision by the U.S. Supreme Court, Alice lived to see the abolition of carceral institutions such as psychiatric hospitals, nursing homes, and prisons. Instead of court-mandated conservatorships, supported decision-making al-lowed people to thrive with autonomy. Decades of activism by disabled people and their coconspirators led to community-based care grounded in disability justice principles. Successive natural disasters, pandemics, wars, and mass migrations produced the largest percentage of disabled people in recorded history. The confluence of these forces created a reimagined society that dismantled notions of enforced productivity and toxic individualism. This allowed Alice the freedom and supports to do everything she wanted during the latter half of her life.

In 2032, inspired by the Linda Lindas, Alice became a performer and songwriter for the punk rock band Rage Against the Ableism. The band, famous for wearing Aggretsuko masks and thrashing against injustice, spawned five records in twelve years. Her songs, such as "Ableism Is Trash," "Fuck You, Pay Me," and "S.T.F.U. White People," are still performed in karaoke pods today, from Memphis to Mars.

With the progression of her disability, Alice moved to a zero-gravity capsule on the moon in 2045 as a member of the second Crips in Space cohort of scientists, creators, and explorers.

During the past two decades, Alice receded from public life, preferring to amplify and support the next generation of disabled cyborgs.

"Good shit takes time," Alice wrote in her first memoir, *Year of the Tiger* (Vintage Books, 2022). She took her time with both her work and the pleasures of life, as someone who did not find success until her late forties. Known for throwing excellent parties, curating disability media and culture exceptionally well, savoring a good latte and pastry, being a benevolent Bossy Boss to close friends and comrades, and messing around at all hours of the night, Alice is survived by her sisters, Emily and Grace; family friend Rani Singh; and a few precious unnamed others. Her sisters will continue her legacy by archiving her materials at the Society of Disabled Oracles and redistributing her assets within the community. She is also survived by her holocats Blueberry, Claude, Cinnamon, Meowmee Jr., Mittens, and Phil.

Instead of flowers, donations can be made to your local

animal shelter, food bank, library, or mutual-aid collective. For the latest information on the multidimensional interstellar memorial organized by the Cabal, a preselected group of Alice's friends and family, go to the Disability Visibility orb. It will be a weeklong online and in-person dance party, film festival, feast, orgy, and celebration. Please contact the Cabal for permissions, requests, or questions, as members know her wishes best and want to prevent any inaccurate coverage of Alice's life and work.

Enjoy all of Alice's good shit, and may you create some good shit as well.

Acknowledgments

When I answered my "Proust-ish Questionnaire" (page 213), I said I am the greatest love of my life. It would be logical at this point to thank myself for holding my shit together during the writing and editing of this book. Thank you, Alice, for recognizing two years ago that it was time to be bold like a tiger and propose a memoir with your year approaching in 2022. Thank you for looking back and ahead while living through an interminable pandemic that pushed you to the brink. Thank you for making the time to sit, think, dream, rage, and laugh. You did it, bitch! Now good luck promoting the fuck out of it.

The real truth is that this book is a collective endeavor and there are many people to recognize. First, my parents, Henry and Bobby, and my sisters, Emily and Grace. The Wongs are such a weird and funny family. They give me a sense of security and support that allows me the freedom to be my extra, extra self. My family has been there from the very beginning and made my life possible. My friends (who know who they are) have been awesome as they rooted for me and gave me the space to grumble, to freak out, and to moan and groan about the process from beginning to end. The genuine enthusiasm from friends for the release of *Year of the Tiger* kept me going and washed away moments of self-doubt, since writing and editing can be very lonely experiences.

I did not share drafts of the manuscript with many people,

but there are six people who took the time to review specific parts and who offered invaluable feedback: Ryan Easterly, Yomi Wrong, Ellen D. Wu, Jaipreet Virdi, Emily Nusbaum, and Alyssa Burgart. Thank you for answering my questions, suggesting edits, and catching some inaccuracies that would have mortified me! There are three people who unknowingly intervened and changed the shape of several chapters. Those chapters deepened significantly thanks to David Masumoto, Nora Shen, and Dixie Shrock, who reached out to me through letters, emails, and texts. I am lucky to be connected to all three of you.

My anthology, *Disability Visibility*, does not contain any artwork, but with this memoir I wanted to stretch myself and have as much fun as possible. Initially I attempted to doodle a few sketches, but I ended up using the Canva app with its fancy fonts and stock images to create various graphics throughout the chapters. I am particularly proud of *Snack Manifesto* (page 64) and *My Disabled Ancestors* (page 310). I used the Procreate app to handwrite the section titles with an Apple Pencil on an iPad mini. These tools contributed to the book along with ye olde reliable laptop. Thank you, apps, hardware, and high-speed internet.

Thank you to the artists and the owners of numerous photos and illustrations who gave permission for their inclusion in *Year of the Tiger*. I also wanted to tell some stories visually and commissioned four fantastic artists who made this book a delight: Sam Schäfer, Hatiye Garip, Lizartistry, and Felicia Liang. Support these artists if you can!

I am fortunate to work with an amazing group of people from Vintage Books. I collaborated with my fantastic cat-loving editor, Anna Kaufman, for a second time, along with editorial assistant Zuleima Ugalde. Our discussions as the book developed were full of care and the best intentions. The design, typefaces, and layout of the book are thanks to Andy

Hughes, head of production; Christopher Zucker, associate director of design; and Debbie Glasserman, interior designer, who made all the visual elements I added look less janky. As a person who struggles with verb-tense usage and who has a tendency to use all caps and em dashes, I am thankful for Kayla Overbey, production editor; Nancy B. Tan, copy editor; and proofreaders Kathy Strickman and Diana Drew. Blessed are the detail-oriented people who are *on it* and *keep things on time*! A book, no matter how interesting, needs to reach an audience. Many thanks to publicist Julie Ertl and marketer Sophie Normil, who have helped spread the Good Word of *Year of the Tiger* to the masses. Thanks also to cover designer Madeline Partner for a beautiful exterior that reflects the ferocity that is this memoir. I look forward to working with many of these fine folks again on my upcoming anthology, *Disability Intimacy*.

There are three more individuals in publishing who I want to highlight: Julia Kardon, Catherine Tung, Jenn Baker, and Rosalie Morales Kearns. My literary agent, Julia Kardon of H.G. Literary, has had my back since my first book proposal. She repeatedly explains (with patience) the details of my contracts and answers my inane questions about the business. She believes in me as a writer/editor and wants to help me fulfill all my ambitions. Julia is also a cat person, which is a sign of her excellence. Catherine Tung was an editor at Vintage Books in 2018; she emailed me out of the blue, asking if I had any interest in editing an anthology. Thanks to Catherine's initial contact and her work as an editor during the first half of *Disability Visibility*'s publication process, I got the opportunity to become an author/editor of three books—something fortyyear-old Alice couldn't imagine. Jenn Baker—writer, podcaster, and senior editor at Amistad Books—was someone I followed on Twitter for several years. I learn about all the best books, new writers of color, and the inner workings of the publishing industry from her. Jenn has been so generous with her time and professional expertise. I consider her a friend and a mentor as I try to push for greater disability diversity in publishing and figure out my next steps in world domination. Rosalie Morales Kearns, the founder of Shade Mountain Press, was another person, like Jenn, who demystified many aspects of the publishing world to me long before I had a book deal with Vintage. I still have a lot to learn!

Finally, I want to give a shout-out to my snail child, Augustus the Slow. A garden snail (*Cornu aspersum*), Augustus joined the Wong family in fall 2021 as the ideal low-maintenance pandemic pet. Watching Augustus slowly munch a piece of napa cabbage or hang upside down, motionless, in a glass habitat for hours brings great contentment. Feeding, observing, and caring for Augustus taught me that doing nothing is everything. Augustus is no longer alive, but I know he lived well. We could all learn a lot from Augustus.

Photo Insert Captions

Page 1: (*Top*) Me as a baby in 1974, just chillin' on my blankie. Note my huge head and fluffy tufts of black hair. Mom always said I had a big head. And I still do. (*Middle*) Me as a wee newborn in 1974. I'm wrapped up in a blanket like a burrito and being held by Mom. (*Bottom*) Me around three or four years old, lazing about on a coffee table at our home in Indianapolis. I look like I'm a million miles away. What is Alice the kid thinking about? Love the '70s decor!

Page 2: (*Top*) I believe this is my fourth birthday party, just as I was about to blow out my candles. My little sister, Emily, is immediately to my left-hand side, and next to her is my childhood buddy Ellen. For kids' parties, Mom made a punch from a gallon of rainbow sherbert and a liter of 7-UP. Mmmmm. (*Middle top*) A holiday feast for either Thanksgiving, Christmas, or a different very special occasion. Two roast ducks marinated in soy sauce overnight and stuffed with green onions, star anise, lots of salt, and maybe ginger, and served with homemade flour pancakes and other savory fillings. Oh, the aroma of roast duck . . . *chef's kiss* (*Middle center*) This photo shows three types of delicious homemade hand-wrapped dumplings. The left four vertical rows are made with wheat flour; the remainder are made with white flour, which has a silkier taste. On the far right are two flat ravioli-shaped dumplings made from excess dough. (*Middle bottom*) Me, at age six or seven, cute as hell and saying hello to a brown rabbit at Eagle Creek Park, where I often went on field trips during elementary school. (*Bottom*) This is one of my favorite photos of my mom and me. Look at the pure joy captured in that moment!

Page 3: (*Top*) The Wong family in front of our modified van. From left to right behind me are Mom, Dad, Grace, and Emily. Any van with a lift costs a lot of money, and this was our second, with a fancier lift and a locking system. It was a big-ass deal. (*Middle left*) Me in my teenage years, wearing an olive leather jacket from The Limited that I thought was the shit. I'm posing next to a tiger sculpture in Chicago's Chinatown. (*Middle right*) Here I am with a disabled U.S. president! (*Bottom left*) My friend Jean Lin sent me this framed article featuring me from the San Francisco edition of the *World Journal* in 2010. I was interviewed about an award I'd received from the city for my activism. At the time I was not yet using a BiPap machine for breathing. (*Bottom right*) About to receive my undergraduate degree in 1997 from Indiana University, Indianapolis.

Page 4: (*Top left*) Now and forever. (*Top right*) Documentation from my previous life in academia at U.C. San Francisco! (*Middle left, top*) This is one of the few remaining mixtapes I've saved. Ellen, my lifelong friend, made it for me in September 1992. No two mixtapes are the same, and they're always better with stickers. (*Middle center*) Thank you, Kalyn Heffernan, of the band Wheelchair Sports Camp, who gave me permission to use two songs as theme music for my *Disability Visibility* podcast: "Hard Out Here for a Gimp" and "Dance Off." Big fan! (*Middle right, top*) I love this illustration by disabled artist Mike Mort. I used it as my podcast's logo in 2017. (*Middle left, bottom*) This arrived as a surprise thank-you gift after I gave a talk about disabled oracles for an event, Assembly for the Future, in 2020. The organizers commissioned this amazing needlepoint portrait of me from artist Tal Fitzpatrick. (*Middle right, bottom*) The cover of my first self-published anthology (e-book only), a minicollection of essays by disabled people in response to the Trump era in October 2018. It was illustrated by Micah Bazant. (*Bottom*) We truly need more books about disability culture for kids. I was delighted to be featured in *We Move Together*, a children's book written by Kelly Fritsch and Anne McGuire and illustrated by Eduardo Trejos. I'm on the far left side of this illustration.

Page 5: (*Top left*) Everyone has a story. (*Top center*) I have a ton of these C.D.s from StoryCorps. Each participant gets to keep a recording of their oral history, and I got to interview more than thirty of my friends between 2014 and 2018. (*Top right*) This is a very cool hand-drawn illustration by Maximilian Demilt, a fifth-grade student at Castle Bridge School in New York City. I spoke to his class in 2020, and afterward his teacher sent this to me. I love it. (*Middle left*) That's me on the wall of the San Francisco Museum of Modern Art on Howard Street! I had a great time being part of French artist J.R.'s *The Chronicles of San Francisco* in 2019. (*Middle center, top*) This was a fun collaboration with artist Abi Oyewole, who made stickers and pins inspired by a hashtag I used on Twitter regarding plastic-straw bans.

(*Middle center*) Yeahhhh, ACCESS, BITCH! Created by Sky Cubacub. I love it so much. (*Middle center, bottom*) Art is activism. Many thanks to artist Haley Brown, who created this graphic for the community organizing that my friends and I are involved in regarding the recall of BiPaps, CPaps, and ventilators by Philips Respironics. (*Bottom left*) Got this sticker from 18 Million Rising, and I totally dig it. (*Bottom middle*) I don't ride paratransit anymore, but this reminds me of the old days. (*Bottom right*) All politics are local. The same can be said for activism. I got involved with a few organizations in the San Francisco Bay area in my twenties and thirties, such as the S.F. In-Home Supportive Services Public Authority. As a past member of the board, I learned a lot about the local and state politics on funding community-based services.

Page 6: (*Top left*) A rare family photo, taken by Eddie Hernandez Photography, 2020. *From left:* Me, Grace, Emily, Mom, and Dad. (*Top right*) This. This is the vibe. Created by Felicia Liang. (*Middle left*) Friends!!! I had a fun time designing merch for Access Is Love, a campaign co-created by Mia Mingus (*top*), Sandy Ho (*bottom*), and me. (*Middle center*) #CommunityAsHome was a 2020 collaboration between artist Ashanti Fortson (*right*) and myself. Ashanti's art is gorgeous! (*Middle right, top*) My sisters and I at a photo booth many years ago. (*Middle right, bottom*) Me in my bedroom at my tiny desk and bookshelf. This is where all the magic happens. (*Bottom left*) Artist Micah Bazant created this graphic for anyone to use, and I am so grateful. (*Bottom right*) Yomi Wrong (*left*) is a longtime friend. Here we are together at a San Francisco Public Library event in 2019.

Page 7: (*Top left*) In 2016 I splurged and asked designer Sky Cubacub (*left*) to make a custom outfit for me (*center*), shown here. Sky and their friend Nina Litoff (*right*) were in town, and they asked photographer Grace DuVal to take some photos. (*Top right*) Ing Wong-Ward (*left*) is one of my disabled ancestors. She and her family came out to San Francisco on vacation, and I was so lucky to have spent time with her. This is us in 2016. (*Middle left*) I have a lot of Darth Vader (and Yoda) in me. This is the closest to cosplay I will get. (*Middle right*) I still haven't seen my book *Disability Visibility* in a bookstore or a library, but I took a few pics celebrating my anthology as I sheltered at home in 2020. (*Bottom left*) StoryCorps used to be located at the San Francisco Public Library, and I spent a lot of time there interviewing friends. Here I'm with facilitators Yosmay del Mazo (*left*) and Geraldine Ah-Sue (*right*). (*Bottom right*) Celebrating the wedding of Rani Singh (*right*), a family friend, in 2015.

Page 8: To Mars and beyond!

Answers to *Year of the Tiger* Crossword

ACROSS

2. Watch it jiggle: MARROW
3. Hot yoga: COFFEE
5. A form of love: ACCESS
9. Northerners: SHANDONGNESE
11. I *heart* __: ME
14. Resistance is futile: CYBORGS
16. A lifeline: MEDICAID
17. #___TheVote: CRIP
18. Cross-training routine: INTERVIEWING
19. It's alive!: EUGENICS

DOWN

1. Cassandra-esque: ORACLE
3. Every day: CATURDAY
4. Care is _____: INFRASTRUCTURE
5. Suck on it: ABLEISM
6. Hoosier city: INDIANAPOLIS
7. "Greetings, Mork!": NANU NANU
8. Not so easy: BREATHING
10. A fave word: FUCK
12. Shady scam: NORMALCY
13. Peachy keen: MASUMOTO
15. Show me the money: DUMPLINGS

Permissions Acknowledgments

"A Mutant from Planet Cripton: An Origin" first appeared in *Nerds of Color*.

"First-Person Political: Musings from an Angry Asian American Disabled Girl" was previously published in *Amerasia Journal* 39, no. 1 (2013): 108–117.

"The Americans with Disabilities Act" first appeared on the *Disability Visibility* podcast on July 26, 2020.

"Did You Enjoy High School?" first appeared on the *Death, Sex & Money* podcast as "Alice Wong on Ruckuses, Rage, and Medicaid" on October 21, 2020.

"My Medicaid, My Life" first appeared in the *New York Times* on May 3, 2017.

"The *Olmstead* Decision and Me" first appeared on the *Disability Visibility Project* blog on June 27, 2019.

"#CripTheVote: Then and Now" first appeared as discussions on episode 99 (September 13, 2017) and episode 1 (March 21, 2021) of the *Disability Visibility* podcast.

"My Day as a Robot" first appeared on the California Foundation for Independent Living Centers' Ability Tools program blog, *Ability Tools*, on May 1, 2018.

"Net Neutrality, Accessibility, and the Disability Community" first appeared on the *MediaJustice* blog on November 22, 2017.

"The Last Straw" first appeared in *Eater* (Vox Media, LLC) on July 19, 2018. eater.com/2018/7/19/17586742/plastic-straw-ban -disabilities

"Ode to a Spit Cup" first appeared in *Body Talk: 37 Voices Explore Our Radical Anatomy*, edited by Kelly Jensen (Chapel Hill, N.C.: Algonquin Young Readers, 2020).

"Let's Recognize Why #AccessIsLove" was originally published as "On Valentine's Day, Let's Recognize Why #AccessIsLove" on the *Rooted in Rights* blog on February 14, 2019.

"The One Percent Disabled Club" first appeared as a discussion on episode 63 (January 21, 2016) of the *Denzel Washington Is the Greatest Actor of All Time Period* podcast.

"Disabled Faces" first appeared on the *Disability Visibility Project* blog on December 9, 2020.

"Westward Ho" first appeared in *Collective Wisdom: Lessons, Inspiration, and Advice from Women over Fifty* by Grace Bonney (New York: Artisan, 2021).

"Storytelling as Activism" was a conference conversation for the Longmore Lecture in Disability Studies, held on April 3, 2018. The Longmore Lecture is hosted by the Paul K. Longmore Institute on Disability at San Francisco State University.

"Diversifying Radio with Disabled Voices" first appeared on Transom on May 10, 2016.

"Choreography of Care" first appeared as a segment on the *Making Contact* radio show on April 13, 2016.

"Podcasting as Storytelling" first appeared on episode 100 (April 3, 2021) of the *Disability Visibility* podcast.

"I'm Disabled and Need a Ventilator to Live. Am I Expendable During This Pandemic?" first appeared on Vox (Vox Media, LLC) on April 4, 2020. vox.com/first-person/2020/4/4/21204261/coronavirus-covid-19-disabled-people-disabilities-triage

"Freedom for Some Is Not Freedom for All" first appeared on the *Disability Visibility Project* blog on June 7, 2020.

"Cooking in Quarantine: Shelter-In-Place Jook" first appeared on Al Jazeera on March 26, 2020.

"It's My Body and I'll Live If I Want To" first appeared on the *With Friends Like These* podcast on March 27, 2020.

"No to Normal" first appeared as a speech for San Francisco's Night of Ideas on January 28, 2021.

"How to Create a More Inclusive Future Post-COVID" first appeared on Mashable as "How to create a more inclusive future post-COVID with disability advocate Alice Wong" on March 3, 2021. © 2021 by Ziff Davis, LLC.

"The Last Disabled Oracle" first appeared as a talk for Assembly for the Future, a collaborative project with The Things We Did Next. A transcript of the talk first appeared on the *Disability Visibility Project* blog as "Message from the Future: Disabled Oracle Society" on August 14, 2020.

Interior

Courtesy of the author and Bobby Wong: pages 1, 5, 9, 11, 13 (*top, bottom*), 16 (*top, bottom*), 17, 25, 26, 30, 32, 55, 56, 57, 61, 64–65, 67, 68, 78, 87, 91, 93, 99, 102–104, 106, 124, 135, 137–39, 142, 157, 163 (*top*), 168, 189, 190, 192, 201, 204, 209, 211, 217, 226, 231 (*left, right*), 254, 258, 260, 265, 278, 286–89, 292–98, 307, 309, 310, 317, 330, 340–41, 350, 352, 356

Pages iv, 132–33: Courtesy of Felicia Liang

Page 37: Courtesy of Grace Wong

Pages 63, 72, 83: Courtesy of Lizartistry

Page 96: Courtesy of Yosmay del Mozo

Page 108: Courtesy of Pete Souza / Obama Presidential Library

Page 119: Courtesy of Allie Cannington

Page 130: Courtesy of Mia Mingus

Pages 158–62, 163 (*bottom*): Artwork and alt-text descriptions courtesy of Sam Schäfer

Pages 176, 178: *The Zoom Portraits: Alice Wong* by Riva Lehrer © Riva Lehrer

Page 200: Courtesy of Ken Stein and Ingrid Tischer; © Ken Stein Photo

Page 250: (*Left*) Courtesy of Cheryl Green, photo credit Oliver Baker; (*center*) courtesy of Geraldine Sue; (*right*) courtesy of Sarika D. Mehta

Page 303: Courtesy of Emily Nusbaum

Pages 318, 334, 346: Courtesy of Hatiye Garip

Insert

Pages 1, 2, 3, 8: Courtesy of the author

Page 4: *Top left:* courtesy of Jane Shi; *middle left, bottom:* courtesy of Tal Fitzpatrick; *middle right, top:* courtesy of Mike Mort; *middle right, bottom:* courtesy of Micah Bazant; *bottom:* illustration by Eduardo Trejos, from *We Move Together*, written by Kelly Fritsch and Anne McGuire, and illustrated by Eduardo Trejos (2021, AK Press) / used by permission; other images courtesy of the author

Page 5: *Top right:* illustration courtesy of Maximilian Demilt; *middle center, top:* courtesy of Abbi Oyewole; *middle center:* courtesy of Rebirth Garments; *middle center, bottom:* courtesy of Haley Brown; other images courtesy of the author

Page 6: *Top left:* Eddie Hernandez Photography, © 2020 by Eddie Hernandez Photography; *middle left, top:* courtesy of Mia Mingus; *middle left, bottom:* courtesy of Sandy Ho; *middle center:* courtesy of Ashanti Fortson, © 2020 by Ashanti Fortson / all rights reserved; *bottom left:* courtesy of Micah Bazant; other images courtesy of the author

Page 7: *Top left:* courtesy of Grace DuVal, © 2021 by Grace DuVal; other images courtesy of the author

NOW ADAPTED
FOR YOUNG ADULTS

Don't miss the urgent and compelling
essay collection edited by **ALICE WONG**

Learn more at PRH.com